The Neighbor

Three Inquiries in Political Theology

SLAVOJ ŽIŽEK

ERIC L. SANTNER

KENNETH REINHARD

The University of Chicago Press   Chicago and London

SLAVOJ ŽIŽEK is professor of philosophy at the University of Ljubljana. His numerous books include *Iraq: The Borrowed Kettle* and *The Puppet and the Dwarf: The Perverse Core of Christianity*.

ERIC L. SANTNER is professor in and chair of the Department of Germanic Studies at the University of Chicago. His most recent book is *On the Psychotheology of Everyday Life: Reflections on Freud and Rosenzweig*.

KENNETH REINHARD is associate professor of English and comparative literature at the University of California, Los Angeles, where he also directed the Center for Jewish Studies. He is coauthor of *After Oedipus: Shakespeare in Psychoanalysis*.

The University of Chicago Press, Chicago 60637
The University of Chicago Press, Ltd., London
© 2005 by The University of Chicago
All rights reserved. Published 2005
Printed in the United States of America

14 13 12 11 10 09 08 07 06   2 3 4 5

ISBN: 0-226-70738-5 (cloth)
ISBN: 0-226-70739-3 (paper)

Library of Congress Cataloging-in-Publication Data

Žižek, Slavoj.
    The neighbor : three inquiries in political theology / Slavoj Žižek,
Eric L. Santner, Kenneth Reinhard.
        p. cm. — (Religion and postmodernism)
        ISBN 0-226-70738-5 (cloth : alk. paper) — ISBN 0-226-70739-3
    (pbk. : alk. paper)
        1. Political theology. 2. Church and social problems. I. Santner,
    Eric L., 1955–. II. Reinhard, Kenneth, 1957–. III. Title. IV. Series.
    BT83.59 .Z59 2006
    177'.7—dc22

                                                           2005016280

Contents

Introduction

In a well-known series of reflections in *Civilization and Its Discontents,* Freud made abundantly clear what he thought about the biblical injunction, first articulated in Leviticus 19:18 and then elaborated in the Christian teaching, to love one's neighbor as oneself. "Let us adopt a naive attitude towards it," Freud proposes, "as though we were hearing it for the first time; we shall be unable then to suppress a feeling of surprise and bewilderment." Freud condenses this surprise and bewilderment in a series of questions and objections that cannot but seem reasonable and commonsensical:

Why would we do it? What good will it do us? But, above all, how shall we achieve it? How can it be possible? My love is something valuable to me which I ought not to throw away without reflection. It imposes duties on me for whose fulfillment I must be ready to make sacrifices. If I love someone, he must deserve it in some way. . . . He deserves it if he is so like me in important ways that I can love myself in him; and he deserves it if he is so much more perfect than myself that I can love my ideal of my own self in him.

Things become even more complex when this neighbor is a perfect stranger:

But if he is a stranger to me and if he cannot attract me by any worth of his own of any significance that he may already have acquired for my emotional life, it will be hard for me to love him. Indeed, I should be wrong to do so, for my love is valued by all my own people as a sign of my preferring them, and it is an injustice to them if I put a stranger on a par with them. But if I am to love him (with this universal love) merely because he, too, is an inhabitant of this earth, like an insect, an earth-worm or a grass-snake, then I fear that only a small modicum of my love will fall to his share.

But things get even worse. "Not merely is this stranger in general unworthy of my love," Freud writes;

I must honestly confess that he has more claim to my hostility and even my hatred. He seems not to have the least trace of love for me and shows me not the slightest consideration. If it will do him any good he has no hesitation in injuring me, nor does he ask himself whether the amount of advantage he gains bears any proportion to the extent of the harm he does to me. Indeed, he need not even obtain an advantage; if he can satisfy any sort of desire by it, he thinks nothing of jeering at me, insulting me, slandering me and showing his superior power; and the more secure he feels and the more helpless I am, the more certainly I can expect him to behave like this to me.

Freud brings his reflections on neighbor-love to a provisional conclusion by appealing to the persistence, in human beings, of a fundamental inclination toward aggression, a primary mutual hostility. As "creatures among whose instinctual endowments is to be reckoned a powerful share of aggressiveness, . . . their neighbor is for them not only a potential helper or sexual object, but also someone who tempts them to satisfy their aggressiveness on him, to exploit his capacity for work without compensation, to use him sexually without his consent, to seize his possessions, to humiliate him, to cause him pain, to torture and to kill him. *Homo homini lupus.*"[1]

Against the background of such remarks, it might well seem to be a fool's undertaking to attempt to make psychoanalysis a key resource in the project of reanimating the ethical urgency and significance of neighbor-love in contemporary society and culture. But that is just what the essays in this volume propose to do. This book's underlying premise—axiom even—is that the Freudian revolution is *stricto sensu internal* to the topic of neighbor and, indeed, provides a crucial point of

---

1. Sigmund Freud, *Civilization and Its Discontents,* trans. James Strachey (New York: W. W. Norton, 1989), 66–69.

reference for the project of rethinking the notion of neighbor in light of the catastrophic experiences of the twentieth century.

After the slaughters of World War II, the Shoah, the gulag, multiple ethnic and religious slaughters, the explosive rise of slums in the last decades, and so on, the notion of neighbor has lost its innocence. To take the extreme case: in what precise sense is the *Muselmann*, the "living dead" of the Nazi concentration camps, still our neighbor? Is "human rights militarism," as the predominant ideological justification of today's military interventions, really sustained by the love for a neighbor? And, in our own societies, is not the multiculturalist notion of tolerance, whose fundamental value is the right not to be harassed, precisely a strategy to keep the intrusive neighbor at a proper distance? In the magnificent chapter 2.C ("*You* Shall Love Your Neighbor") of his *Works of Love*, Søren Kierkegaard develops the claim that the ideal neighbor that we should love is a dead one—the only good neighbor is a dead neighbor. His line of reasoning is surprisingly simple and straightforward: in contrast to poets and lovers, whose object of love is distinguished by its particular outstanding qualities, "to love one's neighbor means equality": "Forsake all distinctions so that you can love your neighbor."[2] However, it is only in death that all distinctions disappear: "Death erases all distinctions, but preference is always related to distinctions."[3]

Is this love for the dead neighbor really just Kierkegaard's theological idiosyncrasy? In some "radical" circles in the United States, there came recently a proposal to "rethink" the rights of necrophiliacs (those who desire to have sex with dead bodies). So the idea was formulated that, in the same way people give permission for their organs to be used for medical purposes in the case of their sudden death, people should also be allowed to grant permission for their bodies to be given to necrophiliacs to play with. Is this proposal not the perfect exemplification of how a particular politically correct stance realizes Kierkegaard's insight into how the only good neighbor is a dead neighbor? A dead neighbor—a corpse—is the ideal sexual partner of a "tolerant" subject trying to avoid either harassing or being harassed: by definition, a corpse cannot be harassed; at the same time, a dead body *does not enjoy,* so the disturbing threat of the partner's excessive enjoyment is also eliminated.

To put it in the simplest way possible, the essays collected here share the basic premise that Freud's discovery of the unconscious gives us the

---

2. Søren Kierkegaard, *Works of Love,* trans. Howard Hong (New York: Harper, 1994), 75.
3. Ibid., 74.

resources to understand, with a new and heretofore unimagined complexity, what is happening when we enter into the proximity of another's desire, a desire that touches on the border regions of life and death and that can therefore assume an inhuman, even monstrous aspect. What if, for example, Kafka's "inhuman" figure Odradek proves to be the exemplary case of the neighbor? The premise of this volume is that only through understanding the eventfulness of such an encounter will it be possible to truly grasp what is at stake now in the commandment to love one's neighbor as oneself.

II

As Jacques Lacan points out, the biblical commandment to love the neighbor represents a complete break from classical ethics: "Nothing is farther from the message of Socrates than *you shall love your neighbor as yourself*, a formula that is remarkably absent from all that he says."[4] With the injunction in the Torah to "love your neighbor as yourself" (Lev. 19:18) and the New Testament's question "who is my neighbor?" (Luke 10:29), the relationship to another person indicated as "the neighbor" (*re'a* in Hebrew, *plesion* in the Greek) comes to define monotheistic ethics in its difference from the Greco-Roman or "pagan" ethics of moderation and temperance as the keys to happiness. Lacan's ultimate point, one already adumbrated in Freud's various warnings about the possibility of neighbor-love, is that the encounter with the neighbor—this new point of orientation in ethical life—points to a beyond of the pleasure principle that still guides the classical ethics of happiness. Judaism opens up a tradition in which an alien traumatic kernel forever persists in my neighbor; the neighbor remains an impenetrable, enigmatic presence that, far from serving my project of self-disciplining moderation and prudence, hystericizes me.

Jewish literature presents numerous examples of the radical ethics of the neighbor, from the Talmud and Midrash, Maimonides and Nachmanides, to Rosenzweig and Levinas; and in Christianity neighbor-love is a central problem to thinkers as diverse as Augustine, William of Ockham, Catherine of Siena, Luther, and Kierkegaard. At the same time, the neighbor has acted as a doctrinal shibboleth for the separation and even opposition of Jewish and Christian ethics and for the emergence of the

---

4. Jacques Lacan, *Le séminaire, livre 8: Le transfert* (Paris: Seuil, 1991), 186.

so-called secular world from the Christian line of interpretation. The New Testament defines itself against what it sees as the narrow legalism of Pharisaic Judaism and initiates the dialectics of new versus old, universal versus particular, and love versus law that will inform ethical theory in modernity. For Immanuel Kant, the commandment to love the neighbor embodies the rigors of ethics as pure practical reason, in which the Good is clearly distinguished from both Jewish law and pagan well-being. Kant's frequent citation of Leviticus 19:18 as an instance of the categorical imperative continues the logic of universalization that began in the New Testament and provides the proof text for the reconciliation between religion and reason.

In both Judaism and Christianity, the commandment in Leviticus 19:18 to "love your neighbor as yourself" functions most canonically as the central law or moral principle par excellence, the ethical essence of true religion, in tandem with the commandment to "love God." But the meaning of neither of these injunctions can be taken as self-evident: just as love of God can be interpreted in terms of many divergent practices, from private meditation to public martyrdom, so the intent and extent of the commandment to love the neighbor are obscure and have frequently been points of radical disagreement and sectarian division, even in mainstream interpretation. For skeptical readers, both religious and secular, the commandment to love the neighbor has seemed far from rational and has, in fact, appeared deeply enigmatic—indeed, as an enigma that calls us to rethink the very nature of subjectivity, responsibility, and community. We might even say that neighbor-love is not a law that can be obeyed literally, nor a theory that can be definitively exemplified, but a rule that can be proved only by its exception. That is, neighbor-love functions more as an obstacle to its own theorization than as a roadmap for ethical life: whereas all ethical imperatives involve some ambiguity and hence require some degree of interpretation (e.g., What constitutes honoring one's parents? Is there a difference between "killing" and "murdering"?), the injunction to "love your neighbor as yourself" involves interpretive and practical aporias in *all* its individual terms, and even more so as an utterance. One cannot attempt to fulfill it without taking the risk of transgressing it. Despite its seemingly universal dissemination, despite its appropriation in the name of various moral and political agendas, something in the call to neighbor-love remains opaque and does not give itself up willingly to univocal interpretation. Yet it remains always in the imperative and presses on us with an urgency that seems to go beyond both its religious origins and its modern appropriations as universal Reason.

To begin, who is my neighbor? In Judaism this question often takes the form of asking whether the neighbor to be loved includes non-Jews along with Jews. Before modernity, however, few Jewish readers understood the injunction to extend beyond the limit of the covenant; and while some medieval exegetes include fellow monotheists among the neighbors, others restrict the commandment's object even more, limiting the neighbor to strictly *observant* fellow Jews. But even the most exclusive account must face the inevitable question of the choice of one particular neighbor over another, for to love any one neighbor is surely to fail to love another. A defining moment in the emergence of Christian universalism comes when the neighbor is asserted to include everyone, Jew and Gentile alike, in the parable of the Good Samaritan: while the Levite and the Cohen pass by the injured man in the road, presumably not recognizing him as a fellow Jew, or perhaps fearful of violating laws of purity through contact with a corpse, the Good Samaritan comes to his aid and proves himself the true neighbor of his neighbor—whether dead or alive.

Secondly, what acts or affects are imposed in the seemingly excessive and even inappropriate injunction to "love" my neighbor (*ahavah,* in Hebrew, which includes romantic and sexual love)? The medieval Rabbi Nachmanides insists that *love* is a figure of speech, an "overstatement." Pointing to the peculiar grammar of the Hebrew phrase, which could be translated awkwardly but literally as "love *to* the neighbor as yourself," he argues that the commandment enjoins love of the neighbor's welfare, not person. Christianity has similarly tried to distance the commandment from any sense of inappropriate affect, usually by emphasizing its close connection with the love of God. Some commentators (notably Kierkegaard), pointing out that love cannot be commanded, cannot be produced by imperative or necessity, argue that the commandment is meant to be confronted as enigma, to be broken through to love of God.

Furthermore, what does the commandment's apparent reflexivity, the call to love the neighbor *as yourself,* imply about the nature of self-love and, by extension, about subjectivity? What is the force of the comparative *kamokah* (again, an unusual formation in this grammatical context)? Neighbor-love has come to serve as a test of the meaning of affiliation, membership, and community insofar as the commandment seems to require a relationship or affective bond of some sort between the other and the self. Is the neighbor understood as an extension of the category of the self, the familial, and the friend, that is, as someone *like* me whom I am obligated to give preferential treatment to; or does it imply the inclusion of the other into my circle of responsibility, extending to the stranger, even the enemy?

Finally, and for the concerns of the present volume most importantly, does the commandment call us to expand the range of our identifications or does it urge us to come closer, become answerable to, an alterity that remains radically inassimilable? In this spirit, one might paraphrase Max Horkheimer's old motto from the late 1930s "If you do not want to talk about Fascism, then shut up about capitalism": if you do not want to talk about Odradek, Gregor Samsa, and the *Muselmann,* then shut up about your love for a neighbor.

In raising these questions, neighbor-love not only opens up a set of fundamental issues that continue to define ethical inquiry in modernity, but also implies a new theological configuration of political theory. The essays in this volume make a preliminary step into this opening.

III

In the first essay, Kenneth Reinhard argues that Freud and Lacan provide the resources for a radical rethinking of the two fundamental categories of Carl Schmitt's political theology, that of the sovereign (as the one who decides on the state of exception) and that of the friend-enemy distinction (as providing the very framework of the field of political life). Rather than simply abandoning the concept of political theology—a common reflex in contemporary liberal thought—Reinhard argues that it ought to be pushed further toward an alternative political theology of the neighbor. In doing so, Reinhard suggests, we might avoid the two alternative ways of *not* encountering the neighbor, which he correlates with the psychic structures of psychosis and neurosis: "Neurosis and psychosis represent two asymmetrical modes of the failure to love the neighbor: whereas the neurotic becomes an autonomous subject of desire in turning away from the impossibility of the command to love the neighbor, the psychotic fails to achieve subjectivity while succeeding in experiencing the other as radically other, loving the neighbor not wisely, but too well." Reinhard proposes that the way out of this bind is to be found in Lacan's elaboration of sexual difference and his notion of the "impossibility" of the sexual relation. Reinhard argues that Lacan's "formula" of masculine sexuation—the pattern according to which a "masculine" subjective structure comes to be stabilized—closely parallel's Schmitt's understanding of the organization of the political field (friend-foe distinction) around the figure of the sovereign and his paradoxical "right" to declare a state of exception. Masculine subjectivity is constituted, in this view, in relation to the fantasy of the primal father: "The sovereign is like the primal father in being stationed at the margins of the state he regulates: it is only insofar as there can be a radical exception to the law that the law can exist and be effective. The primal father and the sovereign occupy the position of extreme dictators whose word both violates the rule of the total state and promises it *totality*, closure, drawing a line between the inside and the outside, the native and the stranger. The subjective decision that results in masculine sexuation is *the choice not to choose,* the decision to remain in a liminal position by both accepting subjection to the law of castration and maintaining the belief in the existence of *at least one* man who has escaped that law, while enforcing it on all others." For Reinhard, Lacan's proposal of an alternative logic for feminine sexuation, one that includes the dimension that Lacan called the *pas-tout,* the not-all, offers the resources for allowing us to pass from the political theology of the friend-enemy to that of the neighbor, a figure located no longer in a field totalized by a sovereign exception, but rather within an infinite series of possible encounters, one without limit and without totalization, a field without the stability of margins.

In the second essay of the volume, Eric Santner takes as his point of departure Walter Benjamin's famous allegory of the chess player in which an automaton, representing historical materialism, is guided in his moves by a wizened dwarf representing, in turn, the resources of theology. Santner raises the question, as simple as it is perplexing, as to the nature of the materiality at stake in such materialism. That is, what sort of materiality must this be if theology is to play a role in its analysis and recomposition? And how should one understand the theology that, in Benjamin's view, would be up to such a task? Santner pursues these questions by way of an engagement with the work of Franz Rosenzweig, the German-Jewish philosopher whose magnum opus, *The Star of Redemption,* was a crucial point of reference for Benjamin's thought in general and for the critique of historicism he proposes in his *Theses,* in particular. Through a reading of Rosenzweig's discussion of the concept of miracles, Santner argues that the materiality at issue in historical materialism needs to be understood as a kind of semiotic density, a signifying stress, constituting the subject's *creatureliness.* For Santner, "becoming creature," the acquisition of the materiality at issue in historical materialism, is linked to the state of exception already elaborated in Reinhard's essay, that is, to exposure to a boundary zone of the Law where the force of law exceeds any normative content, where the meaningfulness of law is traversed by a movement of *designification.* Creaturely life is what gets "(dis)organized" by way of what Benjamin calls the *erregende Schrift,* the exciting script, that gathers around the edges of states of emergency/ exception. Against this background, Santner proposes that a miracle implies a capacity to intervene into this dimension of creaturely life, the possibility of releasing the energies contained there, opening them to genuinely new destinies. It is, Santner argues, through such interventions that one remains faithful to the commandment of neighbor-love.

In the final essay of the volume, Slavoj Žižek argues for an understanding of the injunction to love one's neighbor precisely as a challenge to the so-called ethical turn in contemporary thought, a turn often linked to the thought of Emmanuel Levinas. Žižek's main target in this essay is what he characterizes as an ethics of the "last man"—Friedrich Nietzsche's notion of the "last man" is the point of reference here—the paradigmatic citizen of contemporary Western civilizations who fears an excessive intensity of life as something that might disturb his search for happiness without stress and who, for this reason, rejects "cruel" imposed moral norms as a threat to his fragile balance. For Žižek, a whole series of contemporary commodities and phenomena embodies this anxiety and vulnerability apropos of excess: coffee without caffeine, beer without alcohol, up to the desire to prosecute wars without casualties (nonexistent on our side, invisible on the other side). Žižek proposes a revaluation of the notion of excess, of exposure to excess, one that follows the logic of the Hegelian revision of the Kantian position: Is the status of the subject always limited, dispossessed, and exposed, or is the subject itself a name for this dispossession? From the subject's limitation, we have to move to limit itself as the name for the subject.

For Žižek, this Hegelian sublation of the Kantian position disseminates into the field of political life a crucial dimension of life introduced by the Kantian transcendental turn, that of "inhuman" understood as the very "extimate" feature which makes the human human. Whereas the judgment "he is not human" means simply that this person is external to humanity, animal or divine, the judgment "he is inhuman" means something thoroughly different, namely, that this person is neither simply human nor simply inhuman, but marked by a terrifying excess which, although it negates what we understand as humanity, is inherent to being human. In the pre-Kantian universe, Žižek suggests, humans were simply humans, beings of reason, fighting the excesses of animal lusts and divine madness. With Kant and German Idealism, however, the excess to be fought is absolutely immanent, the core of subjectivity itself (which is why, with German Idealism, the metaphor for the core of subjectivity is Night, "Night of the World," in contrast to the Enlightenment notion of the Light of Reason fighting the darkness around). So when, in the pre-Kantian universe, a hero goes mad, it means he is deprived of his humanity, in other words, the animal passions or divine madness took over. With Kant, on the other hand, madness signals the unconstrained explosion of the very core of a human being. Žižek argues that this dimension is missed in the ethical turn in contemporary thought in general, and in the work of Levinas, in particular. Žižek's further argument is that it is only by insisting on this dimension that it becomes possible to reinvigorate the properly *political* potential of the injunction of neighbor-love.

The essays in this volume were written over the course of several years of intensive conversations between the three contributors. These conversations have never yielded complete agreement or harmony (or even comprehension!). Nonetheless, we have all taken as our fundamental point of departure—as the very matter of thought, *die Sache des Denkens*—the axiom that it is only with the emergence of the psychoanalytic concept of the unconscious—with the emergence of the subject of psychoanalysis—that we can truly grasp the ethical and political complexity introduced into the world by the injunction to love one's neighbor as oneself.

KENNETH REINHARD

Toward a Political Theology of the Neighbor

In *The Concept of the Political* (1932), Carl Schmitt writes: "the specific political distinction to which political actions and motives can be reduced is that between friend and enemy."[1] However, in his book *Political Theology* (1922), Schmitt presented a quite different, even contradictory, logic of the political. There, the structural function of the exception—the sovereign's Godlike ability to declare a state of emergency and act outside the law—implies that the border between the law and lawlessness is permeable and, by extension, that the relationship of interiority (friends) and exteriority (enemies) is unstable. The fact that Schmitt's political theology generates antitheses that it cannot maintain should not invalidate what we can take as its fundamental insight, that the political order is sustained by theological concepts that it cannot completely assimilate. The friend-enemy distinction remains significant when we understand it as a *symptom* of political theology, an attempt to formalize the political against the threat of the theological—that is, as the political's defense against destabilizing aspects of its own theologism.

Rather than abandoning political theology because of these contradictions, we need to push it further. The structural analogy of sovereignty to deity that grants the sovereign God's authority to decree an exception also suggests

---

1. Carl Schmitt, *The Concept of the Political*, trans. George Schwab (Chicago: University of Chicago Press, 1996), 26.

that the sovereign's legitimacy derives in part from the divine claim to the fidelity of love: "you shall love the Lord your God with all your heart and with all your soul and with all your might" (Deut. 6:5).[2] For the political theological tradition represented by Machiavelli, the key question may be whether it is better for the sovereign to be loved or feared. The theology of the Hebrew Bible, however, does not oppose those passionate relationships; God is to be loved *and* feared. In a famous midrash on the giving of the law at Sinai, God holds the mountain over the people and makes them an offer they can't refuse: "If you accept the Torah, it is well; if not, your grave will be right here."[3] The legitimacy of the law established at Sinai is based on a consent in excess of freedom of choice and a love indistinguishable from fear. Hence, we find an affective correlate of the paradoxical topology of sovereignty in the ambivalence that underlies the commandment to love God—a commandment that, like all commandments to love, has at its heart the collision of autonomy and heteronomy. Insofar as this antinomy includes both sides of the double genitive of "love of God," we can propose it as the *mysterium sanctum* underlying political theology, the implicit credo of sovereignty that informs the hierarchy of relations within family, polis, and ecclesia.

But in both Jewish and Christian doxology, love of God is conventionally paired with love of the neighbor, as two essentially linked imperatives or theological-ethical principles. In this essay, I bring the psychoanalytic commentary on the neighbor in the work of Freud and Lacan into relation with the logic of political theology theorized by Schmitt, in order to begin to specify the conditions of a political theology of the neighbor. Freud's writing is centrally relevant to a political theology of the neighbor, as the other side of the political theology of the friend and enemy, most notably in his late works *Civilization and Its Discontents* and *Moses and Monotheism*. However, the neighbor and neighbor-love appear over the entire range of his writings, from his earliest unpublished drafts to Wilhelm Fliess through his last works. Although Lacan's most famous remarks on the neighbor appear in his sem-

2. St. Francis de Sales in the *Treatise on the Love of God* writes, "nothing so much presses man's heart as love; if a man know that he is beloved, be it by whom it may, he is pressed to love in his turn. But if a common man be beloved by a great lord, he is much more pressed; and if by a great monarch, how much more yet?" (book 7, chap. 8; www.ccel.org/d/desales/love/htm/TOC.htm).

3. When the Israelites accept the law, thereby granting it the legitimacy of consent, they say, "All that the Lord has spoken we will do and obey" (נַעֲשֶׂה וְנִשְׁמָע; Ex. 24:7); the word translated as "obey," *shama*, literally means "to hear." Hence, the Rabbinic tradition reads the textual order of "do" and "hear" as implying that the Israelites were committing to the commandments *prior* to having heard or understood them, and for this they are greatly praised. See Hayim Nahman Bialik and Yehoshua Hana Ravnitzky, eds., *The Book of Legends: Sefer Ha-Aggadah, Legends from the Talmud and Midrash* (New York: Schocken, 1992), 79.

inar 7, *The Ethics of Psychoanalysis,* the neighbor and neighbor-love are frequent topics of his writing and seminars. In *Totem and Taboo,* Freud presents a mythical genealogy of the paternal law remarkably similar to Schmitt's theory of sovereignty. Like the sovereign, the father of the primal horde has the singular ability to transgress the law in the very process of embodying and enforcing it. Freud appropriates the narrative of the primal father in order to explain the genesis of the law and to stage a mythical "primal scene" of the origins of the superego's conflicting imperatives for and against enjoyment. In seminar 17, *The Other Side of Psychoanalysis,* Lacan introduces the "discourse of the master" in part as a formalization of the structure of Freud's narrative of the primal horde.[4] And in the years between seminar 17 and seminar 21, Lacan rethought the discourse of the master in the language of symbolic logic and set theory as part of his "formulas of sexuation," where the structural parallels with Schmitt's political theology become most striking.

Indeed, just as Schmitt insists that what is at stake in sovereignty is the ability to *decide* when to declare a state of emergency, without needing any grounds or basis for the decision, so, according to Lacan, to participate in one of the two logics that define sexuation is, paradoxically, to have *chosen* to be a man or a woman.[5] If Schmitt's account of the sovereign exception can be mapped onto the man's side of Lacan's formulas of sexuation, what, we might wonder, are the political implications corresponding to the other choice of sexuation, that of the woman? According to Lacan, the position of the woman entails a different logic, and implies an entirely distinct account of individual and group relations, under the aegis of what he calls the "not-all" (*pas-tout*). Whereas the position of man is held vis-à-vis a totality of Men, Lacan argues that women do not participate in a general category of Woman, but enter into their sexuality "one by one," as part of an infinite series of exceptions that form a radically open set, a "not-all." Can we locate in the not-all a political theology of the neighbor? That is, a mode of political relation that would not be based on the friend-enemy couple, but on the neighbor as a third term, one that is obscured by Schmitt's binary opposition, but that is no less central to religious discourse, sociality, and political theology? I do not mean to argue that we should replace the model of sov-

---

4. Jacques Lacan, *Le séminaire, livre 17: L'envers de la psychanalyse* (Paris: Seuil, 1991), 117–52.

5. "One ultimately situates oneself [in the man's position] by choice—women are free to situate themselves there if it gives them pleasure to do so"; "If it inscribes itself [in the woman's position] . . . it will be a not-whole, insofar as it has the choice of positing itself in Φx or of not being there" (Jacques Lacan, *The Seminar of Jacques Lacan,* book 20: *Encore, 1972–1973: On Feminine Sexuality, the Limits of Love and Knowledge* [New York: W. W. Norton, 1998]), 71, 80).

ereignty based on love of God implicit in Schmitt's political theology with one based on love of neighbor. Rather, my argument is that a political theology of the neighbor must come as a *supplement* to the political theology of the friend and enemy. It is only by considering the principles of love of God and love of neighbor together, as two halves of the same thought, as is the case in both Jewish and Christian doctrine, that we can begin to imagine other possibilities for social and subjective organization.

Political Theology

The argument for the theological foundations of political theory is, of course, very old. In the last century, though, it has been given what we might call a radically conservative inflection through the ideas of Carl Schmitt, who famously writes that "all significant concepts of the modern theory of the state are secularized theological concepts."[6] For Schmitt, political theology is the truth of political theory in two ways. First, Schmitt defines sovereignty not according to its normative juridical and executive functions, but in terms of its extraordinary or exceptional powers. The sovereign is the one who can suspend the law in time of emergency, in part or *in toto*, for the sake of its ultimate restitution and the preservation of the polis. Just as God suspends the laws of nature in miracles, so the sovereign is empowered to interrupt the laws of the state, to decide if and when to act, without the support of precedent or previously determined principles. Second, Schmitt claims that the essential logic of the political lies in the opposition between the categories of "friend" and "enemy," an antithesis not of pathos but of *ethos*. The polis requires the ever-present "real possibility" of war for the concepts

6. Carl Schmitt, *Political Theology: Four Chapters on the Concept of Sovereignty*, trans. George Schwab (Cambridge, MA: MIT Press, 1985), 36. For a useful overview of the idea of political theology, beginning with the Hebrew Bible, although largely from Christian perspectives, see Peter Scott and William T. Cavanaugh, eds., *The Blackwell Companion to Political Theology* (Oxford: Blackwell, 2004). In revisions of earlier works, Schmitt (in *Political Theology II*) and Hans Blumenberg (in *The Legitimacy of the Modern World*) debate the status of "secularization." For Schmitt, Blumenberg's thesis merely concerns legality, not legitimacy, and hence has no historical force; for Blumenberg, Schmitt's account of secularization is merely metaphorical, or based on a structural analogy between theology and politics, and derives its legitimacy not from an existential decision, but from a history of decisions that have already been made. See Hans Blumenberg, *The Legitimacy of the Modern Age* (Cambridge, MA: MIT Press, 1985); and Carl Schmitt, *Politische Theologie II. Die Legende von der Erledigung jeder politischen Theologie* (Berlin: Duncker & Humblot, 1970). Clearly, the question of secularization will be crucial to establishing the conditions of a political theology of the neighbor, but this topic is beyond the scope of this essay.

friend and enemy to retain their validity, and the exceptional decision to go to war constitutes the purest manifestation of the political as such.[7] I would argue, moreover, that there is an implicit link between these two elements of Schmitt's thinking: the ultimate justification of the sovereign's ability to decide on the exception is that it is meant to restore or ratify the essential political distinction between friend and enemy, however tendentious that opposition may be. There are fundamental differences, however, in the topologies implied here: if the principle of the friend-enemy opposition is based on the purity of the demarcation between interior and exterior, the assumption of a strict and recognizable difference between "us" and "them," the principle of sovereign exceptionality involves a more complex spatial logic. Is the sovereign inside or outside the law that he or she may decide to suspend at any moment? Sovereignty, Schmitt argues, is a "borderline" concept—a concept both of the border and at the border of conceptuality. To borrow a term from Lacan, we might describe this topology as one of "extimacy," insofar as the sovereign is paradoxically both inside and outside the law.[8] Moreover, Schmitt's concept of the political is *theological* in its manner of bridging these two topologies: just as in the Bible God's inaugural declaration "let there be light" was an extraordinary and fully arbitrary intervention of creation *ex nihilo* into the "darkness" of primal chaos, a cut that divided the world into stable oppositions of "light" and "darkness," so at the moment of emergency the sovereign transgresses the limits of the law for the sake of the reemergence of the fundamental opposition between friend and enemy that establishes the foundation of the political world.[9]

7. Schmitt refers several times to the friend-enemy determination as a "decision" made both by the state as a whole and existentially, at the level of every soldier on the battlefield: "Only the actual participants can correctly recognize, understand, and judge the concrete situation and settle the extreme case of conflict"; "In its entirety the state as an organized political entity *decides for itself* the friend-enemy distinction" (my emphasis); "The friend, enemy, and combat concepts receive their real meaning precisely because they refer to the real possibility of physical killing. War follows from enmity. War is the existential negation of the enemy"; "What always matters is the possibility of the extreme case taking place, the real war, and the decision whether this situation has or has not arrived. That the extreme case appears to be an exception does not negate its decisive character but confirms it all the more. . . . One can say that the exceptional case has an especially decisive meaning which exposes the core of the matter" (Schmitt, *Concept of the Political*, 27, 29–30, 33, 35.

8. "Perhaps what we have described as the central place, as the intimate exteriority or 'extimacy,' that is the Thing, will help shed light on the question or mystery that remains" (Jacques Lacan, *The Seminar of Jacques Lacan, book 7: The Ethics of Psychoanalysis, 1959–1960*, trans. Dennis Porter [New York: W. W. Norton, 1992], 139). Also see Giorgio Agamben's discussion of this topology in Schmitt (*Homo Sacer: Sovereign Power and Bare Life*, trans. Daniel Heller-Roazen [Stanford, CA: Stanford University Press, 1998], 15–29).

9. Schmitt refers to sovereignty as a "borderline concept" precisely because the sovereign holds an ambiguous position on the border of the law: "Although he stands outside the normally valid legal system, he nevertheless belongs to it" (*Political Theology*, 7).

The figure of the enemy in Schmitt's 1932 *The Concept of the Political* is drained of all animus. The enemy, according to Schmitt, is not evil:

The distinction of friend and enemy denotes the utmost degree of intensity of a union or separation, of an association or dissociation. . . . The political enemy need not be morally evil or aesthetically ugly; he need not appear as an economic competitor, and it may even be advantageous to engage with him in business transactions. But he is, nevertheless, the other, the stranger; and it is sufficient for his nature that he is, in a specifically intense way, existentially something different and alien, so that in the extreme case conflicts with him are possible. . . . Only the actual participants can correctly recognize, understand, and judge the concrete situation and settle the extreme case of conflict. Each participant is in a position to judge whether the adversary intends to negate his opponent's way of life and therefore must be repulsed or fought in order to preserve one's own form of existence.[10]

The political emerges in a process that seems to have, on the one hand, the characteristics of formal logic, the "union or separation" of two groups, friends and enemies; and, on the other, an intensely personal, existential moment of "recognition," "understanding," and "judgment" for the particular subjects involved. The Friend and the Enemy form twin *imagos* for the national and subjective ethos, figures of positive and negative political ontology by which the interior "we" (the "I" and its friends) is identified as such, as distinguished from the exterior "they." If the "extreme case" of battle to the death with the enemy is the formal scene always on the horizon, as in the Hegelian dialectic of intersubjectivity, the *decision* to engage in war is radically contingent, not determined by any necessity. The act of war, in this sense, is the exception that proves the political rule, the self-identity of the state. And it is precisely insofar as this decisive act is always that of an individual subject, the "actual participants" in conflict, that subjectivity too becomes an instance of self-sovereignty.[11]

One problem with this account of the political, where we divide the world into friends we identify with and enemies we define ourselves against, is that it is fragile, liable to break down or even to invert and oscillate in the face of complex situations. But it is precisely in its inadequacy to the world we live in that Schmitt's account of the friend-enemy distinction is most useful: today, we find ourselves in a world from

10. Schmitt, *Concept of the Political*, 26–27.
11. In his illuminating discussion of Schmitt in *Politics of Friendship*, Jacques Derrida writes, "without an enemy, and therefore without friends, where does one then find oneself, *qua* a self?" (*Politics of Friendship*, trans. George Collins [New York: Verso, 1997], 77).

which the political may have already disappeared, or at least has mutated into some strange new shape. A world not anchored by the "us" and "them" oppositions that flourished as recently as the Cold War is one subject to radical instability, both subjectively and politically. The disappearance of the enemy results in something like global psychosis: since the mirroring relationship between Friend and Enemy provides a form of stability, albeit one based on projective identifications and repudiations, the loss of the enemy threatens to destroy what Lacan calls the "imaginary tripod" (*trépied imaginaire*) that props up the psychotic with a sort of pseudo-subjectivity, until something causes it to collapse, resulting in full-blown delusions, hallucinations, and paranoia.[12] Hence, for Schmitt, a world without enemies is much more dangerous than one where one is surrounded by enemies. As Derrida writes, the disappearance of the enemy opens the door for "an unheard-of violence, the evil of a malice knowing neither measure nor ground, an unleashing incommensurable in its unprecedented—therefore monstrous—forms; a violence in the face of which what is called hostility, war, conflict, enmity, cruelty, even hatred, would regain reassuring and ultimately appeasing contours, because they would be *identifiable*."[13] America today is desperately unsure about both its enemies and its friends, and hence deeply uncertain about itself. The rhetoric of the so-called war on terror is a sign of the disappearance of the traditional, localizable enemy: the terrorist does not have the stabilizing function that Schmitt associates with the enemy, but to declare war on him is to attempt to resuscitate the enemy's failing animus.

Derrida's argument in *The Politics of Friendship* is not so much that we have entered into a historical period where the friend-enemy polarity has broken down, but that it is an inherently unstable opposition. Derrida's account of how the enemy and friend come to displace and infect each other in his reading of Schmitt leads him to propose "a step (not) beyond the political":

Let us not forget that the political would precisely be that which thus endlessly *binds* or *opposes* the friend-enemy/enemy-friend couple in the drive or decision of death. . . . A hypothesis, then: and what if another lovence (in friendship or in love) were bound

---

12. Jacques Lacan, "On a Question Preliminary to Any Possible Treatment of Psychosis," *Écrits: A Selection*, trans. Alan Sheridan (New York: W. W. Norton, 1977), 207; partial translation of Lacan, *Écrits* (Paris: Éditions du Seuil, 1966), 566. Lacan argues that it is the appearance of an actual instance of a father, or a "One-father" ("*Un-père*"), in the place of the missing symbolic father that triggers psychotic collapse (*Écrits* [1977], 217; *Écrits* [1966], 577; translation modified).

13. Derrida, *Politics of Friendship*, 83.

to an affirmation of life, to the endless repetition of this affirmation, only in seeking its way . . . in the step beyond the political, or beyond *that* political as the horizon of finitude . . . the *phileîn* beyond the political or another politics for loving.[14]

This other "politics for loving" that Derrida hypothesizes, this love both beyond and not-beyond the political, must still remain in the vicinity of the theological if it is to be significant, in Schmitt's terms, and not merely a fantasy of some purely secular politics. I would like to suggest that such a politics can be located in the figure of the neighbor—the figure that materializes the uncertain division between the friend/family/self and the enemy/stranger/other.

There is an element of this political theology of the neighbor that we can already point to in Derrida's comments on Schmitt's reference to Jesus's call to "love your enemies" in Matthew. For Schmitt, this biblical reference points to a linguistic distinction in Greek and Latin (but not German or English) between the private *inimicos,* who may indeed be loved or hated, and the public *hostis,* the political enemy, who, according to Schmitt, is not an object of affect. But as Derrida points out in a reading of this passage in *The Gift of Death,* the full line from Matthew that Schmitt refers to involves a crucial reference to the neighbor: "Ye have heard that it hath been said, Thou shalt love thy neighbor, and hate thine enemy. But I say unto you, Love your enemies, bless them that curse you . . ." (5:43–44). Jesus cites Leviticus 19:18, the commandment to "love thy neighbor as thyself," but adds to it something not present in the Hebrew Bible, a directive to "hate thine enemy," in order to make it seem that he is undoing a piece of legal vengeance and, in proclaiming Love your enemies, is asserting its opposite. In fact, the biblical passage in Leviticus Jesus refers to has just specifically forbidden vengeance.[15] Jesus acts here as a *sovereign,* in declaring an exception ("love your enemies") to a law ("hate thine enemy") that he himself has confected; Jesus's commandment to love the enemy must be perceived as not merely new, but antinomian, in violation of the preexisting legal code. Jesus's act of suspending a law that did not previously exist is not merely his exercise of the sovereign prerogative of exception, but an act of political-theological creation *ex nihilo,* truly a polemical "miracle."

14. Ibid., 123. Derrida uses the word *lovence* (*aimance*) several times in this text, a coinage, he notes, that also appears in the work of the poet Abdelkebir Khatibi. Derrida defines *lovence* as love in the middle voice, between passive and active, between loving and being loved.

15. Leviticus 19:18: "You shall not take vengeance or bear any grudge against the sons of your own people, but you shall love your neighbor as yourself: I am the Lord" (*Oxford Annotated Bible, Revised Standard Version* [New York: Oxford University Press, 1962], 146).

Although Jesus's rhetorical technique here would seem to be that of par-adoxical reversal, the first part of the verse, the injunction to love the neighbor, is not challenged, but persists, extended in the series of acts of love that follows ("bless them that curse you, do good to them that hate you, and pray for them which despitefully use you"). Indeed, rather than being inverted, it will be purified of particularism and appropriated as a central tenet of the new Christian political theology.

For Schmitt, the line from Matthew is meant to clarify the difference between the public enemy and the various enmities that occur privately and are not part of the political as such. Jesus, he points out, uses the word *inimicus* or *ekhthros* for the enemy we are enjoined to love, and this must be distinguished from the true enemy, the *hostis* or *polemios*. As Derrida indicates, Schmitt's disturbing example is that the Christian state can have Islam as its enemy, but still love the Muslim as its neigh-bor.[16] But Derrida argues that it is precisely in this enemy, the one who constitutes the political for Schmitt, that the trace of the neighbor ma-terializes: "An identifiable enemy—that is, one who is *reliable* to the point of treachery, and thereby familiar. One's fellow man, in sum, who could almost be loved as oneself. . . . This adversary would remain a neighbor, even if he were an evil neighbor against whom war would have to be waged."[17] The implication of Derrida's comment is that the neighbor who is to be loved as ourself cannot be relegated to a private, pre- or extrapolitical realm, insofar as a similar, if not identical, structure of reflexivity also determines the relationship to the public enemy, who, as reliably "identifiable," is loved (or hated) as ourself. Thus, Derrida points out a possibility of "semantic slippage and inversion" in Schmitt's political theology: the enemy can also be a friend, and the friend is sometimes an enemy. The border between them, and between the pub-lic and private realms they are associated with, is "fragile, porous, con-testable," and to this extent "the Schmittian discourse collapses" and against the threat of that ruin, it takes form.[18]

Schmitt's theory of the exception recapitulates the first two structural moments in providential history by describing the sovereign's political miracles as acts of "creation" and "revelation": if "creation" corresponds to the reestablishment of the polis in the superlegal sovereign act that terminates the civic crisis and the threat of chaos, "revelation" is the ar-ticulation of the constitution or civic law that holds open and maps the

16. Derrida, *Politics of Friendship,* 89.
17. Ibid., 83.
18. Ibid., 88.

contours of the political space established by creation. Cast in the light of revelation, the essence of the law is located in its *exceptional* rather than normative function.[19] However, Schmitt does not include among the metaphors that fill out his structural analogy what would traditionally be the final act of the drama of political theology: the eschatological conclusion when the earthly kingdom fashioned and chartered by God falls into ruin through human depredation, to be replaced by a heavenly kingdom that will last forever. For Walter Benjamin, who maintained a dialogue with Schmitt on these issues, redemption is finally the only theological category that has real significance for politics.[20] In his "Theologico-Political Fragment," Benjamin extends the account of allegorical signification he developed in his book on the German *Trauerspiel* to theorize the redemptive logic of political theology: "The order of the profane assists, through being profane, the coming of the Messianic Kingdom. The profane, therefore, although not itself a category of this Kingdom, is a decisive category of its quietest approach. . . . For nature is Messianic by reason of its eternal and total passing away."[21] The world we live in contains figures of redemption not in the examples of charity and acts of neighbor-love we might find here and there, but in the signs of transitoriness that we see everywhere: natural decay, cultural ruin, political disintegration—the eternity of entropy only. Benjamin's account of the political theology of redemption is insistently material and consistently focused on the transformations of temporality. In his late essay "Theses on the Philosophy of History," Benjamin places central importance on redemption, not as a religious correlative for the Marxist dream of a classless society, but as a kind of temporal bomb which the historical materialist can throw into teleological historicism

19. Schmitt argues that "a continuous thread runs through the metaphysical, political, and sociological conceptions that postulate the sovereign as a personal unity and primeval creator." In Leibniz he locates the "clearest philosophical expression" of the "systemic relationship between jurisprudence and theology": "Both have a double principle, reason . . . and scripture, which means a book with positive revelations and directives" (*Political Theology*, 37–38, 47).

20. Eric Santner has argued that the account of *miracle* we find in Rosenzweig and Benjamin can be seen as a critique of Schmitt's political theology: if for Schmitt the sovereign's power of exception is a kind of political "miracle," for Rosenzweig and Benjamin, the miracle is precisely the *interruption* of the exceptionality of sovereignty. See "Miracles Happen," p. 102, in this volume.

21. Walter Benjamin, *Reflections* (New York: Harcourt Brace Jovanovich, 1978), 312–13. Near the conclusion of his *Trauerspiel* book, Benjamin suggests that the *Trauerspiel*'s allegories of natural decay and cultural ruin finally signify redemption: "Ultimately in the death-signs of the baroque direction of allegorical reflection is reversed; on the second part of its wide arc it returns, to redeem. . . . ultimately, the intention does not faithfully rest in the contemplation of bones, but faithlessly leaps forward to the idea of resurrection" (Walter Benjamin, *The Origin of the German Tragic Drama* [London: New Left, 1977], 232–33). Also see Giorgio Agamben's account of the debate between Schmitt and Benjamin in "Gigantomachy Concerning a Void," in *State of Exception*, trans. Kevin Atell (Chicago: University of Chicago Press, 2005), 52–64.

"in order to blast a specific era out of the homogeneous course of history."[22] Redemption is not the final cause of history, but the interruption of the false totality of historical causality and contextualization by acts of critical creation and constellation.

Given Schmitt's right-wing sympathies, it is not surprising that his account of political theology does not invoke the language of redemption, which so frequently serves as a metaphor for political liberation. But it is precisely in redemption that we can find the possibility of a political theology other than that of the friend-enemy dyad—a political theology of the neighbor. In the *Star of Redemption,* his articulation of the three primal elements of human, world, and God into the three basic relationships of creation, revelation, and redemption, Franz Rosenzweig argues that redemption enters into the world through the act of neighbor-love, as the condition for messianic transformation, social revolution, and the radical revaluation of all values.[23] For Rosenzweig, messianic temporality is not indefinitely postponed to the future, but happens now, as an incursion into the presentness of the present by the nearness of the neighbor: "If then a not-yet is inscribed over all redemptive unison, there can only ensue that the end is for the time being represented by the just present moment, the universal and highest by the approximately proximate. The bond of the consummate and redemptive bonding of man and the world is to begin with the neighbor and ever more only the neighbor, the well nigh-nighest [*zunächst der Nächste und immer wieder nur der Nächste, das zu-nächst Nächste*]."[24] For Rosenzweig, love of the neighbor is not merely the first step on the path to redemption, the good deed that might help make the world a better place in some hypothetical future, but its realization *now,* the immanent production of its transcendental conditions. The nearness of the neighbor materializes the imminence of redemption, releasing the here and the now from the fetters of teleology in the infinitesimal calculus of proximity.[25]

---

22. Walter Benjamin, "Theses on the Philosophy of History," in *Illuminations,* trans. Harry Zohn (New York: Harcourt, Brace, 1968), 263.

23. "The effect of the love of 'neighbor' is that 'Anyone' and 'all the world' thus belong together and, for the world of redemption, thereby generate a factuality which wholly corresponds to the reality effected, in creation, through the collaboration of that which is general in a limited sense with that which is distinctive in a limited sense. For the world of redemption, absolute factuality derives from the fact that whoever be momentarily my neighbor represents all the world for me in full validity" (Franz Rosenzweig, *The Star of Redemption,* trans. William Hallo [Notre Dame, IN: University of Notre Dame Press, 1985], 236).

24. Ibid., 234–35; translation of *Der Stern der Erlösung* (Frankfurt: Suhrkamp Verlag, 1988), 262.

25. Recall the last line of Walter Benjamin's "Theses on the Philosophy of History," where he describes the nonhomogeneity of messianic time: "For every second of time was the strait gate through which the Messiah might enter." This immanent messianism disrupts teleological narratives of so-

Giorgio Agamben has linked Schmitt's account of the exceptionality of the sovereign with the seemingly antithetical figure he retrieves from Roman law: the *homo sacer,* the man who can be killed with impunity but cannot be sacrificed. According to Agamben, the axis of the political stretches between sovereign and *homo sacer:* "At the two extreme limits of the [political] order, the sovereign and *homo sacer* present two symmetrical figures that have the same structure and are correlative: the sovereign is the one with respect to whom all men are potentially *homines sacri,* and *homo sacer* is the one with respect to whom all men act as sovereigns."[26] Agamben argues that the *homo sacer* is a figure of the biopolitical ground of the political, humanity reduced to bare (and mere) life that may be taken away with impunity. Sovereignty is exemplified and *universalized* as the conditions of subjectivity, not in the determination of the identity of the Friend and the Enemy and the consequent decision to go to war (as in Schmitt), but in exercising the prerogative to kill the *homo sacer.* Agamben writes that finally *homo sacer* and the sovereign are united by the fact that "in each case we find ourselves confronted with a bare life that has been separated from its context and that, so to speak surviving its death, is for this very reason incompatible with the human world."[27] Eric Santner and Slavoj Žižek have both connected the *homo sacer* and the biblical figure of the neighbor, thus suggesting the further linkage between sovereign and neighbor.[28] This connection helps us clarify the point that the conditions of the political theology of the neighbor cannot be separated from those of the sovereign, but must be understood as their supplement—just as the biblical injunctions to love God and to love the neighbor are combined in both Judaism and Christianity as inseparable, the one finding its fulfillment in the other. Both sovereign and neighbor fall out of the world of the everyday, the situation of regulative law: the sovereign, for the sake of that world, the neighbor, for the sake of its redemption.

---

cial redemption, insisting that messianic temporality is precisely the time of the now (*Jetztzeit*), the moment that is no longer identical to itself or part of a teleological history (Benjamin, *Illuminations,* 264).

26. Agamben, *Homo Sacer,* 84.

27. Ibid., 100.

28. Santner writes that the *Muselmann,* Primo Levi's emblem for the radical evil of the camps and Agamben's exemplar of *homo sacer,* is "the ultimate—and therewith impossible—embodiment of the *neighbor*" ("Miracles Happen," p. 100 in this volume). Žižek argues that the ethical act of the *refuseniks,* the Israeli soldiers who refused to participate in immoral acts against Palestinians, reduced to the state of *homo sacer* in the occupied territories, was to treat the Palestinians "as *neighbors* in the strict Judeo-Christian sense" ("From *Homo Sacer* to the Neighbor," in *Welcome to the Desert of the Real* [London: Verso, 2002], 116).

Schmitt's claim that all political concepts are secularized religious concepts suggests that we should be able to locate a secularized concept of the neighbor in political theory. And indeed, we find two strong gestures toward such a project in texts by Theodor Adorno and Hannah Arendt, examples that will extend our consideration of the political theology of the neighbor. In a remarkable essay on Kierkegaard's *Works of Love,* Adorno is strikingly ambivalent about Kierkegaard's account of love and the neighbor, until he comes to regard it as an example of Kierkegaard's own ambivalence. At first, Adorno criticizes Kierkegaard for his reduction of the neighbor to an abstraction, without specificity or particularity. Adorno is disturbed by Kierkegaard's elimination of the actual neighbor, who becomes merely contingent—anyone can stand for "the general principle of the otherness or the universal human." Indeed, the ideal object of love, according to Kierkegaard, is the *dead* neighbor, precisely because no reciprocity (which reduces love to the economics of gift exchange) can be expected of the dead, nor do they have any of the annoyingly particular traits that interfere with the purity of love for the living.[29] Given these assumptions, Adorno writes, "the overstraining of the transcendence of love threatens, at any given moment, to become transformed into the darkest hatred of man."[30] Yet it is precisely Kierkegaard's "misanthropy," the result of his abandonment of the external world for the internal one, that gives him singular insight into the situation of modern society and its defining absence, the neighbor. According to Adorno,

Kierkegaard is unaware of the demonic consequence that his insistence actually leaves the world to the devil. For what can loving one's neighbor mean, if one can neither help him nor interfere with a setting of the world which makes such help impossible? Kierkegaard's doctrine of impotent mercifulness bring to the fore the deadlock which the concept of the neighbor necessarily meets today. The neighbor no longer exists. In modern society, the relations of men have been "reified" to such an extent that the neighbor cannot behave spontaneously to the neighbor for longer than an instant.[31]

29. Slavoj Žižek, however, is skeptical of Kierkegaard's argument and suggests Kierkegaard's preference for the dead neighbor is for the sake of avoiding the other's jouissance: "the dead neighbor means the neighbor deprived of the annoying excess of *jouissance* which makes him or her unbearable. So it is clear where Kierkegaard cheats: in trying to sell us, as the authentic difficult act of love, what is in fact an escape from the effort of authentic love. Love for the dead neighbor is an easy feast: it basks in its own perfection, indifferent to its object" (*Revolution at the Gates: Žižek on Lenin* [New York: Verso, 2002], 214).

30. Theodor Adorno, "On Kierkegaard's Doctrine of Love," *Studies in Philosophy and Social Science* 8 (1939–1940): 417, 419.

31. Ibid., 420.

For Adorno, Kierkegaard's lack of interest in the particularity of the neighbor signals that his project must be read as social critique: the only neighbor we can love is the dead one, because the neighbor as such is dead, has disappeared from modernity. Adorno suggests that the strength of Kierkegaard's account of neighbor-love derives from its anti-Hegelian historiography; just as Benjamin was able to glean signs of redemption from the natural history of decline, so Adorno argues that Kierkegaard "conceives progress itself as the history of advancing decay."[32] Thus, it is precisely in his elimination of the real neighbor that Kierkegaard points to the social conditions that have made neighbor relations impossible. Kierkegaard's condemnation of "worldly happiness" as impoverished compared with the happiness of eternity is not merely the Christian ideology of deferred pleasure, according to Adorno, but points to the real poverty, "civic inequality," and "universal injustice" that concepts of so-called welfare conceal.[33]

In her study of Hannah Arendt, Seyla Benhabib proposes that Arendt's *The Origins of Totalitarianism* owes key methodological concepts, such as "configuration" and "crystallization of elements," and perhaps even its sense of the word "origin" to Walter Benjamin's *Origins of the German Tragic Drama*, where Benjamin first considers Schmitt's notion of political theology.[34] According to Arendt, what unites fascism and communism, despite drastic differences in their origins and ideologies, is the fact that the collectivization of the people as a mass in modernity, whether called a proletariat, the *Volk,* or a concentration camp, has the paradoxical effect of increasing social isolation and destroying the political as such.[35] In the final chapter of *The Origins of Totalitarianism,* Arendt describes the form of life that follows the disappearance of authentically political sociality as "organized loneliness."[36] The "loneliness" of totalitarian regimes must be distinguished from that of the modern "man of the crowd" of Baudelaire or Poe, the "man without qualities," both alienated and sustained by the endless currents of people circulating along

---

32. Ibid., 424.

33. Ibid., 425.

34. Selya Benhabib, *The Reluctant Modernism of Hannah Arendt* (Thousand Oaks, CA: Sage, 1996), 64.

35. Here Arendt comes close to Schmitt's argument about the "total state," which, however, as Julien Freund argues, is not a theory of totalitarianism, but "hyperstatism in the sense that the state increasingly intervenes in all domains—the economy, culture, etc.—in the form of the welfare state. It no longer deals only with politics but tends to invade all sectors of social life" (Julien Freund, "Schmitt's Political Thought," *Telos* 102 [Winter 1995]: 13). Just as much as for Arendt, the state that goes beyond its rightful business, the determination of friend-enemy distinctions, is no longer authentically political.

36. Hannah Arendt, *The Origins of Totalitarianism* (New York: Harcourt, Brace, 1973), 478.

the urban streets. Totalitarian isolation is more like the loneliness of some strange Leviathan, the multitude fused into a single monstrous body; as Arendt writes of the populace under totalitarianism, "it is as though their plurality had disappeared into One Man of gigantic dimensions." [37] Just as much as it erases the possibility of a social relationship by fostering paranoid structures of suspicion and mutual surveillance, totalitarianism destroys interiority and the discursive conditions necessary for thinking:

All thinking, strictly speaking, is done in solitude and is a dialogue between me and myself; but this dialogue of the two-in-one does not lose contact with the world of my fellow-men because they are represented in the self with whom I lead the dialogue of thought. The problem of solitude is that this two-in-one needs the others in order to become one again: one unchangeable individual whose identity can never be mistaken for that of any other. For the confirmation of my identity I depend entirely upon other people; and it is the great saving grace of companionship for solitary men that it makes them "whole" again, saves them from the dialogue of thought in which one remains always equivocal, restores the identity which makes them speak with the single voice of one unexchangeable person. [38]

Arendt argues that thinking is a *social* discursive process that can only arise in *solitude,* and as such must be distinguished from the loneliness of totalitarian society, which, even in a crowd, only talks to itself. The dialectic of real thought requires that the difference which defines the social be taken on as self-difference, self-alienation: we become singular, "unexchangeable," only insofar as we have allowed ourselves to enter into discourse with internalized "fellow-men." For Arendt, totalitarian loneliness is not simply a function of the disappearance of traditional social relationships of neighboring, but results from the overwhelming *presence* of this neighbor, who is neither fully interiorized nor exteriorized, but whose unbearable closeness makes the self "equivocal," interchangeable rather than singular, and thus threatens its ability to speak to others within a symbolic order.

For Arendt, the primary characteristic of the failure of social relations under totalitarianism is the disappearance of the space between people and the correlative unleashing of "a principle destructive for all human living-together." Unlike tyranny, which is still a form of politics, totalitarianism is the annihilation of the political: "By destroying the space

37. Ibid., 465–66.
38. Ibid., 476.

between men and pressing men against each other, even the productive potentialities of isolation are annihilated. . . . if this practice is compared with that of tyranny, it seems as if a way had been found to set the desert itself into motion, to let loose a sand storm that could cover all parts of the inhabited earth."[39] Arendt's analysis suggests that what is lost in totalitarianism is the spacing proper to the function of the neighbor. To destroy the relation of the neighbor is to eliminate the breathing space that keeps the subject in proper relationship to the Other, neither too close nor too far, but in proximity, the "nearness" that neighboring entails. The emptiness of the social sphere, the "desert" left by tyranny, itself materializes as a horrific "sand storm" in totalitarianism, a solidification of the void that fills up all space, allowing no room for either subject or society.[40]

Whether or not Arendt's account of totalitarianism is an adequate theory of fascism or communism, the distinction she draws between "tyranny" and "totalitarianism" is useful for reflecting on the nature of political theology. If tyranny is still political—and indeed, in some ways embodies the essence of the political—why is totalitarianism no longer political, according to Arendt? The malaise of "loneliness" that she describes under totalitarian conditions might be explainable as a social or cultural symptom, not indicative of a new form (or failure) of politics; but it is precisely the disappearance of the space of the neighbor that for Arendt marks the loss of the political as such. By suggesting that the disappearance of the neighbor, lost in the fused body politic without organs, is the key event in the final dissolution of the political in modernity, Arendt's comments imply that the neighbor is a category of essential concern for political theory and not merely a function of ethics, a category of social relation crucial to the maintenance of the sphere of the political as such.

39. Ibid., 478.

40. Arendt suggests that for Saint Augustine the commandment to neighbor-love denaturalizes the mere "living together" that characterizes unredeemed life, desedimenting the social in order to allow for individuation. That is, neighbor-love paradoxically both requires and effects the "isolation" of the individual—a mode of isolation that is the condition of the higher communion of the heavenly city: "I never love the neighbor for his own sake, only for the sake of divine grace. This indirectness, which is unique to love of neighbor, puts an even more radical stop to the self-evident living together in the earthly city. . . . We are commanded to love our neighbor, to practice mutual love, only because in doing so we love Christ. This indirectness breaks up social relations by turning them into provisional ones. . . . In the city of God these relations are made radically relative by eternity. . . . The indirectness of the mutual relations of believers is just what allows each to grasp the other's whole being which lies in God's presence. In contrast, any worldly community envisions the being of the human race, but not that of the individual. The individual as such can only be grasped in the *isolation* in which the believer stands before God" (Hannah Arendt, *Love and Saint Augustine* [Chicago: University of Chicago Press, 1996], 111; my emphasis).

Psychoanalysis and the Neighbor

Arendt's account of the social and linguistic conditions of totalitarianism can be understood in terms of the phenomenon that Lacan calls "holophrasis," an expression he borrows from linguistics, where it refers to a single word used as a phrase—for example, the exclamation "fire!" Lacan associates holophrasis with psychosis, as well as with psychosomatic afflictions; in both cases, suffering is not organized in the manner of neurotic symptoms, via condensation and displacement, but through the direct petrifaction of the signifier onto the body. In Lacan's early accounts of holophrasis in the 1950s, he argues that it materializes the "limit" between language and the body, "the ambiguous intermediary zone between the symbolic and the imaginary." Later, in the 1960s, he defines holophrasis as the fusion of a primary signifier with the other signifiers in a symbolic system. The gap between these signifiers, S_1 and S_2, is the space where a subject should precipitate, and in a discursive field where there is no such gap, there is no room for subjectivity, only for what Lacan calls a kind of "monolithic" autism.[41]

When the proximity of the neighbor collapses, paranoid delusions and hallucinations emerge, often precisely in the place and the guise of the (missing) neighbor. Consider Lacan's emblematic case in seminar 3, *The Psychoses*, the psychotic woman who hears the utterance "Sow!" when she remarks to her neighbor, "I've just been to the pork butcher's." Lacan emphasizes that the woman's hallucination is triggered by "the intrusion of the neighbor" into the *délire à deux* she shares with her equally psychotic sister: "she receives her own speech from him [the neighbor's lover], but not inverted, her own speech is in the other who is herself, her reflection in the mirror, her counterpart."[42] Rather than receiving her signifiers back from the other in inverted form, according to the neurotic logic of desire and the symptom, her statement returns to her unsymbolized, raw, as aural hallucination. The exclamation "sow!" is

41. In seminar 11 Lacan uses the notion of holophrase, where a single term takes on a wide range of grammatical functions, to explain the psychosomatic effect: "I will go so far as to formulate that, when there is no interval between S_1 and S_2, when the first dyad of signifiers become solidified, holophrased, we have the model for a whole series of cases. . . . This solidity, this mass seizure of the primitive signifying chain, is what forbids the dialectical opening that is manifested in the phenomenon of belief" (Lacan, *The Seminar of Jacques Lacan*, book 11: *The Four Fundamental Concepts of Psychoanalysis*, trans. Alan Sheridan [New York: W. W. Norton, 1981], 237–38). See Alexandre Stevens, "L'holophrase, entre psychose et psychosomatique," *Ornicar?* 42 (1987): 45–79; and Eric Laurent, "Institution of the Phantasm, Phantasms of the Institution," www.ch-freudien-be.org/Papers/Txt/Laurent-fc4.pdf.

42. Jacques Lacan, *The Seminar of Jacques Lacan*, book 3: *The Psychoses, 1955–1956* (New York: W. W. Norton, 1993), 49, 51.

holophrastic, a fused isotope of speech that embodies the social void. The appearance of the real neighbor shatters the insular specularity of her relation with her sister and triggers the emergence of the neighbor in the real, as the grotesque literalization of the distorted limit between imaginary and symbolic.

It is not an accident that Lacan chooses to exemplify psychosis with the delusion of the neighbor. Throughout the seminar, Lacan returns to a comment Freud makes to Fliess in his early Draft H on paranoia, sent with a letter to Fliess in January of 1885, a biblically allusive aphorism that seems to hold the key to the truth about psychosis (at one point in his seminar, Lacan writes it on the board as a kind of scriptural revelation): "In every instance the *delusional idea* is maintained with the same energy with which another, intolerably distressing, idea is warded off from the ego. They [paranoiacs] love their *delusions as they love themselves*. That is the secret." (*Sie lieben also den* Wahn wie sich selbst. *Das ist das Geheimnis.*)[43] Freud's comments adumbrate his later theory of psychosis as the repudiation of an unbearable self-judgment through its projection onto the world; in Lacan's reformulation of this mechanism as psychotic "foreclosure," delusion and hallucination are the return in the real of what has been refused from the symbolic. Psychosis can manifest as a personality disorder, a series of wildly shifting moods or even discrete personae, because the psychotic identifies with the reality he has created through projective repudiation. Hence, it is not that the paranoiac "has" a delusion; he *is* his delusion, the threatening yet coherent account of reality that serves as a carapace against an even more disturbing attack from inside. Thus, Freud writes that the psychotic "loves his delusion as himself" because his self is built out of those very delusions.

Although Freud does not call special attention to it, Lacan emphasizes that the reference here is to Leviticus 19:18, the famous injunction to "love your neighbor as yourself":

There is an echo here, which should be given full weight, of what is said in the commandment, *Love thy neighbor as thyself.* . . . Freud had the profound impression that something in the psychotic's relationship to his delusion goes beyond the workings of the signified and meanings. . . . there is an affection here, an attachment, an essential bringing to presence, the mystery of which remains almost total for us, which is that the delusional, the psychotic, clings to his delusion as to something which is himself.[44]

---

43. Sigmund Freud, *The Standard Edition of the Complete Psychological Works of Sigmund Freud* (London: Hogarth, 1958), 1:212; *Briefe an Wilhelm Fliess* (Frankfort: S. Fischer, 1986), 110.

44. Lacan, *Psychoses*, 216.

It is as if Freud's allusion to the commandment to love the neighbor instantiates the proper symbolic relationship to the other, as a talisman against the appearance of the neighbor in the real: be sure to love your neighbor as yourself, because if you don't, you risk the emergence of the *delusion* of the neighbor in its place, as a horrific holophrasis of the failed social relation that will take the place of your self.

But why does Freud derive the formula for paranoia from the biblical injunction to love the neighbor? Why does he announce it in this epigrammatic, even oracular, voice as "the secret"?[45] Lacan's repeated insistence in his seminar on the psychoses on the centrality of Freud's expression leads to two linked explanations: on the one hand, Freud borrows the syntactical *structure* of the phrase in order to articulate the pathologies of paranoid delusion and their normative implications for the psychology of the subject; on the other, the *significations* that emerge from that structure are linked to what we might call Freud's determination of the psychoanalytic subject as primarily an ethical rather than psychological category, constituted by the weight of reality first encountered as the neighbor. Freud's work on paranoia is a key step in formulating an ethics of psychoanalysis around the encounter with the neighbor at the impossible intersection of family and society, since paranoia crystallizes the traumatic experience of the social in a form imperfectly mediated by the stabilizing triangles of the family. Thus, while paranoia, according to Lacan, is caused by the foreclosure of the primal signifier he calls the "Name-of-the-Father," resulting in the failure to dialecticize the maternal and paternal agencies of the family romance, its symptoms typically cluster around the fundamental term of the social relationship, both element and irritant—the neighbor.[46]

The allusion to the biblical neighbor in Freud's Draft H draws our attention to the similarities between the paranoiac's relationship to his or her delusion and that of the subject of cognition to the figure Freud calls the *Nebenmensch* (an unusual German word meaning something like "the next-man" or "adjoining-person") a few months later in the long draft to Fliess entitled the *Project for a Scientific Psychology:*

---

45. In his announcement of the "secret" of delusion, Freud takes the theatrical tone he will assume when he proclaims, six months later to the day, that the "secret" of psychoanalysis had been revealed to him in his dream of Irma's injection, which he hoped would be commemorated with a plaque.

46. For another example, see Freud's 1896 study of defense, "Analysis of a Case of Chronic Paranoia," where he exemplifies paranoid symptomology through the hallucinations and "interpretive delusions" that convinced a young woman that "she was despised by her neighbors" and the subject of their gossip (Freud, *Standard Edition,* 3:174–85).

Let us suppose that the object which furnishes the perception resembles the subject—a *fellow human-being* [*Nebenmensch*]. If so, the theoretical interest [taken in it] is also explained by the fact that *such* an object [*ein solches Objekt*] was simultaneously the [subject's] first satisfying object and further his first hostile object, as well as his sole helping power. For this reason it is in relation to a fellow human-being that a human-being learns to cognize [*Am Nebenmenschen lernt darum der Mensch erkennen*]. Then the perceptual complexes proceeding from this fellow human-being will in part be new and non-comparable—his *features* [*seine Züge*], for instance, in the visual sphere; but other visual perceptions—e.g. those of the movements of his hands—will coincide in the subject with memories of quite similar visual impressions of his own, of his own body, [memories] which are associated with memories of movements experienced by himself. Other perceptions of the object too—if, for instance, he screams—will awaken the memory of his [the subject's] own screaming and at the same time of his own experiences of pain. Thus the complex of the fellow human-being [*Komplex des Nebenmenschen*] falls apart into two components, of which one makes an impression by its constant structure and stays together as a *thing* [*als Ding*], while the other can be *understood* by the activity of memory—that is, it can be traced back to information from [the subject's] own body.[47]

The subject learns to think in relation to its perceptions of the Nebenmensch, a neighboring human being, a fellow creature (not, it seems, the parents, nor a complete stranger, but perhaps, from the sound of its screams, another child), in a scene where the family romance and the social contract find their common root and their mutual contradiction. The Nebenmensch is the neighbor as "the adjoining person" standing between the subject and its primary maternal object, the uncanny complex of perceptions through which subjective reality divides into the representable world of cognition and the "unassimilable" element that Freud calls *das Ding*, "the thing." Freud's comments on *das Ding* here and in his later essay "Negation" are two central textual points of reference for Lacan's reconception of "the real" in the 1960s. In seminar 7, *The Ethics of Psychoanalysis*, Lacan defines *das Ding* as the encounter with something in the other that is completely alien—an intrusive foreignness that goes beyond the compositions of self and other, and their politicizations as "friend" and "enemy." The Thing materializes the constitutive ambiguity of the primal object, the trauma of its uncertain

47. Freud, *Standard Edition*, 1:331 (translation modified); Sigmund Freud, *Aus den Anfängen der Psychoanalyse* (London: Imago, 1950), 415–16. Words and phrases in square brackets, except those taken from the original German text, are interpollated by the editors of the *Standard Edition*.

disposition between excessive presence and radical absence. Lacan describes the encounter with the Nebenmensch as a mode of *mediation;* the Thing is that part of the other that is "mute," but the neighbor speaks and thus forms a template for the subject's emergence: "It is through the intermediary of the *Nebenmensch* as speaking subject that everything that has to do with the thought processes is able to take shape in the subjectivity of the subject."[48] The subject accumulates as the retraversed paths of associative representations that both draw toward and away from the Thing encysted in the Nebenmensch, standing between the subject and the void left by the inevitable withdrawal of maternal succor.[49]

According to Freud, cognition emerges literally "vis-à-vis" the Nebenmensch: some strange *Zug* (feature or trait, but equally line or stroke) in the neighbor's face both initiates and limits the comparison of its attributes with traces from earlier memories through the linked processes Freud distinguishes as "judging" and "remembering." According to Freud, judgment is the act of "dissection" which cuts away unfamiliar, hence uncategorizable, components of the Nebenmensch from familiar ones, establishing a correlation between the Nebenmensch and the subject's first ambivalent experience of an object. Memory, on the other hand, sifts and collates the attributes which have emerged from judgment and, by comparing them with mnemonic traces of the subject's experience of his or her own body, introduces a second similarity, now between the Nebenmensch and the subject. This secondary identification is reflected in the echo between *Mensch* and *Nebenmensch* in Freud's aphoristic phrase *"Am Nebenmenschen lernt darum der Mensch erkennen"* [In relation to a fellow human-being, a human-being learns to cognize]. Indeed, it is precisely a self whose being lies in the indirection of its knowledge that emerges in the aftermath of the encounter with the Nebenmensch. Moreover, whereas the affinity established in judgment between the Nebenmensch and the primordial object is based on an act of winnowing the singular "thing," the real kernel of perception, from its predicates or movements, the comparison between the Nebenmensch and the subject in memory involves only elements which had already

---

48. Lacan comments on Freud's articulation of the mediating function of the *Nebenmensch* later in the seminar: "the formula is striking to the extent that it expresses powerfully the idea of a beside yet alike, separation and identity" (Lacan, *Ethics of Psychoanalysis,* 39, 51).

49. Ibid., 52. The Thing is both the *occasion* for representation and that which *resists* representation, an excess or leftover that informs Lacan's developing notion of the *objet a* in the following seminars.

been established as comparable, as within the field of representation. In this sense, while judgment originally constellates the neighbor as both "helpful" and "hostile," affiliated with the primordial occasion of both love and hate, memory integrates that ambivalence into an imaginary and symbolic network by casting the neighbor as the reflection of the subject's body, as "like" the self.

To the extent that the Nebenmensch is the "next person," merely contiguous with the subject and its maternal source of both pleasure and unpleasure, it represents any and every other person to whom the subject is bound in a relationship of competitive similarity, an imaginary "equality" enforced—more or less—as distributive justice in the social world by civil and moral codes. But insofar as the Nebenmensch is always *this* next person, always embodied in a particular person who fills the arbitrary place of the neighbor, it materializes an uncanniness within the social relationship, an enjoyment that resists sympathetic identification and "understanding," linking the self and other instead in a bond of mutual aggression. In this sense, the Nebenmensch embodies both sides of the reality principle: on the one hand, it functions in the service of the pleasure principle, striving to achieve constancy by enforcing the minimum level of restriction necessary to maintain both body and body politic; and on the other, as the agent of the death drive, it threatens to subvert the social order by manifesting the excluded scandal of the real that subtends it. Thus, rather than standing for a secondary realm of social mediation and abstract intellection that reflects (or reflects on) a more fundamental world of maternal and paternal objects and desires, the Nebenmensch marks the incommensurability between representation and what exceeds it, the antagonism that lodges an impossibility at the heart of both social and familial relationships.

We can perhaps better account for the ethical weight of Freud's description of the encounter with the Nebenmensch by understanding this dynamic as a kind of translation and even transvaluation of the Levitical injunction to "love thy neighbor as thyself," a phrase, we recall, Freud had alluded to in his discussion of paranoia a few months before writing the *Project for a Scientific Psychology*. In Freud's account of cognition, the dual processes of judgment and memory echo and rearticulate the double gesture of the commandment to "love thy neighbor" / "as thyself." In the act of *judgment,* the subject experiences the Nebenmensch with the sundering intensity of its ambivalent love for the primal object. In *memory,* the subject turns that affect onto itself, incorporating the alterity of the Nebenmensch through specular identification.

Thus, in the birth of cognitive thinking and memory out of ethical judgment, the subject loves (and hates) his neighbor "as himself"—as a self, however, already inhabited by the alterity of the neighbor.

Freud writes that "people become paranoiac over things [*Dinge*] that they cannot put up with" and instead project onto the external world.[50] In seminar 7, *The Ethics of Psychoanalysis*, Lacan specifies those "things" as *das Ding* by suggesting that the "moving force of paranoia is essentially the rejection of a certain support in the symbolic order, of that specific support around which the division between the two sides of the relationship to *das Ding* operates."[51] By failing to segregate the unsymbolized real from symbolic reality, a division which, according to the paternal imperative, ought to be established by "judgment," the thing-aspect of the Nebenmensch is not fully separated from its attributes and bleeds over into the realm of cognition in the form of delusions and hallucinations. Thus, whereas the neurotic subject responds to the call to *judge* the Nebenmensch, symbolizing the difference between the Thing and its attributes and identifying with that difference, the paranoiac *fails to judge* the Nebenmensch and, refusing to articulate the space of symbolic difference, is lost in the specter of real-ized signifiers, the materiality and grammatical patterns of language deprived of signification.[52]

Lacan argues that the chain of signifiers that constitutes the subject in their movement around the Thing functions according to the reality principle, through which the incursions of unbearable stimulation are both endured (reality testing as *sampling* reality) and avoided (reality testing as *repudiation* of reality):

What one finds in *das Ding* is the true secret. For the reality principle has a secret that . . . is paradoxical. If Freud speaks of the reality principle, it is in order to reveal to us that from a certain point of view it is always defeated; it only manages to affirm itself at the margin. And this is so by reason of a kind of pressure that one might say, if things didn't, in fact, go much further, Freud calls not "the vital needs" . . . but *die Not des Lebens* in the German text. An infinitely stronger phrase. Something that *wishes*. "Need" and not "needs" [*Le besoin et non pas les besoins*]. Pressure, urgency. The

50. Freud, *Standard Edition*, 1:207; *Briefe*, 106–7.
51. Lacan, *Ethics of Psychoanalysis*, 54.
52. In his late essay "Negation," Freud describes two distinct moments of judgment: the first, "judgement of attribution," in which the world is divided into the "good" and the "bad" by a primal act of affirmation, *Bejahung*; and the second, "judgement of existence," in which the rediscovery of the lost object is confirmed by negation, *Verneinung* (*Standard Edition*, 19:235). Lacan argues that psychotic foreclosure involves the failure of the primal act of judgment as judgment of attribution in his essay "On a Question Preliminary to Any Possible Treatment of Psychosis" (*Écrits*, [1977], 200–201).

state of *Not* is the state of emergency in life [*l'état d'urgence de la vie*]. . . . As soon as we try to articulate the reality principle so as to make it depend on the physical world to which Freud's purpose seems to require us to relate it, it is clear that it functions, in fact, to isolate the subject from reality.[53]

Echoing Freud's announcement of the "secret" of paranoia in the grammar of neighbor-love, Lacan declares that *das Ding* is the "true secret" of the Nebenmensch and the reality principle. Far from being merely a mechanism through which the pleasure principle's tendency for immediate satisfaction is modified in order to bring it into accord with the requirements of reality, Lacan argues that the reality principle functions "to isolate the subject from reality." But this process is only partly successful; that aspect of reality that cannot be represented leaks through, as the *real* of life. In Lacan's striking biopolitical formulation here, the encounter with *das Ding* in the Nebenmensch, the materialization of radical urgency beyond biological necessity, constitutes a "state of emergency," *l'état d'urgence*. Moreover, this emergency figures not only in life, but *as* life: for the speaking subject, life itself is an ongoing crisis in matter, in which disequilibrium and non-self-identity are no longer the exception but have become the norm.[54] Lacan's use of a political vocabulary here suggests that, even before the constitution of a body politic, the subject's body is *already* political, insofar as it is the site of a crisis that requires a determining *choice:* "It is then in relation to the original *Ding* that the first orientation, the first choice, the first seat of subjective orientation takes place."[55] The Thing in the Nebenmensch is the emergency through which the subject arises as self-sovereign; that is, a decision that will determine and legitimate the specific forms in which it will live must have been made, a decision made from the heterological space of the unconscious.

Lacan associates this primordial choice with what Freud calls the "choice of neurosis," *Neurosenwahl,* and describes three modalities in which this choice may unfold: as hysteria, where the primary object pro-

53. Lacan, *Ethics of Psychoanalysis,* 46; *Le séminaire, livre 7: L'éthique de la psychanalyse* (Paris: Seuil, 1986), 58.

54. My thinking here is informed by Eric Santner's comments on the "constitutive 'too much-ness' that characterizes the psyche." Santner writes, "in the view I am distilling from the work of Freud and Rosenzweig, God is above all the name for the pressure to be alive to the world, to open to the too much of pressure generated in large measure by the uncanny presence of my neighbor" (*On the Psychotheology of Everyday Life: Reflections on Freud and Rosenzweig* [Chicago: University of Chicago Press, 2001], 8–9).

55. Lacan, *Ethics of Psychoanalysis,* 54

vided insufficient satisfaction; as obsessional neurosis, where the object gave too much satisfaction; or as paranoia, which involves what Freud calls *Versagen des Glaubens,* a loss of faith in the neighbor's Thing: "the paranoid doesn't believe in that first stranger in relation to whom the subject is obliged to take his bearings."[56] Lacan argues that Freud's notion of *Glauben* here goes beyond the psychological or even epistemological sense of "confidence" or "certainty": "The use of the term belief [*la croyance*] seems to me to be emphasized in a less psychological sense than first seems to be the case. The radical attitude of the paranoid, as designated by Freud, concerns the deepest level of the relationship of man to reality, namely what is articulated as faith [*la foi*]. Here you can see easily how the connection with a different perspective is created that comes to meet it."[57] Although the hallucinatory symptomology of paranoia is often imagined as believing in things that aren't real, in fact, Lacan argues, it is quite the opposite: the paranoiac *fails to believe,* not in one reality or another, but in the transcendental element (the Name of the Father) that should demarcate the difference between *das Ding* and the world of representation and hold the space between them open. By suggesting that *Glauben* here implies a discourse closer to religion than psychology, Lacan discloses the other side of Freud's "secret" of paranoia: when Freud writes that the paranoiac's secret is that he "loves his delusion as himself," "delusion" has literally taken the place of the "neighbor" from the injunction in the Book of Leviticus. Lacan here points to Freud's allusion to the biblical neighbor and further connects it with Freud's notion of the Nebenmensch: when the paranoiac breaks faith with the neighbor and refuses to encounter the Thing, the resulting delusions and hallucinations which swarm in the place of the missing mediator represent a failure of judgment.

In Draft H Freud narrates another case that exemplifies this tendency for paranoid symptoms to attach to the figure of the neighbor. Freud describes the paranoid symptoms developed by one of his patients in her relationships with two sorts of neighbors, inside and outside the house. The woman's paranoia originated with the "enigmatic man" who for awhile boarded with her brother, sister, and herself, a "fellow worker" or comrade [*einen Genossen*] "on the most companionable and sociable terms" with this family of siblings. After the boarder left, however, the woman confided to her sister that he had one day made sexual advances

56. Ibid., 53–54; *L'éthique de la psychanalyse,* 67.
57. Lacan, *Ethics of Psychoanalysis,* 54; *L'éthique de la psychanalyse,* 67.

to her, and her paranoia developed as a delusion that her female neighbors were gossiping about her relationship with the man:

She had been tidying up the rooms while he was still in bed. He called her to his side, and when she unsuspectingly went, put his penis in her hand. There was no sequel to the scene; soon afterward the stranger [*der Fremde*] left.

In the course of the next few years [she] fell ill, began to complain, and eventually developed unmistakable delusions of observation and persecution with the following content. The women neighbors [*Nachbarinnen*] were pitying her for having been jilted and for still waiting for this man to come back; they were always making hints of that kind to her, kept saying all kinds of things to her about the man, and so on.[58]

Freud links the woman's delusions of her neighbors' gossip with her self-reproaches for having enjoyed the sexual advance of the boarder, accusations which, in being projected onto an external agent, Freud reasons, are kept from her ego: "the judgment about her had been transposed outward." But, we might object, if the woman's paranoia serves as a defense against criticism, clearly she suffers no less in externally objectifying it by means of projection. We should understand Freud's explanation as implying not so much that her delusion protects her from being the target of criticism, whether her own or that of others, but that her paranoia relieves her of the burden of being critical, from the responsibility of judging rather than the opprobrium of being judged. That is, insofar as the woman's paranoia lies in her refusal to accede to the imperative to judge the Nebenmensch, something in the Nebenmensch returns—not, however, in the figurative symptoms in which the repressed returns in neurosis, but real-ized in the judgment of the social neighbor.

Hence the woman's self-reproach, her "Vorwurf," for enjoying rather than judging the boarder's advances, is itself, in Freud's later expression, "verworfen," foreclosed or repudiated in the form of the gossip of the *Nachbarinnen*. But the neighbor is not confined to the exterior of the household; rather, if the neighbor constitutes the "secret," *das Geheimnis,* of paranoia, it is an uncanny secret that threatens to disturb the home, *das Heim,* from within. For insofar as the male boarder who serves as the occasion of her delusion is here referred to as her *Genossen,* her fellow worker or comrade, the function of the neighbor is already located inside the house. Etymologically, the *Genossen* is the one with whom we enjoy—in this case, the companion with whom the woman shares her bread and home. Like the English word "boarder," which derives both

58. Freud, *Standard Edition,* 1:207–8; *Briefe,* 107–8.

from the table on which we eat and the edge or margin that separates inside from outside, this *Genossen* is the element of exteriority that has infiltrated the domestic space.[59] As the neighbor within the house, uncomfortably proximate to the family hearth, the boarder becomes *der Fremde* after the sexual assault, the internal stranger who signals transgressive enjoyment that disturbs the home's tranquility and disrupts the very distinction between inside and outside on which the household is built. The external neighbors, the *Nachbarinnen* around whose glances and gossip the woman's symptoms collect, are the projection of the foreclosed internal neighbor, the boarder whose enjoyment had already troubled the borders of the home.

Insofar as the paranoiac forecloses the signifier of the paternal law that regulates the partition between the symbolic and the real, we could say that paranoia involves the failure to accede to the imperative to judge the Nebenmensch *qua* commandment. Hence, Freud's formulation of the structure of paranoia as "they love their delusion as themselves" reflects the paranoiac's refusal of the "thou shalt" implicit in the Levitical injunction, reducing the imperative to a statement, a mere description of reality bereft of the commandment that configures it in a symbolic order.[60] Whereas for the neurotic, the agency of the Name-of-the-Father mediates the subject's relationship with its primary maternal object, the psychotic's lack of this paternal metaphor reveals the overwhelming presence of *das Ding*, no longer shielded by the spacing required for refiguration or substitution. Hence, the paranoiac's too immediate experience of *das Ding* as it materializes in such objects as the neighbor's probing gaze and mocking gossip disrupts the familial structures of subjectivity. On the other hand, the neurotic subject, the subject as such, finds its place within the family circle demarcated by the Oedipus complex only at the cost of attenuating the social relation, which, in the face of the unbearable proximity of the neighbor, gives way to a social order itself modeled on the family. Whereas hysteria, according to Lacan, is the pathological variant of the normative familial neurosis that

59. The *Oxford English Dictionary* argues that *boarder,* although originally deriving from two distinct substantives, one meaning a plank or a table and the other meaning a rim or side, was already blended into one root in Old English (*Compact Edition of the Oxford English Dictionary* [New York: Oxford University Press, 1971], 238).

60. See Kierkegaard's commentary on the fact that love in the injunction to love the neighbor is in the form of an imperative, a duty. According to Kierkegaard, the only love that can be eternal, free of anxiety, jealousy, and hatred, is love that is commanded. Hence, paradoxically, neighbor-love is more free, more independent, than the spontaneous love based on preferential desire, which is merely the illusion of choice (Søren Kierkegaard, *Works of Love* [Princeton, NJ: Princeton University Press, 1995], 17–43).

manifests the impossibility of a sexual relationship, paranoia—ranging from what Freud calls "normal delusions of observation" to full-blown psychotic schizophrenia—indicates the impossibility constitutive of the social relationship: the unbearable proximity of community's fundamental particle, the neighbor.[61]

Lacan's repeated insistence on the "mystery" of Freud's utterance, "They love *their delusions as they love themselves*," suggests that he is intrigued by Freud's claim to have found "the secret" of paranoia not only in terms of the hidden content it might reveal, but also *as* mystery, occlusion of knowledge. Freud is himself clearly interested in the original injunction's grammatical structure, its formal cadence, in which the parallelism between *neighbor* and *self* prepares for his substitution of *delusion* for *neighbor*. But whereas both the original scriptural text and Freud's modifications of it in Draft H (and implicitly in the *Project for a Scientific Psychology*) seem to suggest the dialectical reciprocity and substitutability of their terms (whether between *self* and *neighbor* for the subject of the Levitical injunction, *self* and *Nebenmensch* for the normal neurotic, or *self* and *delusion* in the formula of paranoia), this apparent symmetry is misleading. The paranoid projection is not the result of a representational or figurative act; on the contrary, it is precisely the tropological function of the *as* that the paranoiac rejects in loving his delusion *as himself*—as Lacan writes, "He *literally* loves it like himself."[62] In refusing to tolerate the proximity of the Nebenmensch, the paranoiac literalizes what *should have been* a figure according to the paternal imperative and fixates on a real neighbor, not as a trope of the Nebenmensch, but as the refusal to trope as such.[63]

We can map the structure of psychosis described by Freud and Lacan across the dual axes of political theology: on the one hand, we have seen how the symptoms of psychosis, especially in its paranoid manifestations, tend to cluster along what we can think of as the horizontal axis defined by the imperative to *love the neighbor*. The vicious gossip and penetrating gaze of the neighbor become the site of overwhelming af-

---

61. Freud, *Standard Edition*, 1:208.
62. Lacan, *Psychoses*, 218; my emphasis.
63. Lacan returns to Freud's statement later in the psychoses seminar: "The characteristic of alienating degradation, of madness, that connotes the remnants of this practice which have been lost at the sociological plane provides us with an analogy with what takes place in the psychotic and gives meaning to the sentence from Freud I quoted to you the other day, namely, that the psychotic loves his delusion like himself. The psychotic can only apprehend the Other in the relation with the signifier, he lingers over a mere shell, an envelope, a shadow, the form of speech. The psychotic's Eros is located where speech is absent. It is there that he finds his supreme love" (*Psychoses*, 254).

fect—love, hate, and fear commingled in fragments of the social relationship. On the other hand, the presence or absence of the primary signifier of the symbolic order that Lacan calls "the Name-of-the-Father," the determining condition of psychosis, correlates with the vertical relationship implied by the commandment to *love God,* the theological imperative underlying the exceptional powers of sovereignty. In his reading of Racine's *Athaliah,* Lacan describes this signifier as the "quilting point" [*le point de capiton*] that organizes the symbolic structure of the play: "everything radiates out from and is organized around this signifier," which, in the paradigmatic case of *Athaliah,* is "fear," in the phrase "fear of God." Lacan writes that this signifier is "particularly ambivalent," easily shifting into its correlative divine affect, love; unlike the classical fear of the gods, "The fear of *God* . . . is the principle of wisdom and the foundation of the love of God. Moreover, this tradition is precisely our own."[64] Lacan argues that we live in a world radically transformed by the advent of monotheism and the condensation in it of a primal signifier that anchors us in a relationship with an exceptional God. And, according to Lacan, this has nothing to do with whether or not a particular individual believes: monotheism enacts a material and historical break that is absolute and irrecusable and that structures subjectivity thereafter. In Freud's discussion of the case of Daniel Paul Schreber, we see that for Dr. Schreber "love of God" in its most obscene literal form (the fantasy of being fucked by God) takes the place of his failed relationship to the symbolic order and his inability to assume his position in it as judge. According to Lacan, it is significant that this failure, in Schreber's case and many others, occurs in the *political* sphere:

Further still, the father's relation to this law [promulgated by the Name-of-the-Father] must be considered in itself, for one will find in it the reason for that paradox, by which the ravaging effects of the paternal figure are to be observed with particular frequency in cases where the father really has the function of a legislator or, at least has the upper hand, whether in fact he is one of those fathers who makes the laws or whether he poses as the pillar of the faith, as a paragon of integrity and devotion, as virtuous or as a virtuoso, by serving a work of salvation, of whatever object or lack of object, of nation or of birth, of safeguard or salubrity, of legacy or legality, of the pure, the impure or of empire [*du pur, du pire ou de l'empire*], all ideals that provide him with all too many opportunities of being in a posture of undeserving, inadequacy, even

---

64. Lacan, *Psychoses,* 266. In the Hebrew Bible, the word translated as *fear* of God, *yirah,* is closely associated with *love* of God. See Psalms 118:4, "Let those who fear the Lord declare, 'His steadfast love is eternal.'"

of fraud, and, in short, of excluding the Name-of-the-Father from its position in the signifier.[65]

The signifier of the Father is "sovereign" in its rule over the subject precisely insofar as it is the *exception* to the rules that govern the movement of signification. There is a point, at least hypothetically, when the subject hovers between neurosis and psychosis, even perhaps a zero degree where "primal repression," the installation of the paternal signifier, and "foreclosure," the *failure* to install such a signifier, have not yet been distinguished.[66] And this is the point when the subject is called upon to decide whether primal repression or foreclosure will define the political economy of his or her psyche.

Lacan poses the distinction between neurosis and psychosis as a question of love: "Where does the difference between someone who is psychotic and someone who isn't come from? It comes from the fact that for the psychotic a love relation that abolishes him as subject is possible insofar as it allows a radical heterogeneity of the Other. But this love is also a dead love."[67] Although the psychotic fails to separate himself from the other's signifiers, because of the unbearable intensity of the affect they arouse, it is this inability that at the same time enables him to experience the Other in its purity, or "radical heterogeneity." Unlike the model of love for the dead neighbor that Kierkegaard presents as exemplary of love, the psychotic's love is itself dead, petrified in the fullness of its encounter with the real Other. Whereas such an encounter with the absolute alterity of the neighbor is paradigmatic of ethics for Levinas, for Lacan it is neither ethical nor real love. Neurosis and psychosis represent two asymmetrical modes of the failure to love the neighbor: whereas the neurotic becomes an autonomous subject of desire in turn-

---

65. Lacan, "On a Question Preliminary to Any Possible Treatment of Psychosis," *Écrits* (1977), 218–19; *Écrits* (1966), 579.

66. The signifier of the "Name-of-the-Father" is equivalent to what Lacan later calls "S_1," the signifier of what Freud calls "primal repression." In an exchange with Jean Hyppolite during his seminar of 1953–54, Lacan describes the structure of *Verwerfung*, the mechanism of the psychotic's "foreclosure" of a primal signifier, in terms that are virtually indistinguishable from those of primal repression—presumably the exact opposite of foreclosure: "originally, for repression to be possible, there must be a beyond of repression, something final, already primitively constituted, an initial nucleus of the repressed . . . it is the centre of attraction, calling up all the subsequent repressions. I'd say that that is the very essence of the Freudian discovery." It is as if in its radical exceptionality, the signifier that will become the key mark of interpellation in paternal authority for the subject, variously characterized as "The-Name-of-the-Father," the "phallus as signifier," and "S_1," approaches a zero degree where it is indistinguishable from its diametrical opposite, the psychotic's *lack* of such a signifier (*The Seminar of Jacques Lacan*, book 1: *Freud's Papers on Technique, 1953–1954* [New York: W. W. Norton, 1988], 43).

67. Lacan, *Psychoses*, 253.

ing away from the impossibility of the command to love the neighbor, the psychotic fails to achieve subjectivity while succeeding in experiencing the other as radically other, loving the neighbor not wisely, but too well.

Toward a Political Theology of the Neighbor

The political theology described by Schmitt has precise thematic and topological analogues in Freud and Lacan that will allow us to approach more closely the question of a political theology of the neighbor. First, recall Freud's revision of Darwin's account of the mythical primal horde in *Totem and Taboo*. Faced with "a violent and jealous father who keeps all the females for himself" and forbids his sons any sexual access to them, the brothers one day band together to kill and devour their father. They discover the power that arises from collectivity: "united, they had the courage to do and succeeded in doing what would have been impossible for them individually."[68] But their ambivalence toward their father prevents them from gaining access to the forbidden *jouissance* (represented by the women), even though the father is dead: "They hated their father, who presented such a formidable obstacle to their craving for power and their sexual desires; but they loved and admired him too. . . . A sense of guilt made its appearance, which in this instance coincided with the remorse felt by the whole group."[69] The sons enter into a mode of melancholic mourning, whereby they identify with the lost object, simultaneously loving and hating the father, but now as part of themselves. This way, as Freud famously remarks, "The dead father became stronger than the living one had been." The sons hate themselves for the murder of the father they loved and hate the father who has become part of themselves. Hence, the cannibal feast by which they consummated their victory literalized the introjection of the father as the superego—an obscene and self-punishing agency whose enforcement of the law has become absolute. Now, carrying the father's ever-vigilant prohibition within them, the brothers prohibit themselves the free enjoyment for which they had killed the father. Freud's myth establishes the prototype for the structure of modern sociality, based on the intrinsic substitutability of its members—not, however, in the structure of the primal horde, but in its demise, in the generations of new filial

68. Freud, *Standard Edition,* 13:141.
69. Ibid., 143.

bands "composed of members with equal rights" and with equal (self-) restrictions.[70]

This narrative of the origin of the superego in the intergenerational transmission of guilt is familiar to us. But Freud's myth also contains the structural contours of a primitive Schmittian political theology.[71] The primal father holds the place of the sovereign at the border of the law: both inside it, as its embodiment and the principle of its enforcement, and outside, the great exception, the one person who is not himself subject to prohibition, but freely enjoys. Murdering and consuming the father apotheosizes him, in the sense that his function becomes transcendentalized, rather than located in a particular set of individuals and contingent circumstances. Freud describes the totemism that underwrites this originary constitution of the political in theological terms, as the establishment of a "covenant" between the father and the sons: "He promised them everything that a childish imagination may expect from a father—protection, care, indulgence—while on their side they undertook to respect his life, that is to say, not to repeat the deed which had brought destruction on their real father."[72] Freud will renarrativize this structure in his last great book, *Moses and Monotheism,* and both versions of the myth resonate, of course, with the Passion story of Christianity, the murder and resurrection of Jesus, meant to both expiate and repeat the murder of the primal father. In *Moses and Monotheism,* the rational Egyptian Moses is murdered and replaced by the Semitic Moses, the representative of the jealous desert God of the burning bush. Slavoj Žižek points out that this ferocious, prohibitory God that emerges in *Moses and Monotheism* is *not* the return of the presymbolic father of the primal horde, the originary father of jouissance. Rather, this Moses reincarnated as the father-God is pure will, as Lacan points out, will without jouissance—both ferocious and ignorant of the jouissance represented by the primal father.[73] Žižek argues that Freud's account of the father in these texts provides a theological background for Schmitt's understanding of political antagonism. Moreover, Žižek suggests that this father as sheer will opens up the possibility of both modern science *and* modern accounts of sexual difference:

70. Ibid., 141.

71. Slavoj Žižek describes the theological background to Schmitt's theory of the exception through a fine reading of the shifts in Freud's account of the father and the genesis of the law between *Totem and Taboo* and *Moses and Monotheism* ("Carl Schmitt in the Age of Post-Politics," in *The Challenge of Carl Schmitt,* ed. Chantal Mouffe (New York: Verso, 1999), 22–27.

72. Freud, *Standard Edition,* 13:144.

73. See Lacan, *Ethics of Psychoanalysis,* 167–78; and seminar 17, *L'envers de la psychanalyse,* 155–66.

The paradox that one has to bear in mind here is that this God of groundless Willing and ferocious "irrational" rage is the God who, by means of His Prohibition, accomplishes the destruction of the old sexualized Wisdom, and thus opens up the space for the desexualized "abstract" knowledge of modern science. The paradox lies in the fact that there is "objective" scientific knowledge (in the modern, post-Cartesian sense of the term) only if the universe of scientific knowledge is itself supplemented and sustained by this excessive "irrational" figure of the "real father." . . . Pre-modern Aristotelian and medieval knowledge was not yet "objective" rational scientific knowledge precisely because it lacked this excessive element of God *qua* the subjectivity of pure "irrational" willing. . . . The further paradox is that this "irrational" God *qua* the prohibitory paternal figure also opens up the space for the entire development of modernity, up to the deconstructionist notion that our sexual identity is a contingent sociosymbolic formation: the moment this prohibitory figure recedes, we are back with Jungian neo-obscurantist notions of masculine and feminine eternal archetypes which thrive today. . . . paradoxically, the domain of symbolic rules, if it is to count as such, has to be grounded in some tautological authority *beyond rules,* which says: "It is so because I say it is so!"[74]

If this third aspect of the father as ferocious yet ignorant of jouissance is the "real" father, his function is to maintain the distinction, the breathing space, between the other two paternal manifestations: the ravenously sexual presymbolic or "imaginary" father of the primal horde and the "symbolic" father, internalized as the memory of his name, who replaces him and legislates access to jouissance, doling it out according to a strict economy of guilt. The figure of the reasonable, logical father, the Egyptian Moses, who reoccupies the place of this symbolic father, depends upon these other two fathers, imaginary and real, to embody and mark the place of the jouissance on whose suspension (rather than elimination) the rational order of knowledge, difference, and structure itself is predicated and differentiated from the premodern account of knowledge as correspondence (or what Lacan calls the assumption of a "sexual relationship" between heaven and earth, spirit and matter). This third father of willed ignorance of jouissance defines the order that allows the separation between what Žižek calls the imaginary or "Jungian" notion of sexual essence and its symbolic "deconstruction" in performative models of gender positionality. Hence the Freudo-Lacanian account of the three fathers, in demonstrating the conditions of the emergence of neutral scientific knowledge and its distinction from the magical thinking of essential reciprocity, also shows how the two dominant non-

74. "Carl Schmitt in the Age of Post-Politics," 26.

psychoanalytic notions of gender emerge: gender as biological or even cosmic necessity, on the one hand, and gender as fluid continuum of cultural possibilities, on the other.

But we can also find at least the beginnings of an expression of a third, properly psychoanalytic model of sexual difference in the scenario of the primal horde, one that is conditioned by a logic that assumes neither (biological-cosmic) necessity nor (cultural-ludic) possibility, but only the *impossibility* of fully inhabiting sexual identity that makes every concrete instance of sexuation a function of radical contingency. Although Freud does not present the myth of the primal horde as a narrative of sexual difference, it is clear that it is heavily inflected by the masculine conditions of sexuation: to be a man in the wake of the murder of the primal father is to take on the functions of both the singular father and the plural sons and to be divided between their contradictory imperatives. On the one hand, a man assumes his sexuality as an individual, but interchangeable, member of a group of sons, whose possibilities of jouissance are strictly limited, not only to women outside the immediate family "horde," but by the guilt and reparative renunciation that vitiates all later attempts at sexual encounters. The sons form a collective with equal rights, insofar as they are all equally *prohibited* from the untrammeled access to jouissance that they imagine the father once enjoyed. On the other hand, this filial position of self-denial is mitigated by the other aspect of the introjected paternal agency: each son participates in the legend of the Great Father who once *did* enjoy fully, and each represents for himself the possibility of the father's greatness being restored.

For Lacan, Freud's myth of the primal horde expresses the ethical paradox that constitutes modernity: even though we no longer believe in the living authority of a moral code that derives from the now debunked religious law, we still obey it. As he comments in his seminar *The Ethics of Psychoanalysis*, "Although the obstacle is removed as a result of the murder [of the father], *jouissance* is still prohibited; not only that, but the prohibition is reinforced . . . whoever attempts to submit to the moral law sees the demands of his superego grow increasingly meticulous and increasingly cruel."[75] The internalization of the paternal agency of criticism and renunciation constitutes the masculine subject, on the one hand, as a self-limiting system: the drives are attenuated and regulated not only insofar as we cede their satisfaction to the agency of the primordial father who still claims them for his exclusive usufruct, but also on account of the guilt we suffer for our ill will toward the father we still

75. Lacan, *Ethics of Psychoanalysis*, 176.

love. On the other hand, there is an excess of prohibition over transgression that prevents the subjective system from attaining homeostasis—the more we give up jouissance, the more we punish ourselves.[76] According to Lacan, the cultural mechanism that responds to and embodies this traumatic ambivalence is the imperative to *love God:*

> But if for us God is dead, it is because he always has been dead, and that's what Freud says. He has never been the father except in the mythology of the son, or, in other words, in that of the commandment that commands that he, the father, be loved, and in the drama of the passion which reveals that there is a resurrection after death. That is to say, the man who made incarnate the death of God still exists. He still exists with the commandment which orders him to love God. That's the place where Freud stops, and he stops at the same time . . . at the place that concerns the love of one's neighbor, which is something that appears to be insurmountable for us, indeed incomprehensible.[77]

The commandment to love God is itself the instantiation, the only true materialization, of the still-living father—his resurrection or installation as undead in the position of absolute sovereign, both inside and beyond the world of moral law he regulates.[78] Whereas the classical assumption about ethics is that pleasure, well-being, and happiness all lead to the greater good, Lacan argues that for Freud, on the contrary, the idea of the Good is a screen against jouissance, a vestige of the paternal prohibition of enjoyment.

---

76. In *Civilization and Its Discontents,* Freud explains this increase in self-directed aggressivity: "The effect of instinctual renunciation on the conscience then is that every piece of aggression whose satisfaction the subject gives up is taken over by the super-ego and increases the latter's aggressiveness (against the ego) . . . the original severity of the super-ego does not—or does not so much—represent the severity which one has experienced from it [the object], or which one attributes to it; it represents rather one's own aggressiveness towards it" (*Standard Edition,* 21:129–30).

77. Lacan, *Ethics of Psychoanalysis,* 177–78.

78. Lacan argues that Freud "stops" before the commandment to love God insofar as he is able to revalue and purify it, in the manner of Spinoza, of its pathological ambivalence, as *amor intellectualis Dei* (*Ethics of Psychoanalysis,* 180). In the concluding words of seminar 11, four years later, Lacan suggests that this model of the "intellectual love of God" is an attempt to avoid sacrificing to the Other, "*the dark God*": "It is the eternal meaning of the sacrifice, to which no one can resist, unless animated by that faith, so difficult to sustain, which perhaps, one man alone has been able to formulate in a plausible way—namely, Spinoza, with his *Amor intellectualis Dei.*" Although this is a "heroic" project, its renunciation of desire, or quietism, ultimately does not represent the way of psychoanalysis; nor does its antithesis, the project to sustain pure desire, which Lacan finds equally in Kant and Sade. Rather, the "impure desire" of psychoanalysis is "a desire to obtain absolute difference, a desire which intervenes when, confronted with the primary signifier, the subject is, for the first time, in a position to subject himself to it. There only may the signification of a limitless love emerge, because it is outside the limits of the law, where alone it may live" (*Four Fundamental Concepts,* 275–76).

And whereas Lacan's comment suggests that Freud's work reiterates the structural centrality of the commandment to love God, as a reminder of the father's exception to the law of prohibition he ordains, Freud pulls back from the commandment to love the neighbor, where, according to Lacan, he perceives and reacts against the traces within the law of the obscene transgression the commandment would seem designed to limit. This, Lacan suggests, is a sign of Freud's moral fiber: "the whole Aristotelian conception of the good is alive in this man who is a true man; he tells us the most sensitive and reasonable things about what it is worth sharing the good that is our love with. But what escapes him is perhaps the fact that precisely because we take that path we miss the opening on to *jouissance*. It is in the nature of the good to be altruistic. But that's not the love of thy neighbor." [79] Freud rejects the injunction to love the neighbor for the best moral reasons: my love is precious, and I owe it to family and friends first; moreover, my neighbor is malicious, unloving, and unlovable. But the cost of this response is that he misses something real in it, what Lacan calls "the difficult way, love for one's neighbor." And if Freud "stops" at the thought of the consequences of his discovery of the obscenity of the law, it is with even greater horror that he encounters the truth of the commandment to love the neighbor that he finds, Lacan suggests, *in the same place.* The position of the subject is precisely at the intersection of these two commandments to love, where they come together, forming an ethical pivot. If the subject is called to face one or the other, he or she nevertheless remains in the place determined by both. The neighbor (as what Freud had called in the *Project for a Scientific Psychology* the Nebenmensch) bears within it the "thing," the kernel of jouissance that is both foreign, strange, and unrecognizable in the other and intimate to me—the secret of my own traumatic drives. As Lacan writes, "we cannot avoid the formula that *jouissance* is evil. Freud leads us by the hand to this point: it is evil because it involves the evil of the neighbor [*le mal du prochain*]." [80] What troubles Freud in the injunction to love the neighbor is precisely the fact that it condenses his own most disturbing insights about the nature of the superego, both urging and prohibiting the violence of jouissance in a single utterance. For Freud, the neighbor materializes the fundamental antagonism both within and between the familial and the social, the

79. Lacan, *Ethics of Psychoanalysis*, 186–87. For more on Lacan's comments in this seminar on the relationship between the commandments to love God and to love the neighbor, see Kenneth Reinhard, "Freud, My Neighbor," *American Imago* 54, no. 2 (1997): 165–95.

80. Lacan, *Ethics of Psychoanalysis*, 184 (translation modified); *L'éthique de la psychanalyse*, 217.

"strangeness" that haunts the subject of practical reason. The antagonism *between* the familial and the social is what inspires the project of converting the one into the other, but the antagonism that the neighbor deposits *within* each, as their negative intersection, prevents the success of any such translation. Familial desire does not precede and condition social responsibility, but vice versa: the response to the neighbor is not the sublation, but the *cause* of Oedipal love.

At this point in his seminar, Lacan presents the problematic of neighbor-love as a double bind for which there is no clear solution. He suggests a modification of a classic Kantian test case of ethical reason to explain his sense of the situation. In Kant's example, we are asked to decide whether to obey a despot who demands that we testify falsely against someone who will be put to death because of our testimony, or be put to death ourselves for our disobedience. For Kant, it is clear that we must die rather than testify falsely, since the biblical law against false testimony constitutes a truly categorical imperative for practical reason (we cannot imagine, according to Kant, a coherent world that would approve of false testimony). Lacan wonders how things are changed if it is a question not of perjury, but of presenting *true* testimony that will nevertheless condemn our fellow man, if, for example, "I am summoned to inform on my neighbor or my brother for activities that are prejudicial to the security of the state." Here, I am caught between two equally urgent duties, to love my neighbor and to support the general good represented by national interests. But how is my decision affected by the fact that in testifying truthfully perhaps I am satisfying a desire, unconscious or not, to kill my neighbor? Or, perhaps even more disturbing, how do I calculate the possibility that being betrayed might be in accordance with my neighbor's jouissance?

And I who stand here right now and bear witness to the idea that there is no law of the good except in evil and through evil, should I bear such witness? This Law makes my neighbor's *jouissance* the point on which, in bearing witness in this case, the meaning of my duty oscillates. Must I go toward my duty of truth insofar as it preserves the authentic place of my *jouissance,* even if it remains empty? Or must I resign myself to this lie, which, by making me substitute forcefully the good for the principle of my *jouissance,* commands me to blow alternatively hot and cold? Either I retreat from betraying my neighbor [*prochain*] so as to spare my fellow man [*semblable*] or I shelter behind my fellow man so as to give up my own *jouissance.*[81]

81. Lacan, *Ethics of Psychoanalysis,* 190 (translation modified); *L'éthique de la psychanalyse,* 223.

To testify against the other, in the name of Truth, may indeed support my jouissance, which may include condemning my neighbor to death. But insofar as to do so would require that I speak from the place and in the name of the Law, I am thereby evacuating the conditions necessary to my jouissance, which can only be sustained by and as transgression. On the other hand, to refuse to testify, for the sake of saving the other person's life, is to treat him as my "fellow man," *mon semblable,* whose good (self-preservation, satisfaction of needs) I imagine in the mirror of my own ego. And this is to fail to encounter him as "my neighbor," *mon prochain,* whose jouissance I cannot presume to know and which I may in fact betray along with the moral law in not testifying against him. The subject of jouissance is in a deadlock from which the ethics of practical reason provides no escape. To be loyal to the paternal law is to betray the neighbor, and to encounter the neighbor who stands nakedly before me is to give up on the conditions of sociality itself.

This is the same paradox that emerges in any sustained encounter with Emmanuel Levinas's thinking, which has been the primary site recently for a renewed interest in ethical critical theory. For Levinas, ethics is based on my radically asymmetrical and nonreciprocal relationship to the other as the "neighbor" to whom I owe a debt that can never be amortized and for which I am unjustly persecuted. No one can take my place, assume my ethical burden, but I am called to assume the place of all others. Politics, on the other hand, is a relationship among equals, subjects equivalent to each other, each having the same rights and responsibilities, each intrinsically *substitutable*—this particular other's claim must be put in perspective by this other other's claim, and indeed by *all* others. Politics for Levinas is a question of distributive justice, and as such it implies a reciprocal and symmetrical relationship among *fellow citizens.* Although Levinas's work has been made into a theory of moral conscience for postcolonial and multicultural studies, the ethical basis for political criticism, the crucial point that is often passed over (indeed, that Levinas himself seems to forget) is that there can be *no relationship* between ethics and politics in Levinas's theory. This fundamental disjunction between the conditions of ethics (and the neighbor) and politics (and the citizen, on the model of "fraternity") should preclude any attempt to draw political consequences from Levinas's theory of the neighbor.[82] What is truly radical in Levinas's thought is precisely this im-

---

82. Although Howard Caygill is more convinced of the harmonious connections between politics and ethics in Levinas's thought than I am, he points out that the political in Levinas is not congruent with the assumptions of liberalism and, indeed, remains a troubling element in his work:

passe, the fact of the unbridgeable gap between ethics and politics: insofar as ethics involves the encounter of the *two* of the neighbor and the
self, it cannot conceive of the *three,* the symbolic representation and mediation on which politics is based; ethics is inherently apolitical, must
willfully ignore what would be fair or for the general good. To shift the
other as neighbor into mediation with the other in the polis is precisely
to *give up* on ethics; moreover, to try to bring politics to the immediate
level of the singular face of the other, to see the other as a singularity,
can only mean to give up on politics. Slavoj Žižek counters the political
appropriation of Levinas by radicalizing his insight into the incommensurability between politics and ethics, which he presents as the opposition between justice and love: "Others are primordially an (ethically) indifferent multitude, and love is a violent gesture of cutting into this
multitude and privileging a One as the neighbor, thus introducing a radical imbalance into the whole. In contrast to love, justice begins when I
remember the faceless many left in shadow in this privileging of the
One. Justice and love are thus structurally incompatible. . . . What this
means is that the third is not secondary: it is always-already here, and
the primordial ethical obligation is towards this Third who is *not* here in
the face-to-face relationship."[83] Žižek argues that only by *limiting* our
obligation to the singular other and shifting into the perspective of the
political Other, the third, can we locate ethics on the grounds of the universal, rather than one version or another of particularism. When we
hold onto this insight, despite its inconvenience for the project of an
ethical critical theory, we encounter what is truly radical in Levinas. This
is also where his thought approaches Lacan's insight that there is no
such thing as a sexual relationship, which, in its impossibility, is itself
the very rock of the real. The political is the condition of the ethical, the
only ground by which we can approach ethics, and not vice versa. The
love of the neighbor cannot be generalized into a universal social love,
but it is only from the perspective of the political in its radical nonrelationship with ethics that love as such can emerge: as I will argue below,
the *two* can only be created by passing through the *three.* It is only when
we understand the neighbor in Levinas in terms of the fundamental aporia of the ethical and the political in his thinking—an aporia that resists

---

"War and the political assume a proximity in Levinas's thought that were it recognized would prove
extremely uncomfortable for liberal readers accustomed to keeping war—as the alleged pathology
of civility—separate from peace. The proximity of war and politics is a thought that brings Levinas
closer to the thought of Clausewitz and Carl Schmitt than to the liberal ethical theory that issued
from Kant" (Howard Caygill, *Levinas and the Political* [New York: Routledge, 2002], 3).

83. Slavoj Žižek, "Smashing the Neighbor's Face."

any attempt to appropriate either term for the service of the other—that we encounter the resources he provides for a political theology of the neighbor.

As Lacan comes increasingly to terms with the impasse that he will ultimately formulate as "the impossibility of the sexual relationship" in the 1970s, he reframes the question of sexual difference in terms of two pairs of logical "formulas of sexuation." The contradictions between universal statement and existential exception that inscribe "man" and "woman" in these formulas will serve as a template for my development of a political theology of the neighbor in the nonrelationship between ethics and politics. Although Lacan continues to draw on his earlier models of sexual difference (formulated primarily in terms of "being" or "having" the phallus), his transformation of those models in the later years of his seminar has profound implications for all aspects of his thinking. What we might call the reality of sexual difference in his earlier paradigm was the *symbolic,* based on the phallus as the signifier of lack that constituted both men and women as split subjects, "castrated," albeit in fundamentally asymmetrical ways.[84] In his later writings, the reality of sexual difference becomes *the real* in ways that alter Lacan's understanding of this central concept. Lacan's notion of "the real" shifts over the years of his seminar, both in terms of its relationship with the other two elements of his fundamental topology (made up of the imaginary, symbolic, and real) and in terms of its significations and resistance to signification. By way of a simplified chronology, we can say that, whereas in the 1950s the real was simply "reality," the manifold of sensory perception of the external world in relation to which the symbolic subject emerges; and in the 1960s the real was primarily "trauma," the lack in the Other or inconsistencies in the symbolic order around which the subject as reaction formation collected; in the 1970s the real is the *impossible,* most frequently manifesting in Lacan's axiomatic declaration of *the impossibility of a sexual relationship.* Lacan's theory of sexuation must be understood as the corollary of this new account of the real: there are subjects called "men" and subjects called "women" precisely because of the abyss of the real that separates them and that divides each from itself. Men and women swerve away from the impossibility of their relationship in different ways, and each relates instead to a substitute (a signifier or object) in lieu of meeting with another subject. Moreover, Lacan enigmatically suggests that although intersubjective sexual relations are impossible, love "makes up for" or "supplements" this impossibility.

84. See, for example, Lacan's essay "The Signification of the Phallus," *Écrits* (1977), 281–91.

But this declaration and what Lacan means by "love" remain ambiguous: are we to understand that love is the consoling *illusion* that there is something more than sex, which we experience only as failed? or nonexistent? Or is Lacan suggesting that love is *not* an illusion, but the union of disjunctive elements in a new whole, greater than the parts, that does indeed compensate us for the failure of sex with something of value? Or does he mean that love is something more than either of those readings would suggest, that there is something *real* in love, correlative to the real of the impossibility of the sexual relationship, but neither identical to it nor to its dissimulation?

Before pursuing this question of love, which must clearly be fundamental to a political theology of the neighbor, we need to say something more about the formulations of man and woman, which for Lacan are the consequence of the impossibility of a sexual relationship, and their relation to Freud's model of sovereignty in the primal horde. To be a man or a woman is to be inscribed within what we might call a theory not of sex but of *sets*. The difference between men and women—the *real* difference, rather than the distortive, imaginary one reflected in biology or the symbolic one determined by culture—lies in the nature of the participation of an element, "a man" or "a woman," in the set of which it is a member, "man" or "woman." Lacan uses the language of symbolic logic to express sexuation as a particular modality of the relationship of an element and the set of which it is a member: in each case a *universal quantifier*, symbolized by $\forall$ and meaning "all" or "every" element of the set, is juxtaposed with an *existential quantifier*, symbolized by $\exists$, which means "there is one" or "there is at least one" such element.

In figure 1, the bottom formula on the side of men should be read, "All speaking beings inscribed here are subjected to the phallic function." That is, to be a man is to be under the universal thrall of the phallus as signifier; and the name for the limitations that this signifier imposes is "castration," the price of entry into the technologies of symbolic mediation, which promise some partial and limited measure of enjoyment, in giving up the greater enjoyment mythically attributed to the father of the primal horde. To write oneself as "man" is to enter into a social contract where access to unmediated jouissance, the "impossible" traumatic enjoyment associated with the overwhelming presence of the mother's body, is sacrificed for the sake of the symbolic substitutions and displacements of culture and the remnant of jouissance that it promises. The crucial function of the phallus, Φx, is precisely that *all men* are subjected to it, which implies that a set is posited called "all men," a set that is characterized by its totality and the homogeneity of its members, as

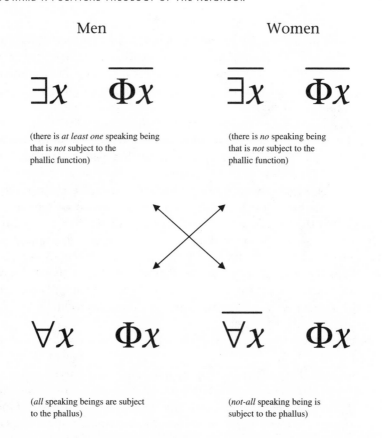

Men

Women

$\exists x \quad \overline{\Phi x}$

$\overline{\exists x} \quad \overline{\Phi x}$

(there is *at least one* speaking being that is *not* subject to the phallic function)

(there is *no* speaking being that is *not* subject to the phallic function)

$\forall x \quad \Phi x$

$\overline{\forall x} \quad \overline{\Phi x}$

(*all* speaking beings are subject to the phallus)

(*not-all* speaking being is subject to the phallus)

Figure 1

castrated subjects. An individual man is always more or less an *example* of the closed set of Man; each man participates synecdochally in an idea of Man, which he equally represents and falls short of. This is the democratic principle par excellence, the assumption that "all men are created equal," that they are interchangeable to the extent that they are both *represented* and *limited* by a single universal law.

Yet although castration is the inexorable condition of entering the rule of the symbolic order as a man, there is an *exception* which, Lacan says, proves the rule: the formula on the top left of figure 1 indicates "there is a speaking being inscribed here who is *not* subject to the phallic function." In political terms, we could say that this existential formulation represents the nondemocratic truth that is internal to democracy, the exception that constitutes both the transcendental condition and immanent horizon of the democratic rule of law. Lacan connects this exceptionality with Freud's myth of the father of the primal horde from *Totem and Taboo:* in the unconscious, this uncastrated man supports the illusion of "having it all," the possibility of unlimited enjoyment, that enables men to bear their own castration. As if to suggest that this Father almost constitutes his own species distinct from that of *Homo sapiens,* Lacan coins the name "homoinzun" for him, a homonymic holophrasis of *au moins un,* "at least one," as in the formula "there exists *at least one* speaking being who is not subject to castration":

I will dare to say, all the same, that people had a few more ideas in their heads when they demonstrated the existence of God. It's evident that God exists, but not any more than you do! That doesn't get us very far. So, what's finally involved is the question of existence. What is it that really interests us in this *"there exists,"* with respect to the signifier? That is that there exists *at least one* for whom that business of castration doesn't work, and it is because of this that what is called the Father has been invented. That's why the Father exists at least as much as God, which is to say, not very much.

. . . Inasmuch as *there exists one,* it follows that all the others can function, that is, with reference to this exception, to this *"there exists."* [85]

Lacan here points out that the cultural question of God's existence is not entirely a metaphysical or religious speculation. Rather, it signals the more material problem, at the level of the signifier, of the existence of a Father who is *not* subject to the law of castration. Just as in Freud's myth of the primal horde there must be, at least hypothetically, one man whose jouissance is not limited, Lacan argues that in the order of the signifier there must be at least one signifier that is not subject to its laws—an "exception," the singular signifier that remains rigid, intransigent, and around which all the other signifiers revolve. The myth of the murder of the primal father is Freud's attempt to secularize the function

---

85. "J'oserai dire que les gens avaient quand même un tout petit peu plus d'idées dans la tête quand ils démontraient l'existence de Dieu. C'est évident que Dieu existe, mais pas plus que vous! Ça va pas loin. Enfin ceci pour mettre au point ce qu'il en est de l'existence. Qu'est-ce qui peut bien nous intéresser concernant cet *il existe* en matière de signifiant ? Ça serait qu'il en existe *au moins un* pour qui ça ne fonctionne pas cette affaire de castration, et c'est bien pour ça qu'on l'a inventé, c'est ce qui s'appelle le Père, c'est pourquoi le Père existe au moins autant que Dieu, c'est-à-dire pas beaucoup. . . . Donc à partir de ce *qu'il existe un,* c'est à partir de là que tous les autres peuvent fonctionner, c'est en référence à cette exception, à cet il *existe*" (Jacques Lacan, *Le séminaire, livre 19: . . . ou pire, 1971–1972* [unpublished transcript, December 8, 1971], my translation).

of God and provide the imaginary support of this exceptional signifier: both God and the Father exist (or better, *ek*-sist, as Lacan writes, following Heidegger) at the limit of the worlds of existence they orchestrate. Hence, both God and the Father *persist* with the structural necessity of not being castrated, of being whole, the existential exception to a universal rule. So whereas the speaking being that inscribes itself on the side of "man" is defined as the *individual example* of a *universal set* or principle (the phallus), the closure of that set is itself the function of an exception, a transcendental term that both exceeds and enforces its limits.

In describing the way in which a subject emerges in writing itself in either one set of logical functions or the other, Lacan consistently refers to the "choice" of sexuation. We see here what we might call the "decisionist" aspect of Lacan's account of sexuation: "one ultimately situates oneself there [in the man's or woman's position] by choice."[86] By this, Lacan does not mean to claim that the subject selects its gender from a subjective position prior to such a choice, since no intentional agency yet exists at such a hypothetical preoriginary moment. Nor should we read Lacan's assertion as implying that the choice is the selection from a continuum of polymorphic gender positions, contingent masquerades, or metamorphic forms of drag. Nor should we assume from Lacan's language of choice that sexuation can be retracted, revised, or repeated at a later date. The signifiers "man" and "woman" express the fact of a radical decision, a cut that divides the one from the other and each in itself, but not as a historical or phenomenological condition. Indeed, to be a man or a woman is not to assume an identity but, as we have said, to *fail* to take on identity as self-sameness, self-certainty. And this constitutive failure is both a consequence of the fundamental impossibility of the sexual relationship and its hypostasized repetition.

To borrow Alain Badiou's terms, we might say that sexuation is an *event* in being—not a static situation, but an encounter involving a "pure choice," which retroactively is named as either "man" or "woman." For Badiou, a real choice is one that has "no basis in any objective difference," but is between what he calls "indiscernibles": "It is then a question of an absolutely pure choice, free from any presupposition other than that of having to choose. . . . If there is no value by which

86. Lacan, *Encore*, 73. Also see Lacan's comments in his seminar of the next year, *Les non-dupes errent:* "'the sexed being authorizes itself.' It's in this sense that, that he has the choice, I mean that by which one limits oneself, finally, in order to classify them as male or female, in the civil state, finally, that doesn't change the fact that he has the choice" ["l'être sexué ne s'autorise que de lui-même." C'est en ce sens que, qu'il a le choix, je veux dire que ce à quoi on se limite, enfin, pour les classer mâle ou féminin, dans l'état civil, enfin, ça, ça n'empêche pas qu'il a le choix] (April 9, 1974).

to discriminate what you have to choose, it is your freedom as such which provides the norm, to the point where it effectively becomes indistinguishable from chance. The indiscernible is the subtraction that establishes a point of coincidence between chance and freedom."[87] Such a decision between indiscernibles through subtraction describes the nature of the choice of sexuation the subject makes, according to Lacan. The terms man and woman are constituted in relation to the subtraction of a third term, the phallus, which each is equally deprived of and dominated by. If we can imagine the mythical primal scene where a proto-subject faces the choice between Lacan's two sets of formulas of sexuation, the choice would be between apparent *indiscernibles:* both men and women are absolutely subject to the phallic function, and in each case there is an exception to that rule. In traditional Aristotelian logic, the pairs of logical assertions that define men and women would be, in fact, equivalent: the universal statement that "All speaking beings are subject to the phallus" (male) is not logically different from the negative existential formulation on the woman's side: "There is no speaking being who is not subject to the phallus." The first makes a global assertion using an affirmative universal quantifier ("all x are castrated"), and the second indicates that there is no exception to the phallic function, in a double negative existential quantifier ("no x is not castrated"). In the case of the man, the existential assertion "there *is* a man who is not subject to the phallic law of castration" posits an exception to the universal without suspending its universality. And similarly, on the woman's side the universal quantifier is negated, also positing the possibility of an exception. But if, on the most formal level, it appears that there is almost no difference between men and women—each is the product of logically equivalent contradictions between universal and existential quantifiers—to have made the choice is to *produce* difference as such. In the "trajectory of truth" that, according to Badiou, proceeds by way of subtraction, while the choice among "indiscernibles" is the act that produces a subject, the truth that results from that choice is "generic": "Indiscernible in its act or as subject, a truth is generic in its result or being."[88] *Générique,* of course, is a form of the word *genre* in French, which means not only "kind" but also "gender." Hence, from the choice that is made on the basis of no discernible difference, sexual difference, which Badiou understands as difference as such, emerges.

87. Alain Badiou, *Theoretical Writings* (New York: Continuum, 2004), 112–13.

88. Ibid., 114; translation of Alain Badiou, "Conférence sur la soustraction," in *Conditions* (Paris: Seuil, 1992), 192.

Indeed, the *emergence* of sexuality in the speaking-being can be characterized as what Schmitt calls an *emergency,* an exigency to which the protosubject responds by choosing to write itself, in absolutely irrevocable and incomparable ways, under the signifier "man" *or* the signifier "woman." The positions represented by these two signifiers are indiscernible, but must be chosen between, on the basis of inexorable conditions that are undecidable for the normative law. Schmitt's theory of the sovereign as the one who decides on the exception, the extreme contingency where the constitution is suspended, helps explain Lacan's claims that sexuality is both an exception to a rule and a choice. Schmitt's notion of the sovereign as a "border concept," both within and beyond the law, describes the situation of the subject who will have located himself as a man in Lacan's logics of sexuation: just as the universal rule of the phallus is expressed in the lower left side of Lacan's diagram, so this determination is contradicted by an existential exception, embodied by the primal father, inscribed on the upper left side of the formulas of sexuation. The sovereign is like the primal father in being stationed at the margins of the state he regulates: it is only insofar as there can be a radical exception to the law that the law can exist and be effective. The primal father and the sovereign occupy the position of extreme dictators whose word both violates the rule of the total state and promises it *totality,* closure, drawing a line between the inside and the outside, the native and the stranger. The subjective decision that results in masculine sexuation is *the choice not to choose,* the decision to remain in a liminal position by both accepting subjection to the law of castration and maintaining the belief in the existence of *at least one* man who has escaped that law, while enforcing it on all others.[89]

But there is still the question of the woman's sexuation, that is, the consequences of the other decision, which, we might say, involves *the choice to choose,* the decision not only to take responsibility for the irrevocably past choice that brought a woman into the open community of women, but also for the infinite series of contingent decisions that follow from it. To begin with, how do we make sense of the negative universal quantifier on the upper half of the woman's side of Lacan's formulas (see figure 1), "there is *no* speaking being who locates herself on this side who is *not* subject to the phallus"? How is the double negative of the existential formulation different from its counterpart on the

89. This is closely related to the logic of fetishism described by Octave Mannoni in "Je sais bien mais quand même . . . ," in *Clefs pour l'imaginaire* (Paris: Seuil, 1968). Slavoj Žižek has commented on this logic in several places; see *For They Know Not What They Do: Enjoyment as a Political Factor* (New York: Verso, 1991), 245–53.

man's side, the universal affirmative formulation of castration? In classical logic, the negation of a universal (the bottom half of the woman's side of the diagram, "not-all speaking beings are subject to the phallus") would imply the existence of an exception to the rule of castration. Thus, we might expect that, as on the man's side, there is "at least one" woman who is not castrated. But the doubly negative existential assertion on the woman's side is different from the positive universal assertion of castration precisely insofar as it directly contradicts that possibility and insists that there *cannot* be an exception to the law of the phallus.[90] It is as if the woman's side of the formulas anticipates the question of the possibility of an exception—Why shouldn't there be, as for the man, an "exception that proves the rule," a Great Mother who escapes castration?—and flatly negates that question: there is *no exception* to the rule of the phallus for the woman. If this is the case, then what is the status of the "not-all" on the bottom right side of the equation: "not-all speaking beings are subject to the phallus"? For Lacan, the stakes riding on the not-all are very high:

One of the following two things is true: either what I write has no meaning at all . . . or when I write $\overline{\forall x} \, \Phi x$, a never-before-seen function in which the negation is placed on the quantifier, which should be read *pas-tout*, it means that when any speaking being whatsoever situates itself under the banner "women," it is on the basis of the following—that it grounds itself as being *pas-tout* in situating itself in the phallic function. That is what defines what? Woman precisely, except that Woman [La *femme*] can only be written with a bar through it. There's no such thing as Woman, Woman with a capital W indicating the universal [*Il n'y a pas* La *femme, article défini pour désigner l'universel*]. There's no such thing as woman because in her essence . . . she is not all [pas tout].[91]

The logical consistency of Lacan's entire discourse depends on the status of the not-all; if there is *knowledge* in these signifiers, it is only because there is *truth* in the not-all, which, however, in its singularity, subtracts something from the totality of knowledge. Lacan's account of the not-all is in part negative: he maintains that the "not-all" does *not* mean that not all women are under the law of the phallus—that is, that some perhaps escape castration and in some way preserve their jouissance intact. Nor does it mean that not *all of* a woman is castrated, that some part

90. See Alain Badiou's close discussion of this question in his essay "Sujet et Infini," in *Conditions* (Paris: Seuil, 1992), 288–89.
91. Lacan, *Encore,* 72–73 (translation slightly modified); *Le séminaire, livre 20: Encore* (Paris: Seuil, 1975), 68.

of her being or her body remains unscathed, free of the signifier's cut. Unlike the case of men, for whom there *is* a unified category, "all men," that they are identified as being members of, women are *radically singular,* not examples of a class or members of a closed set, but *each one an exception.* They are an exception, however, not to a "rule," but to an open set, an infinite series of particular women, into which each woman enters "one by one." As Lacan says, "You know that the not-all has been essential to me in marking that there is no such thing as *the Woman,* which is, namely, that there are only, if I may say, different ones, and in some way, [they enter] one by one; and that all that is in some way dominated by the privileged function of this, nonetheless, that there isn't one to represent the statement that interdicts, namely the absolutely-no. There you have it."[92]

There is, then, no common denominator for subjects who locate themselves as women, no way of characterizing "women in general," contrary to popular misconceptions about feminine essence and unlike the case for men, who *are* determined by the assumption that there is a totality of the set Man. No authentic positive characterization of Woman in general is possible. One should talk only about individual beings, who enter into the logic of the not-all one at a time, each as if for the first time. The relationship between particular elements of the open set of women is metonymic rather than synecdochal: one woman cannot substitute or stand for another and is not in a relationship of equality with another, but can only *stand next to* another, in an unending series that has no characteristics that unify it. There is no figure of the sovereign woman who might adjudicate the claims of individual women to participate in feminine sexuality and determine the boundaries of the set. In the language of set theory, a man belongs to and is included in the subset of humanity called "all men," a set that constitutes a unified group, guaranteed by the transcendental exceptionality of the primal Father. A woman, however, belongs to the subset of women without being included in it, insofar as that subset has no border that would determine membership and delimit inside from outside. Men are part of the group Man insofar as they are all equivalent in their failure to represent the primal Father: the set of "all men" functions according to the principles of group formation around a leader that Freud describes in *Group Psychol-*

---

92. "Vous savez que le pas-tout m'a très essentiellement servi à marquer qu'il n'y a pas de *la femme,* c'est à savoir qu'il n'y en a, si je puis dire, que diverses et en quelque sorte une par une, et que tout cela se trouve en quelque sorte dominé par la fonction privilégiée de ceci, qu'il n'y en a néanmoins pas une à représenter le dire qui interdit, à savoir l'absolument—non. Voilà" (Lacan, *Le séminaire, livre 21: Les non-dupes errent* [unpublished transcript, May 14, 1974], my translation).

ogy and the Analysis of the Ego. And although women are no less irrecus-
ably marked by the phallus, the terms of their reprieve are not given by
a transcendental sovereign who represents the possibility of eventual
satisfaction, but *immanently,* in the contingencies of their particular in-
habitations of the not-all.

Lacan clearly distinguishes woman's not-all from psychotic foreclosure, which it might seem superficially to resemble, insofar as each involves the nonfunctioning or suspension of the paternal signifier and
consequent nontotalization of the field of signifiers. Foreclosure, Lacan
argues, is a question of language, of saying or not saying the Name of the
Father. This contingency of the symbolic order can lead either to normative (neurotic) subjectivity or to the psychotic's failure to become a
subject. The not-all, however, operates at the level of the real, rather
than the symbolic, as the *impossibility* of saying something or, better, the
impossibility of *writing* (that is, formalizing) the sexual relationship. The
phallic function is by no means foreclosed in the case of women; rather,
Lacan describes the not-all as a principle of "discordance" vis-à-vis the
phallus. Whereas the psychotic forecloses the phallic function, failing to
submit to its sovereignty, the woman's not-all defines something more
like a nonaccord or noncompliance with the phallic function, submis-
sion to it with reserve, with a reservation that hinges precisely on
the impossibility of the sexual relationship that the phallic function
both represents and dissimulates.[93] The psychotic's refusal of the paternal signifier correlates with the *collapse* of the space of the neighbor;
the woman's demurral, on the other hand, *opens up* the space of the
neighbor.

Is this all to say that the neighbor is a woman? Should we risk claiming that, if the subject of the political theology of sovereignty is man, the
subject of the political theology of the neighbor is woman? First of all,
we must be careful not to make the false assumption that these modes
of political organization are topo-theological options that we can choose
between. A political theology of the neighbor cannot replace the political theology of the sovereign, but can only supplement it, both in the
sense of pointing to some structural lack and descriptive deficiency in
traditional political theology that the figure of the neighbor might compensate for and in the sense of pointing to something heterogeneous to

93. Lacan, *Le séminaire, livre 19: . . . ou pire* (December 8, 1971). "Our not-all is discordance. But
what is foreclosure? Surely, it is to be located in a different register than that of discordance. . . . There
is only foreclosure when there is speaking. . . . Foreclosure has to do with the fact that something
may or may not be spoken. And of that of which nothing can be said, it can only be concluded with
a question on the Real" (my translation).

political theology, something other than itself in its very core, that manifests and finds its phenomenology in the neighbor. Moreover, it would be even more misleading to imagine that we have made a historical transition from the epoch of the (modern) All to that of the (postmodern) Not-All, characterized by increasingly feminine and neighborly values. Such modes of political messianism, whether gradualist or apocalyptic, would propose the neighbor as the path to completing political theology by restoring its missing feminine complement. In addition, just as the sexual relationship between men and women remains fundamentally impossible, so there can be no theoretical paradigm that simply combines these modalities in a unified field theory. We must avoid the fantasmatic structures such accounts imply, both as wishful illusions and as veils cloaking the irreducible trauma of the neighbor's jouissance. The political theology of the neighbor is the *decompletion* of the political theology of sovereignty, the *supplement* that both supplies something that was lacking and inserts something heteronomous into political economy. As Eric Santner has argued, if the politics of sovereignty is defined by the exception, the neighbor constitutes the exception to the exception, the interruption of sovereignty. The politics of the Not-All can be thought of as the decision to say no to the superegoic insistence on All, on jouissance as an *obligation;* as Slavoj Žižek has recently formulated it, this is to reserve the right *not to enjoy,* to desist from the insistence of the sovereign exception. If there is a mode by which Sovereign and Neighbor come together, it can only be by means not of sex, but of love—that is, as the production of something new, what Alain Badiou calls a new open set, a new open part of a world.

In a discussion of Lacan's notion of the "infinity of the not-all" in feminine sexuality, Alain Badiou writes, "the not-all, far from allowing us to extract from it the affirmation that there exists one who is not under the effect of castration, indicates, on the contrary, a particular mode of that effect, namely that it is 'somewhere' and not everywhere. The for-all [*pour-tout*] of the position man is also an everywhere [*partout*]. The somewhere, and not everywhere, of the woman's position is called: not-all."[94] According to Badiou, in the case of women, the universal law of castration is localized as a subset of feminine sexuality, which is itself an *open set,* infinite in scope. The "not-all" does not contradict the fact that

---

94. "le pas-toute, loin qu'on puisse en extraire l'affirmation qu'existe une qui n'est pas sous l'effect de la castration, indique au contraire un mode particulier de cet effet, à savoir qu'il est 'quelque part' et non partout. Le pour-tout de la position homme est aussi un partout. Le quelque part, et non partout, de la position femme se dit: pas-toute" (Alain Badiou, "Sujet et Infini," 291). Badiou is commenting on remarks Lacan makes in the first session of his seminar 19, . . . *ou pire* (1971–1972).

there is no exception to the phallic law within that closed set, but rather, we might say, quietly insists that this is "not all" there is to a woman. Whereas for men the law of the phallus is both inexorable and ubiquitous, for a woman the universality of castration is itself a closed subset within the open set of her subjectivity. Thus, woman's sexuality requires an idea of *infinity*—a theological concept that only mathematics can fully secularize—unlike the claim of "totality" ("the set of all men exists") that determines men's sexuality. And since dialectical relationship is impossible between finite and infinite entities, this, according to Badiou, is what makes a sexual relationship between men and women impossible. Badiou argues that Lacan's use of set theory in these later seminars remains "pre-Cantorian," insofar as his account of the infinity of feminine sexuality does not require its actual existence, but merely its negative virtuality in the finite. Lacan's point is that the infinite of the pas-tout is inaccessible, it is infinite *to men,* not in itself. According to Badiou, however, the *reality* of the infinite must be established mathematically, and it cannot be other than through a pure *decision,* that is, axiomatically: "Silently, in the infinite element of her *jouissance,* a woman must have decided that in regard to the first, phallic, *jouissance,* there exists an inaccessible point that in effect supplements it and determines her as not-all with regard to the phallic function."[95] For Badiou, the actual infinity of woman's jouissance implies that one cannot give a satisfactory account of sexual difference based solely on the phallic function; another function is required, which he calls the "generic function, or the function of humanity."[96]

We will discuss the "generic" set in a moment, but first let's follow Badiou's argument about love and humanity in his essay "What Is Love?" According to Badiou, it is only through *love* that the truth of sexual difference and the impossibility of the sexual relationship emerges, in relationship to the category *humanity:* "The existence of love makes it appear retroactively that, in the disjunction, the female position is oddly the bearer of love's relation to humanity." For a woman, according to Badiou, the human world (made up by the truth procedures of science, art, love, and politics) is only valuable insofar as there is love; when love is present, it infuses itself throughout the field of humanity, linking and correlating its elements. For the man, this is not the case; the truth procedures of life are independent of each other, love is only one field among four in which life unfolds. If for men these elements of human-

95. Alain Badiou, "Sujet et Infini," 297–98.
96. Ibid., 304.

ity are metaphors of each other, each representing the whole of Humanity, for women the elements of life are threads that are meaningless in isolation and that only love can tie into a knot. Thus, in retroactively determining the real of sexual difference, love *creates* Humanity. Badiou writes, "the feminine representation of humanity is at the same time conditional and knotting, which authorizes a more total perception *and* in that case a more abrupt right to inhumanity. However, the masculine representation is at the same time symbolic and separative, which can entail not only indifference but also a greater ability to conclude."[97] According to the masculine paradigm, the link that binds humanity under the conditions of love is that of *metaphor,* the paternal metaphor that inflates the sphere of humanity by defining *similarities* between men and between discursive spheres of life. According to the feminine syntagm, humanity is the *knotting* of various discursive strands and truth procedures, where each element remains both irreducibly itself and intimately imbricated in the others. In Badiou's account, the masculine mode concludes by means of the symbolic technology of mourning, piece-by-piece symbolizing and desymbolizing. The feminine mode, however, is not exactly melancholic, which we might expect according to a Freudian account of their opposition, but allows for separation not only through untying, but through the violent cut that is *inhuman* precisely in getting at the dead heart of the human. Each mode—metaphor and knot—represents different possibilities of binding and unbinding the universalism of humanity: the former, by totalizing; the latter, by infinitizing.

Earlier I borrowed Badiou's terms to describe sexuation as an "event" in being that requires a decision: a choice must be made between positions without positive difference, terms that are virtually indiscernible, in order to establish difference as such—the *two* of sexual difference. However, we can now refine that characterization by further utilizing Badiou's terms and concepts. If the choice of sexuation that is called "man" constructs what Badiou calls a new "situation" from the trauma of the imperative to choose, we can infer that the choice of sexuation called "woman" names an *event,* and as such is *not* constructible, cannot be defined or discerned according to the rules of the set in which it is included. This is to say that woman constitutes what Badiou (following the mathematician Paul Cohen) calls a *generic* set, which Badiou, without further comment, symbolizes as ♀.[98] A "generic set" is included in a sit-

97. Alain Badiou, "What Is Love?" *Umbr(a)* 1 (1996): 52.
98. Cohen uses *G* to symbolize the generic set. Badiou writes, "By a dilection whose origin I leave to the reader to discover, I will choose for this inscription the symbol ♀" (*L'être et l'événement* [Paris:

uation without belonging to it, without being proper to it or presented in it; that is, without being discernible in the terms of the situation. The process of a truth, according to Badiou, is the elaboration of a subset of elements that, although invisible and insignificant from the perspective of the situation, remain faithful to the event and testify to its truth. There are no positive predicates other than this fidelity that unify the elements of generic sets, and they remain *open,* as "sets made up of in-finitely many members that share no common characteristic and con-form to no common rule."⁹⁹ To say directly what Badiou implies by us-ing the symbol ♀ to designate the generic set, the paradigmatic instance of such a set is the set of *not-all women.* Furthermore, we should pay at-tention to the directly political implications of this mathematical no-tion; as Peter Hallward suggests, the axiom of the generic set "justifies the *possibility* . . . of joining 'entirely disparate sets together in unnatural union.'"¹⁰⁰ That is, because the generic set has no positive characteristics other than a connection which is elaborated between it and the event to which it testifies, *new* sets that have no principle of identity can be made by combining generic sets. These new sets can be *unnatural* sets or com-munities that depend on nothing to hold them together and which can-not even be perceived from any position outside the set—*neighborhoods,* we might say, that exist within the political without being determined by citizenship, nationality, or any other legal or autochthonous status. Hence, the logic of the not-all suggests an *infinite* set of possibilities of social inclusion and association distinct from the principles of represen-tation, equality, and totality that determine the conceptual closure of the political theology of the sovereign. Moreover, we can take the risk of further extrapolating from Badiou's account to suggest that such a truth-process, or linked set of fidelities, opens up the space of the political to the love of the neighbor.¹⁰¹ According to Badiou, if the political truth

Seuil, 1988], 392). I am deeply indebted here to Peter Hallward's comments on the generic set in his book *Badiou: A Subject to Truth* (Minneapolis: University of Minnesota Press, 2003).

99. Hallward, *Badiou,* 132.

100. Hallward, *Badiou,* 132; quoting John Randolph Lucas, *Conceptual Roots of Mathematics* (London: Routledge, 2000), 333.

101. Badiou's account of the political has an interesting relationship to Schmitt's. Badiou begins where Schmitt ends, in the sense that he posits that "a fundamental datum of ontology is that the state of the situation always exceeds the situation itself. There are always more parts than ele-ments. . . . This question is really that of power. The power of the State is always superior to that of the situation." But if this superiority of power over situation—an incalculable, errant, intrinsically *infinite* disequilibrium—echoes Schmitt's account of the sovereign's theological ability to declare a state of exception and to act in excess of the laws of nature and the land, the political event per se begins, according to Badiou, only at a secondary phase. It begins in its ability to *interrupt* "the sub-jective errancy of the power of the State," which thereby configures the State as a situation, measures

procedure moves *from the infinite to the one*—the "oneness" of equality that arises when a measure has been given to the disequilibrium of sovereign power—the truth procedure in the case of *love* moves in the opposite direction, *from the one to the infinite,* through the mediation of the two of sexual difference.[102] Badiou writes, "In this sense—and I leave the reader to meditate upon this—politics is love's numerical inverse. In other words, love begins where politics ends."[103] That is, if politics describes a movement from the infinite to the one, by way of three, love describes the movement from the one to the infinite, by way of two (see fig. 2).

Politics   Love

Infinite → 3 → One   //   One → 2 → Infinite

The Neighbor

Figure 2

The political theology of the neighbor opens up where the one truth procedure passes into the other, love into politics or politics into love, precisely at the point of contact of the two "ones" and the two "infinites," the seam where the equality and sameness of the political encounters the singularity and difference of love (see fig. 3). If we think of the relationship between "politics" and "love" in figure 3 as that of the two sides of a Möbius strip, the neighbor marks the point where the strip twists and the one merges into the other—a position with no intrinsic "place" of its own, but always shifting along the continuum created by the ligature of the political and the amorous (see fig. 4). Because the three of politics remains forever incommensurable with the two of love, this moving point must be thought of not as the positive intersection of overlapping sets or topological surfaces, but as the approach of het-

---

its power, and in doing so achieves a degree of "freedom" by putting the state at a distance from its own power.

102. Or, more precisely, through three modalities of the infinite, one of which corresponds to Schmitt's infinite disequilibrium of the sovereign's ability to declare the exception to the situation. Badiou's three modalities of the infinite in politics are (1) the infinite of the situation of collectivity, (2) the infinite disproportion of state power over the collective, and (3) the infinite distance of the freedom opened by fixing a measure to state power ("Politics as Truth Procedure," in *Theoretical Writings,* 157).

103. Ibid., 159–60.

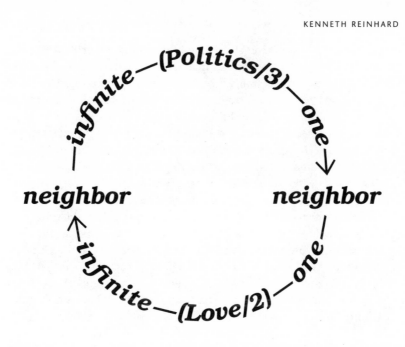

Figure 3

eronomous truth procedures in an infinite calculus of proximity that we name "the neighbor." The question of the role—if any—that the theological plays or can play in Badiou's thinking (a philosophy matched in modernity in its concrete universality and systematic multiplicity perhaps only by that of Rosenzweig) remains open. Badiou does not grant religion the dignity of the four basic truth procedures he describes—pol-

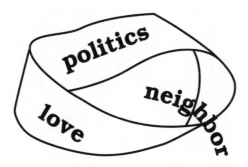

Figure 4

itics, science, art, and love; clearly Badiou's notion of "fidelity" is to be sharply distinguished from any simple notion of religious belief. But perhaps, to follow Badiou's suggestion that we should "meditate" on the fact that "love begins where politics ends," one way to do so would be to propose a political theology of the neighbor.

In a series of lectures delivered at the University of California, Los Angeles, and the University of California, Irvine, in fall 2003 and spring 2004, Alain Badiou presented new theories of love and the neighbor. For Badiou, the question of the neighbor is fundamentally the question of the *neighborhood:* just as there is no possible formulation of a sexual relationship, so two elements in a set, or two people in a world, cannot be directly linked as "neighbors," but only asserted as being in the same neighborhood. And what is a neighborhood? Rather than a definition based on topological nearness or shared points of identification, Badiou describes neighboring in terms of "openness." A neighborhood is an *open* area in a world: a place, subset, or element where there is no boundary, no difference, between the inside of the thing and the thing itself. Similarly, an element can belong to a set without being included in that set; there can still be a something that demarcates a difference between it and the set itself.[104] That is, merely to be on the inside of something is not the same as being included in or interior to that thing or community. For example, a Mexican gardener in Southern California who is an illegal alien is part of the subset called the workforce without being included in that subset, that is, without being proper to it. Badiou calls a set where there is no difference between it and what is interior to it *open*. Hence, to say that one element is neighbor to another is to assert that they are included in a common open set, that there is no difference between each and the set which it is interior to. Furthermore, since the union of two open sets is another open set, the union of two neighborhoods is itself open and thus presents new possibilities of neighboring.

To assert that two elements are "in the same neighborhood," that they are in the interior of the same open place, is not to make an obser-

104. Badiou distinguishes between "membership" and "inclusion" in a set in *L'être et l'événement:* "membership" is the originary relation of set theory, whereby a multiple (a set of elements, all multiples in themselves) is counted as *belonging* to another multiple (another set). According to the "power set axiom" of classical set theory, however, every set is made up not only of its elements or subsets but also of the *set* of all its elements, which must be considered as distinct from and excessive to those elements or subsets themselves. This set of all the subsets of a set does not belong to the set but is *included* in that set and thereby marks an ontological gap in the set—and, for Badiou, in being itself (*L'être et l'événement* [Paris: Éditions du Seuil, 1988], 95–107).

vation or an interpretation, according to Badiou; it is a *decision,* one that involves work, a force and *forcing* rather than the passivity that "being open" might suggest. This work is the construction of a common open area, a new place of universality. The question of the neighborhood, finally, is subjective, a question that calls for a decision to be in the interior of a place and that requires fidelity and work to remain open. We may choose, Badiou insists. Either we can point to our objective differences, the things that separate us from the world, the differences that wall off an inside from an outside, or we can expose ourselves to the world. If our particularity and individuality are what we preserve in the first choice, the decision to be in a neighborhood—located in a particular place, but *open*—is for the sake of universality. And insofar as the union of open sets is itself open, an unlimited number of open sets can be united without being closed or totalized. Hence, the neighborhood opens on *infinity,* endlessly linking new elements in new subsets according to new decisions and fidelities. The political theology of the sovereign elaborated by Schmitt is based on a logic of the boundary; even if the limit is always transgressed in the sovereign's incipient decision to suspend the law, transgression is the exception that proves and reasserts the limit's rule. Badiou's notion of the neighborhood, as a set where *no boundary* separates the set and its members and *no limit* is drawn between inside and outside, can contribute to the elaboration of a political theology of the neighbor. And just as much as the political theology of the sovereign is based on an arbitrary, nondetermined moment of choice, so the opening of a political theology of the neighbor requires a purely subjective act, a *decision.*

For Badiou, *love* is the decision to create a new open set, to knot two interiorities into a new logic of world, a new *neighborhood.* Whereas Lacan argues that love is the supplement for the radical lack of the sexual relationship, for Badiou this supplementarity must be understood not as the (imaginary) dissimulation of or (symbolic) compensation for the sexual failure, but as the real encounter that occurs precisely on the basis of the impossibility of the sexual relation and that retroactively *creates* sexual difference.[105] According to Badiou,

---

105. The complicated question arises here as to the degree of difference between Badiou's position and Lacan's. For Badiou, Lacan's account of love is "pessimistic": he argues that Lacan's statement that love makes up for the lack of a sexual relationship makes love into no more than a poor substitute for sexual nonrelationship. However, it is not clear to me that this fairly represents everything that Lacan says about love. I would suggest that for Lacan there are at least two modes of love, one that is an illusion that merely disguises the truth of nonrelationship and another that involves a real encounter. But this is an elaborate issue that cannot be taken up in full here.

There is at least one non-null term that enters in its place in rapport with the two sexed positions. We will inscribe this term, supposed local mediator of global non-rapport, under the letter *u*. . . . So I advance what I could call the humanistic thesis, which is that the two positions M and W share a multitude of predicatives allowing for detailing almost to infinity their common membership in Humanity. This thesis in reality hearkens back to the non-rapport, to support a detailed description: that what the two terms have in common makes a sort of acceptable approximation of a rapport. It is clear that if there is certainly an element which ties up the two non-related terms in the space of non-rapport, it is certain that this element is absolutely indeterminate, indescribable, uncomposable.[106]

For Badiou, it is only on the basis of love that the fact of two sexes can retroactively be established; it is not that sexual difference is the basis for love, but that *love is the condition of sexual difference,* love *makes* the sexes two. The point *u* of love, unlike the *objet a* of desire, establishes the conditions for an encounter that produces an authentic *twoness*—rather than the false attempts of the Romantic notion of love to create an imaginary "one" (mystical union) or the Christian notion of love to create a symbolic "three" (a child)—through which desire supports itself. The truth of love occurs on the site of the failure of sex—love is itself the truth of sex, in the sense that it creates *the two* that sex fails to bring together in relationship. Badiou writes, "love is the only available experience of a Two counted from itself, of an immanent Two. Each singular love has this of the universal—that, were it ignored by everyone, it contributed on its part, while limping along as long as it could, to establish that the Two can be thought in its place, a place supported partially by the hegemony of the One as well as by the inclusion of the Three." On the ground of the real, between the "One" of the family and the "Three" of the political, love works to find and hold fast to a Two, an immanent two, two-as-such, the result of neither addition nor subtraction, a Two that does not fall into One or reach up to Three, but to infinity: "One, Two, infinity: such is the numericity of the amorous procedure. It structures the becoming of a generic truth. What truth? The truth of the situation *insofar as there exist two disjunct positions.*"[107] If the situation, the state of affairs, the status quo of a particular world, presents itself *as if* it were unified, love is what "fractures" that imaginary unity, brings out the universal truth of disjunction in a particular situation. The world

106. Badiou, "The Scene of Two," *Lacanian Ink* 21 (2003): 48.
107. Badiou, "What Is Love?" 45.

that love opens, the new neighborhood, *within* the political and *beyond* the familial, is the only place where the two may be encountered as such. Badiou suggests that to love the neighbor is to create a new open space, a new *universality* in a particular place.

In a talk on the topic of "Psychoanalysis in the City," Jacques-Alain Miller commented on Lacan's notion of the not-all in terms of changing world political reality. According to Miller, the theory of psychoanalytic practice that Lacan inherited from Freud was situated in a world in which the function of the father and the politics of patriarchy were still dominant, but that is no longer the case.[108] Miller follows Antonio Negri's description of the current historical moment as no longer "disciplinary," in the Foucauldian sense, but a new time of *empire:* "What [Negri] calls *impero,* empire, is a regime that no longer proceeds by prohibition and repression and which, thus, renders transgression and the very idea of revolution and liberation problematic."[109] Miller describes the "machines" that produce the civilizations of Discipline and Empire in terms of Lacan's formulas of sexuation and as a shift from the logic of "all" to that of "not-all":

The function of the father is in effect linked to the structure that Lacan discovered in masculine sexuation. A structure that comprises an all with a supplementary and antinomic element that poses a limit, and which allows the all to be constituted precisely as such, which poses the limit and thus allows for organization and stability. This structure is the very matrix of the hierarchical relation. The not-all is not an all that includes a lack, but on the contrary a series in development without limit and without totalization. This is why the term of globalization is a vacillating term for us, since it is precisely a question of there being no longer any all and, in the current process, what constitutes the all, and what constitutes a limit, is threatened and staggers. What is called globalization is a process of detotalization that puts all the "totalitarian" structures to the test. It is a process by which no element is provided with an attribute it can be as-

108. "The entire Freudian conceptual apparatus retains the mark of the disciplinary epoch: interdiction, repression, censorship . . . which is what permitted a junction between psychoanalysis and Marxism, in the form of Freudo-Marxism or the 1968 style of contestation. . . . Lacan conceptualized psychoanalysis during the disciplinary epoch, but . . . he also anticipated the psychoanalysis of the imperial epoch" (Jacques-Alain Miller, "Milanese Intuitions [1]," *Mental Online: International Journal of Mental Health and Applied Psychoanalysis* 11 [May 2003]: 13, www.mental-nls.com).

109. Describing the current postdisciplinary era, Miller writes, "Everything is now an affair of arrangement. We no longer dream of what is outside. There is nothing but trajectories, arrangements and regimes of jouissance. The Borromean knot is already an effort to find a way out of a structure based on binary opposition and the disciplinary organization that this cleavage implies" (ibid., 14).

sured of by principle and forever. We do not have the security of the attribute, but its attributes, its properties, its accomplishments are precarious. The not-all implies precariousness for the element.[110]

The formulas of man's sexuation also describe the political logic of the Freudo-Marxist era, when the world was understood as a totality, species were defined in terms of genera, and entities were assumed to be possessed of stable properties. According to Miller, the new globalism expresses not only the logic of the not-all, but also specifically feminine qualities: "the rise in society of values said to be feminine, those of compassion, of the promotion of listening practices, of the politics of proximity, all of which must from now on affect political leaders. The spectacle of the world may be becoming decipherable, more decipherable if we relate it to the machine of the not-all."[111] Miller's formulation of the relationship of the masculine "all" and feminine "not-all" reflects some aspects of the relationship we described between the love of God (structured under the Name of the Father) and the love of the Neighbor (the encounter with the Thing) and gives us some more indication of what the political theology of the not-all might be like. Although we may not share Miller's confidence that the world we find ourselves in today is one that supports "feminine values" and psychoanalytic "listening practices" any more than during the modern "disciplinary" phase of the regime of capitalism, we can take his essay as a confirmation of the expediency of developing a political theology of the neighbor in the topology of the not-all.

We must be cautious, however, about accepting the positive value of the "politics of proximity" that Miller calls for, despite its evocation of the relationship of nearness or neighborliness. Proximity in Levinas represents the infinite approach of the other, the other whose otherness "obsesses" me, excluding all other concerns, yet maintained at a certain distance from the self in order to prevent its assimilation to selfsameness. In this sense, proximity as an absolute value is changeless, static, what we might call a figure of "bad infinity." What is excluded here is the question of a community of such neighbors, the *neighborhood* that is infinite in its openness, its lack of boundaries, and its *lack of* obsession with the otherness of the other. Moreover, Miller sees the not-all

110. Jacques-Alain Miller, "Milanese Intuitions (2)," *Mental Online* 12 (May 2003): 11–12, www.mental-nls.com.

111. Ibid., 12.

as a historical development from the All, the progression from an era of "Man" to one of "women." Although at times this may have some descriptive value, I am inclined to see the All and the not-all as logical events rather than chronological situations, simultaneous rather than sequential, and to see them together as defining a structure that always determines political theology, rather than as the supersession of one by the other. Finally, Miller's characterization of the logic of the not-all as that of "globalization" risks losing the *universalism* of the political theology of the neighbor. As Eric Santner points out in *On the Psychotheology of Everyday Life*, a truly psychoanalytic universalism is opposed to "globalism," at least in its current dominant understanding: "for global consciousness, every stranger is ultimately just like me, ultimately familiar. . . . For the psychoanalytic conception of universality . . . it is just the reverse: the possibility of a 'We,' of communality, is granted on the basis of the fact that every familiar is ultimately strange and that, indeed, I am even in a crucial sense a stranger to myself." [112]

How can we find the place of the neighbor between the two of love and the three of politics? According to Lacan, it is only by way of the three, by beginning with the political. Lacan argues that the injunction to "love the neighbor as yourself" is precisely the elaboration of the three and the emergence of a new two from out of it; "it's only because we count to three that we can count to two": "If I have said that religion is that of which one can make the most true . . . I'm going to draw your attention to what I've yakked on about for quite a while, right? that you shall love your neighbor as yourself—does that mean you will be three, yes or no? Yeah. The Borromean knot can only be made of three. The imaginary and the symbolic are not enough, a third element is needed, and I designate it the real." [113] Why are *three loves* implied by the injunction, rather than two (love of my neighbor, love of myself)? Love of myself is *imaginary*, the specular reflection on myself that constitutes the narcissistic ego in the mirror stage; and love of the neighbor is *real*, insofar as the neighbor harbors the strange kernel of enjoyment Freud and Lacan call the Thing. However, this twoness cannot be reached directly and does not subsist on its own, Lacan argues, except by passing by way

---

112. Santner, *On the Psychotheology of Everyday Life*, 5–6.
113. Lacan, *Les non-dupes errent*, December 11, 1973. Lacan argues that when we add one signifier (or number) to another, we do not get two, but *three*, since we also need to take into account the "decoding" or computation that was involved. Hence, even the primary relationship that the master's discourse describes, between S_1 and S_2, involves the *relationship* between them, indicated as $ (the subject). See Badiou, *Le nombre et les nombres* (Paris: Seuil, 1990).

love of God

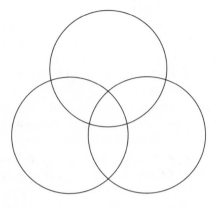

love of self   *love of neighbor*

Figure 5

of the third love, never superseded, the *love of God,* which is the model of symbolic love, the love of the father that sustains the symbolic order. Hence, love of the neighbor *includes within it* the love of God, and together they constitute the Borromean knot of political theology (see fig. 5). Drawing such a knot on the board during a session of his seminar of 1973–74, entitled *Les non-dupes errent,* Lacan comments,

If we take the symbolic as playing the role of the means [*moyen*] between the Real and the Imaginary . . . we are thus at the heart of that love which I just spoke about under the name of divine love. . . . The symbolic taken as love . . . is under the form of this commandment, which praises to the skies being and love. Insofar as it joins something as being and as love, these two things can only be said to support the Real on the one hand and the Imaginary on the other. . . . This is where the dimension of *love your neighbor as yourself* comes from. I've got to say it: be a dupe and you won't err.[114]

The Borromean knot is characterized by the fact that each loop holds together the other two; to cut one is to unravel the connection between the other two. In terms of the three loves, this implies that the relation-

114. Lacan, *Les non-dupes errent,* December 18, 1973.

ship between any two terms requires the third: the subject loves the neighbor only by means of the love of God, and loves God only by means of the love of the neighbor. Moreover, these relationships involve what Lacan characterizes as a kind of salutary *"dupery"*: the nondupes err, according to Lacan, insofar as they believe themselves free of the traps of fantasy, the eruptions of the unconscious, and most of all, the chains of religious ideology. It is only those who know themselves "duped" by these structures, ensnared in their logic, who are able to find a kind of nonerrance. Lacan comments to the analysts and academics in his seminar, "I know quite well you're not believers, right? But you are all the more conned, because even if you aren't believers . . . you believe. I'm not saying that you assume it: *it assumes you.*" [115] For Lacan, the force of religious discourse is not contingent on whether or not we believe in God, whether we take commandments such as "love your neighbor as yourself" seriously as binding, as *law,* or dismiss them as naive moral recommendations. Our subjectivity is itself a function of the intransigent signifiers called "scripture," which, needless to say, are often mobilized for dupery, knavery, and some of the worst crimes perpetrated against humanity. Nevertheless, these signifiers are weighted with a reality that is ignored only at the cost of even greater errors, foolery, and suffering. To be a dupe is, of course, not a guarantee of nonerrance: a "fool for God" is still a fool. But to fail to take the risk of dupery by resorting to the lures of cynical reason is surely to err.

I would like to suggest here a possible schematization that may help us describe the contours of the political theology of the neighbor (see fig. 6). If we think of these circles as both threads in a Borromean knot and the intersecting sets of a Venn diagram, the following implications emerge. The intersection of the self and the neighbor is negative, the abyss of the other's jouissance that inhabits me, in the form of the *objet a,* the remnant of the primordial Thing. The intersection of the self and God is the primal signifier, the Name of the Father, by which the subject is interpellated into the symbolic order, taken up into the All that is defined by the law of castration: $\forall x \, \Phi x$. The intersection of the neighbor and God is the place of the not-all, the field of the subject who chooses to inscribe herself as "woman," $\overline{\forall x} \, \Phi x$. And the empty place in

---

115. Ibid. The name of this year of Lacan's seminar puns on the famous undelivered seminar of ten years earlier, "Les Noms du Père," which, after a first session, Lacan cancelled, refusing to ever take it up again. The seminar called *Les non-dupes errent* is a way for Lacan to put something in the place of "the Names of the Father" without literally breaking his vow to leave it unspoken. It is as if Lacan is warning us against imagining that knowledge of the paternal signifiers would allow us to escape from their grasp, reminding us that we must find a more subtle strategy if we wish not to err.

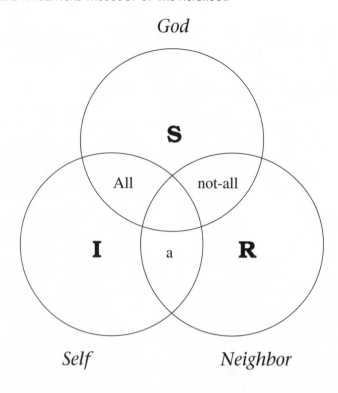

God

S

All   not-all

I   a   R

Self   *Neighbor*

Figure 6

the center, the point of intersection of God, Self, and Neighbor? We might be tempted to locate the phallus there, as the signifier of lack whose vicissitudes link the symbolic, imaginary, and real. But perhaps it is better to leave it open, in order to allow it to signify precisely the Open, the set that is identical with its interior.

To conclude, let me propose six theses concerning the political theology of the neighbor.

1. The political theology of the neighbor is supplementary to the political theology of the sovereign. As such, it is not merely an addition to the theory of sovereignty, but *decompletes* it by subtracting something from the field of the political and naming it the neighbor.

2. The political theology of the neighbor opens up between the family and the polis; it is an act of spacing that maintains the minimum distance required to resist holophrastic fusion (totalitarianism) and possessive individualism (liberal democracy). The space it clears is open, infinite.

3. The political theology of the neighbor thinks the universal from the situation of differences. The condition of the particular comes to stand for the possibility of the universal, not in the reduction of differences, but by determining what is *singularly universal* in them. Hence, justice is not a function of equalizing differences, but depends on sublimating in thought the different to the condition of the same.

4. The political theology of the neighbor materializes the deadlock of ethics and politics. It assumes their radical incommensurability and finds its resources in their disjunction. The knowledge sought by the political theology of the neighbor is not symbolic or imaginary, but knowledge in the real.

5. The political theology of the neighbor is not descriptive but prescriptive. It speaks in the imperative, but without affect, aspiring to the condition of mathematics: "Let x = the neighbor, y = myself, and z = God . . ." It speaks in the name of a law that has been drained of its jouissance and remains as pure structure.

6. The temporality of the political theology of the neighbor is a present tense messianism; it dilates the time of the now by resisting both historicism and progressivism. It is a profane science through which redemption may make its quietest approach.

ERIC L. SANTNER

Miracles Happen: Benjamin, Rosenzweig, Freud, and the Matter of the Neighbor

Most readers of this essay will no doubt be familiar with the famous allegory with which Walter Benjamin begins his theses "On the Concept of History." This opaque little text, written during the first years of World War II, shortly before Benjamin's death, concerns the relation between historical materialism and theology. The former is figured as a chess-playing automaton in Turkish attire who is able to defeat all opponents; beneath the table, hidden by a series of mirrors, sits a hunchbacked dwarf who, as the real chess master manipulating the puppet with a series of strings, holds the place of a theology about which secular, enlightened subjects have grown ashamed. One of the difficulties presented by the allegory is, of course, that in its final self-interpretive moment, it is the puppet—historical materialism—that is endowed with intentionality, agency, and the capacity to exploit the resources of theology: "The puppet called 'historical materialism' is to win all the time. It can easily be a match for anyone *if it enlists the services of theology*, which today, as we know, is small and ugly and has to keep out of sight."[1] At some level, this allegory condenses the entirety

1. Walter Benjamin, "On the Concept of History," trans. Harry Zohn, in *Walter Benjamin: Selected Writings*, vol. 4, *1938–40*, ed. Howard Eiland and Michael W.

of Benjamin's philosophical, political, and literary-critical project. At its core we find two interrelated questions. First, what sort of *materiality* is at issue in historical materialism if it is to be informed and oriented by theology? And second, what must this theology look like if it is to be up to such a task? As I see it, our understanding of Benjamin stands or falls with our capacity to engage with these questions. My hunch is that this engagement might best be served by way of a detour through the work of Franz Rosenzweig, the philosopher whose own efforts to construct a "modernist" theology laid a significant piece of the groundwork for Benjamin's approach. In the following, I will make this detour by following the tracks of a central theme in Rosenzweig's work, the question as to the viability of the concept of *miracle* in a post-Enlightenment age.

I

Some twenty years before Benjamin composed his allegory of historical materialism, Rosenzweig wrote an allegory that in its own way addressed a certain shame that had come to disfigure the features of modern theological thought. The introduction to the second volume of Rosenzweig's magnum opus, *The Star of Redemption*—a work composed during and shortly after World War I—bears the title "On the Possibility of Experiencing Miracles" and begins with the following narrative (taking a quote from Goethe's *Faust* as its point of departure):

If miracle is really the favorite child of belief, then its father has been neglecting his paternal duties badly, at least for some time. For at least a hundred years the child has been nothing but a source of embarrassment to the nurse which he had ordered for it—to theology. She would have gladly been rid of it if only—well if only a degree of consideration for the father had not forbidden it during his lifetime. But time solves all problems. The old man cannot live forever. And thereupon the nurse will know what she must do with this poor little worm which can neither live nor die under its own power; she has already made the preparations.[2]

Jennings (Cambridge, MA: Harvard University Press, 2003), 389. Until recently, the accepted English title of this text was "Theses on the Philosophy of History," the title used in the collection of Benjamin's essays edited by Hannah Arendt, *Illuminations*. For the sake of brevity and because this is the title most familiar to readers of Benjamin in English, I will continue to refer to this text as the "Theses."

2. Franz Rosenzweig, *The Star of Redemption*, trans. William Hallo (Notre Dame, IN: University of Notre Dame Press, 1985), 93. Subsequent references are given in the text.

Given the conventional identification of the Enlightenment with the triumph of reason over superstition, it should come as no surprise that Rosenzweig's account of this state of affairs—the gradual attenuation of the concept of miracle, its place within our form of life—takes the form of a brief history of the Enlightenment, or, as he prefers, a history of a staggered *series* of enlightenment moments culminating in the embarrassment which now shadows the very word *miracle*. As Rosenzweig puts it, "there is not just one enlightenment but a number of enlightenments. One after another, they periodically represent for the belief that has entered the world that knowledge with which it must contend" (*Star,* 97).

The first in this series is the triumph of philosophy over myth in antiquity, a triumph that Nietzsche would famously characterize as that of Socrates over Dionysus. The second "enlightenment" refers to the Renaissance and Reformation, in which the calcified legacies of Aristotle (above all in scholasticism) were supplanted by the privileging of direct, experimental encounter with nature, on the one hand, and of spiritual experience authorized only by scripture and the strength of faith, on the other. For Rosenzweig, the eighteenth-century moment we have come to refer to as the Enlightenment signals the moment when the trust in the reliability of experience and the historical/scriptural record of experience itself begins, in its turn, to appear as a form of naive belief. In each case, what at first occupies the place of knowledge over against belief comes to be retroactively posited as a groundless form of belief. As Rosenzweig summarizes this series, "the enlightenment of antiquity had directed its criticism against the dreams of mythology, that of the Renaissance against the webs of intellect [*die Gespinste der Vernunft*]. The new enlightenment directed it against the gullibility of experience [*die Leichtgläubigkeit der Erfahrung*]. As critique of experience, it became, slowly but surely, a historical critique" (*Star,* 98). It is only at this point, Rosenzweig insists, that miracles truly become a problem for both knowledge and faith; since miracles ultimately depend on the testimony of witnesses— the ultimate witness being the martyr—once testimony was laid open to critical historical analysis, the credibility of miracles, the very ones that fill the pages of scripture and had so long served as a support for faith, could not long survive.

At the heart of what Rosenzweig refers to as historical critique, or the "historical *Weltanschauung*," is the demand, understood as the voice of reason itself, to free oneself from the weight of tradition, from the so-called truths of the past which, because they belong to a concrete historical context and horizon of experience, can no longer make binding claims upon the present and future. "Revelation," if it can still be called that, must be an immanent feature of, must in some sense be nothing but, the self-education of human reason itself, *"mankind's exit from its self-incurred immaturity,"* as Kant famously put it.[3] The past becomes identified with dogmatic invention, mythic projection, or at the very least, a historical specificity that places radical limits on its cultural, political, and moral relevance for the present; it is by definition subject to the suspicions and doubts of the critical faculty of reason which is now posited as the ultimate arbiter of what shall count as being authoritative for human society. As Aleida Assmann has succinctly put it, *"Aufklärung bedeutet Traditionsbruch"* (Enlightenment means break with tradition / break-up of tradition).[4] With the historical enlightenment, then, the last vestiges of the view according to which knowing meant in some sense to *inherit* knowledge, are expunged.[5] This liberation from the past was, Rosenzweig suggests, already well underway in German Pietism, which, beginning in the latter part of the seventeenth century, had already elaborated a new concept of belief that no longer depended on the historical objectivity of miracles. This view would come to be consolidated by Friedrich Schleiermacher in a theology of *Erlebnis* that posited the present intensity of religious feeling as the crucial warrant of faith.

For Rosenzweig, the authentication of faith by way of religious *feeling* rather than the "heteronomy" of scriptural *testimony* was profoundly connected to another crucial tenet of the historical enlightenment: the belief in progress. In secular culture, the break with the dogmatic hold of tradition opened a new confidence in human capacities to understand and master the recalcitrance of the natural world and the social, moral, and political obstacles to a rational organization of society. "Just so, for its part," Rosenzweig writes, "the new belief fastened the present moment of the inner breakthrough of grace to the confidence of its future

---

3. Immanuel Kant, "An Answer to the Question: What Is Enlightenment?" quoted in *What Is Enlightenment? Eighteenth-Century Answers and Twentieth-Century Questions*, ed. James Schmidt (Berkeley: University of California Press, 1996), 58.

4. Aleida Assmann, *Arbeit am nationalen Gedächtnis. Eine kurze Geschichte der deutschen Bildungsidee* (Frankfurt: Campus, 1993), 32. Jean-Joseph Goux has recently offered his own quite powerful genealogy of this enlightenment gesture of self-orphaning. Positing its emergence in the figure of Oedipus, who confronts the Sphinx without recourse to the traditional/mythic conventions of initiatory ordeal, he locates its modern culmination in the *cogito* of Descartes: "Opposed to any genealogical position that attaches the individual to a line of succession (noble or initiatory) and that bases the existence of a subject only on its relation to an ancestral chain that it continues, the Cartesian gesture is the formidable claim of a subject who has broken away from his inheritance, proclaiming his absolute autonomy and basing his legitimacy on himself alone" (Goux, *Oedipus, Philosopher*, trans. Catherine Porter [Stanford, CA: Stanford University Press, 1993], 160–61).

5. One of the paradoxes of the Enlightenment is that the break with tradition needed to be *cultivated* and one form that this culture took was that of Freemasonry, in which one had to be *initiated* into the sublime mysteries revealed in this break with the illusions of tradition.

implementation in life. . . . This hope in the future realm of morality became the star to which belief hitched its world course" (*Star*, 100). The progressive movement toward the *telos* of a future kingdom of morality—*das zukünftige Reich der Sittlichkeit*—thus became the guidepost, albeit in different idioms, for knowledge as well as for belief. Both thereby opened on to the new bourgeois ideology of scientific and moral progress through *Bildung*.

The mandate of *Bildung*, or self-education and self-cultivation, though emerging out of a new and radical valorization of present and future at the expense of the past, included, of course, an explicit demand for historical research. This research, whereby the past would be, so to speak, "surrendered to cognition" (*Star*, 99), would serve in the end to further free the present from its moorings in tradition. To this very purpose, theology after 1800 became *historical theology*. As Paul Mendes-Flohr has put it, "historical theology sought to neutralize the past, to tame it and its claims on the present, in order to secure the autonomy of the present."[6] Nietzsche's own infamous "claim" about the death of God is, ultimately, one concerning this "dialectic of enlightenment" as a dynamic *within* Christianity itself. In Nietzsche's view, the ascetic ideal internal to Christianity eventually takes aim at God Himself, culminating in an "honest atheism" that dismantles the presuppositions of the possibility of experiencing miracles:

What, in all strictness, has really *conquered* the Christian God? . . . Christian morality itself, the concept of truthfulness taken more and more strictly, the confessional subtlety of the Christian conscience translated and sublimated into the scientific conscience, into intellectual cleanliness at any price. To view nature as if it were a proof of the goodness and providence of a God; to interpret history to the glory of a divine reason, as the perpetual witness to a moral world order and moral intentions; to interpret one's own experiences, as pious men long interpreted them, as if everything were preordained, everything a sign, everything sent for salvation of the soul—that now belongs to the *past*, that has conscience *against* it. . . . In this way Christianity *as a dogma* was destroyed by its own morality.[7]

6. Paul Mendes-Flohr, "Rosenzweig's Concept of Miracle," in *Jüdisches Denken in einer Welt ohne Gott. Festschrift für Stephane Moses*, ed. Jens Mattern, Gabriel Motzkin, and Shimon Sandbank (Berlin: Verlag Vorwerk 8, 2000), 57. This entire essay is deeply indebted to Mendes-Flohr's discussion as well as to numerous conversations in private and in the context of a team-taught seminar on Rosenzweig at the University of Chicago in the winter quarter 2002.

7. Friedrich Nietzsche, *On the Genealogy of Morals*, trans. Walter Kaufmann (New York: Vintage, 1969), 160–61. For a brilliant reading of this passage in the larger context of Nietzsche's elaboration of the nihilism in which it culminates, see Alenka Zupancic, *The Shortest Shadow: Nietzsche's Philosophy of the Two* (Cambridge, MA: MIT Press, 2003).

Perhaps the most concise summary of this state of affairs is provided by Serenus Zeitblom, the narrator of Thomas Mann's great novel *Doktor Faustus,* a novel that was, of course, largely based on Nietzsche's own biography and the "event" of Nietzsche in European culture more generally. After joining his friend Adrian Leverkühn at the University of Halle, where the latter was studying theology, Zeitblom quickly registers the sense of crisis in the theological faculty at the turn of the century:

In its [theology's] conservative form, holding tight to revelation and traditional exegesis, it has attempted to "save" whatever elements of biblical religion could be saved; and on the other, liberal, side, theology has accepted the historical-critical methods of profane historical science and "abandoned" its most important beliefs—miracles, large portions of Christology, the physical resurrection of Jesus, and more besides—to scientific criticism. What sort of science is that, which has such a precarious, coerced relationship with reason and is threatened with ruin by the very compromise it makes with it? . . . In its affirmation of culture and ready compliance with the ideals of bourgeois society, it demotes religion to a function of man's humaneness and waters down the ecstatic and paradoxical elements inherent in religious genius to ethical progressiveness. . . . And so, it is said, although the scientific superiority of liberal theology is incontestable, its theological position is weak, for its moralism and humanism lack any insight into *the demonic character of human existence.*[8]

Of course, Mann's narrator quickly warns of the dangers theology runs if it seeks a way out of this impasse by incorporating the terms of so-called *Lebensphilosophie:* "The civilized mind, however—one may call it bourgeois, or simply leave it at civilized—cannot shake off the sense of something uncanny. For by its very nature, theology, once it is linked with the spirit of Life Philosophy, with irrationalism, runs the risk of becoming demonology."[9] As I understand it, Rosenzweig's project was dedicated to elaborating an entirely new conception of the "demonic"—as well of "miracle"—that would allow theology to move beyond the limits of historicism without thereby succumbing to the irrationalism—the fanatical, quasi-mystical *Schwärmerei*—of any sort of *Lebensphilosophie.*[10]

8. Thomas Mann, *Doktor Faustus: The Life of the German Composer Adrian Leverkühn as Told by a Friend,* trans. John E. Woods (New York: Vintage, 1999), 99; my emphasis.
9. Ibid.
10. One might argue, of course, that such was also the goal of Mann's hero, Adrian Leverkühn, in the realm of aesthetics, in general, and music, in particular. In his essay published in this volume, Slavoj Žižek suggests that the dimension of the "demonic" in question here emerged in the wake of the Kantian revolution of thought and therewith belongs to that constellation that Rosenzweig liked to refer to as "1800." What is in question here is "a terrifying excess which, although it negates what we understand as 'humanity,' is inherent to being-human." "In the pre-Kantian universe," Žižek con-

To return for a moment to Benjamin's allegory, we might summarize the gist of Rosenzweig's contribution to its interpretation as follows: a theology that has lost sight of a "demonic" or "inhuman" dimension immanent to the human—and a concept of miracle correlative to it—could never be of any use to historical materialism, because it has itself already become a version of the historicist perspective that materialism was supposed to supplant (Benjamin's *Theses* are, among other things, a radical critique of historicism). This deadlock may hold the key, however, to the paradoxical moment we've already noted in Benjamin's allegory, the moment when the location of agency becomes undecidable in the relation between automaton and dwarf, in other words, when it becomes unclear who is really in charge of the game. The lesson of that uncertainty is, I would suggest, that if materialism is to find its orientation from theology, as Benjamin indicates, this must be a theology that has itself already turned toward materialism as its necessary supplement in a post-Enlightenment age. There must, in other words, be an ongoing exchange of properties, of activity and passivity, between the two. And indeed, this is precisely what Rosenzweig, albeit in somewhat different terms, suggests:

> for the sake of its very status as science, philosophy [historical materialism, in Benjamin's allegory] requires "theologians" to philosophize—theologians, however, now likewise in a new sense. For . . . the theologian whom philosophy requires for the sake of its scientific status is himself a theologian who requires philosophy—for the sake of his integrity. . . . They are dependent on each other and so generate jointly a new type, be it philosopher or theologian, situated between theology and philosophy. (*Star,* 106)

This interstitial space is the locus of what Rosenzweig came to understand as the "new thinking."[11]

For Rosenzweig, philosophy can enter into this new relationship with theology only if it can hold the place of the "materialist" dimension which had been neglected in liberal theology, namely the dimension of *creation:*

---

tinues, "humans were simply humans, beings of reason, fighting the excesses of animal lusts and divine madness, but since Kant and German Idealism, the excess to be fought is absolutely immanent, the very core of subjectivity itself." (Žižek, "Neighbors and Other Monsters," p. 160 in this volume).

11. Rosenzweig used this term in an essay of the same name which he wrote to clarify certain points made in the *Star.* See "The New Thinking," in *Franz Rosenzweig: Philosophical and Theological Writings,* trans. Paul W. Franks and Michael L. Morgan (Indianapolis: Hackett, 2000). Benjamin's work, qua "new thinking," cannot, therefore, be divided up into separate clusters or phases, the one metaphysical/theological, the other materialist/Marxist. The "creaturely" materiality in question for Benjamin was one that required theology to conceptualize.

Thus creation has once more to be placed next to the experience of revelation in the full gravity of its substantiality [*in vollem Schwergewicht ihrer Gegenständlichkeit*]. More than this: the only connection which hope is able to establish between revelation and redemption, and which today is felt to be the essential core of belief, is the trust in the coming of an ethical kingdom of eventual redemption; revelation itself, together with its involvement in and foundation upon this trust, *must once more be built into the concept of creation.* . . . Here, then, lies the point from which philosophy can begin to reconstruct the whole edifice of theology. It was creation which theology neglected in the nineteenth century in its obsession with the idea of a vitally present revelation. And precisely creation is now the gate through which philosophy enters into the house of theology. (*Star,* 103; my emphasis)

II

Rosenzweig's understanding of such a philosophy of creation (or perhaps better, creatureliness)—which I am here attempting to link to Benjamin's conception of historical materialism—must be understood against the background of what he characterizes as the fundamentally *semiotic* structure of miracles. "A miracle," as Rosenzweig puts it in the *Star,* "is essentially a 'sign'" [*Das Wunder ist wesentlich "Zeichen";* trans. modified]. While today one can imagine a miracle only as a breach of natural law of some sort, "for the consciousness of erstwhile humanity," Rosenzweig writes, "miracle was based on an entirely different circumstance, namely, on its having been predicted, not on its deviation from the course of nature as this had previously been fixed by law." As Rosenzweig succinctly puts it, "Miracle and prophecy belong together" (*Star,* 95). In the first instance, Rosenzweig is thinking here of the efforts made by both Judaism and Christianity to anchor the ultimate miracle—that of revelation—in prior "predictions" or signs. "To lend the character of a portent to their miracles of revelation is . . . of supreme importance both to Scripture and to the New Testament. The former does so through the promise to the patriarchs, the latter through the prophecies of the prophets" (*Star,* 96).[12] The crucial distinction here is, thus, between prophecy and sorcery:

12. One of Rosenzweig's many claims about Islam is that the Koran is not organized around this semiotic structure of prefiguration and fulfillment: "Mohammed came upon the idea of revelation and took it over as such a find is wont to be taken over, that is, without generating it out of its presuppositions. The Koran is a 'Talmud' not based on a 'Bible,' a 'New' Testament not based on an 'Old' Testament. Islam has only revelation, not prophecy. In it, therefore, the miracle of revelation is not a 'sign,' it is not the revelation of divine providence, active in creation, as a 'plan of salvation.' Rather the Koran is a miracle in itself, and thus a magical miracle" (*Star,* 116).

Sorcery and portent [*Zeichen*] lie on different planes. . . . The magician turns on the course of the world in active intervention. . . . He attacks God's providence and seeks by audacity, guile, or coercion to extort from it what is unforeseen and unforeseeable by it, what is willed by his own will. The prophet, on the other hand, unveils, as he foresees it, what is willed by providence. What would be sorcery in the hands of the magician, becomes portent in the mouth of the prophet. And by pronouncing the portent, the prophet proves the dominion of providence which the magician denies. He proves it, for how would it be possible to foresee the future if it were not "provided"? And therefore it is incumbent to outdo the heathen miracle, to supplant its spell, which carries out the command of man's own might, with the portent which demonstrates God's providence. (*Star,* 95)

The distinction between magical and providential miracle, between sorcery and sign-event, plays a crucial role in the so-called waters of Meribah episode recounted in Numbers 20. There, one will recall, Moses and Aaron are once more faced with the rebellious lament of the Israelites, who complain of the hardships of their wanderings: "'And why have you made us come up out of Egypt, to bring us to this evil place? It is no place for grain, or figs, or vines, or pomegranates; and there is no water to drink.'" Moses and Aaron withdraw from the assembly and supplicate God, who thereupon tells Moses: "'Take the rod and assemble the congregation, you and Aaron your brother, and tell the rock before their eyes to yield its water; so you shall bring water out of the rock for them; so you shall give drink to the congregation and their cattle.'" What Moses does, however, amounts to a rupture of this arc of promise and fulfillment; instead of bearing witness to the providential sign of God, he performs, instead, a purely magical miracle: "And Moses and Aaron gathered the assembly together before the rock, and he said to them, 'Hear now, you rebels; shall we bring forth water for you out of this rock?' And Moses lifted up his hand and struck the rock with his rod twice, and water came forth abundantly, and the congregation drank, and their cattle." It is against this background that we can understand the otherwise perplexing extremity of God's punishment: "And the Lord said to Moses and Aaron, 'Because you did not believe in me, to sanctify me in the eyes of the people of Israel, therefore you shall not bring this assembly in the land which I have given them.'" [13]

13. Robert Paul has noted yet another significant feature of this episode. Emphasizing the symbolic dimension of the children of Israel's thirst, Paul comments: "At the waters of Meribah, Moses disobeys the paternal injunction to speak, to use language, and reverts to a preoedipal demand for the breast and its withheld bounty. It is thus for a symbolic incestuous infraction of the oedipal law of the father that Moses is punished." The "regression" from sign to sorcery is correlated here with

Now it was precisely this semiotic understanding of revelatory miracle (in contrast to "pagan" magic), of miracle as a specific sort of *event of meaning*, that led Rosenzweig to his genealogy of the historical worldview in the first place, to the claim, that is, that the emergence of a fundamental distrust in and critique of historical testimony had been the ultimate cause of the embarrassment attending to miracles in modernity. With the historical enlightenment, the coordination of prediction and fulfillment that forms the semiotic structure of providence—including the thought that our coming was in some sense expected on this earth— begins to falter. To recall, once more, Nietzsche's precise and devastating account of this state of affairs:

To view nature as if it were a proof of the goodness and providence of a God; to interpret history to the glory of a divine reason, *as the perpetual witness* [my emphasis] to a moral world order and moral intentions; to interpret one's own experiences, as pious men long interpreted them, as if everything were preordained, *everything a sign* [my emphasis], everything sent for salvation of the soul—that now belongs to the *past,* that has conscience *against* it.[14]

As Mendes-Flohr has put it in rather more sober terms, "this [historical] critique . . . would undermine the various religious traditions that are founded on the testimony borne by those who actually witnessed the miracles—the original eyewitnesses—and by those who believed in 'the credibility of those who had transmitted the miracle to them.' . . . The transmission of the witness is embodied in a religious tradition—its teachings as well as rites—and *it is that witness that ultimately endows that tradition with its auctoritas.*"[15] In modernity, Rosenzweig suggests, it can only be philosophy—or as I read Benjamin, a certain understanding of historical materialism—that can reconstitute the semiotic structure of miracles according to which, as Rosenzweig puts it, "prediction, the expectation of a miracle, always remains the actually constitutive factor, while the miracle itself is but the factor of realization" (*Star*, 96). Here, again, Mendes-Flohr:

Eclipsed by the historical enlightenment, the witness of the past which had endowed miracle with the objective power of knowledge was no longer available. It is, alas, ir-

---

one from oedipal to preoedipal modes of demand/desire and satisfaction (*Moses and Civilization: The Meaning behind Freud's Myth* [New Haven, CT: Yale University Press, 1996], 106).

14. Nietzsche, *On the Genealogy of Morals,* 160.

15. Mendes-Flohr, "Rosenzweig's Concept of Miracle," 56; my emphasis.

retrievably lost in the rubble of time created by historicism. If miracle is, nonetheless, to be salvaged from these ruins, Rosenzweig contends, it would be necessary to furnish a credible substitute for the witness of the past. The crucial dimension of the prophecy of miracle, witnessed in the past by Scripture, will be supplied by philosophy, or rather the "new thinking."[16]

What I am proposing, however, is that the new thinking does not so much eliminate the function of the witness as compel us to rethink the very nature of the past, the nature of historical testimony itself. What is at stake in the interstitial space between theology and philosophy—in the "new thinking"—is not so much a dismissal of the "witness of the past" as a new conceptualization of the nature of that which registers itself in historical experience, a rethinking of that which in such experience, in its dense, "creaturely" materiality, calls out toward the future, constitutes—"temporalizes"—the dimension of futurity as a mode of response to a peculiar sort of ex-citation transmitted by the past (one needs to hear/read *excitation* in its derivation from *ex-citare,* a calling out or summoning forth). But this is a past that has, so to speak, never achieved ontological consistency, that in some sense *has not yet been* but remains stuck in a spectral, protocosmic dimension. Philosophy—or the "new thinking"—becomes the elaboration of the logic of such excitations, the historical truth of which can come to serve as a new locus of prophecy in modernity.[17] Thinking becomes a mode of attentiveness to a peculiar sort of address or apostrophe—to a *signifying stress*—immanent to our creaturely life. To use a Heideggerian locution, our *thrownness* into the world does not simply mean that we always find ourselves in the midst of a social formation that we did not choose (our language, our family, our society, our class, our gender, and so on); it means, more importantly, that this social formation in which we find ourselves immersed is itself permeated by inconsistency and incompleteness, is itself haunted by a lack by which we are, in some peculiar way, addressed, "excited," to which we are in some fashion answerable. The anxiety correl-

16. Ibid., 58.
17. In the *Star,* Rosenzweig tends to link the notions of creation and creature to the temporal dimension of the past. As he puts it, the significance of death for the being of creaturely life is that death "first stamps every created thing with the ineradicable stamp of creatureliness, the word 'has been'" (156). My argument here is that Rosenzweig's "theory" of the protocosmos compels us to understand the pastness of this creaturely past as one that includes the dimension of trauma, that is, of a past that in some sense has *not* been. In this sense, the term "historical truth" resonates as well with Freud's use of the term in *Moses and Monotheism.* There Freud argues that the Jewish tradition bears witness to a traumatic past pertaining to the inaugural violence of its origins, a violence that did not take place at the level of a verifiable event. For a detailed discussion of *Moses and Monotheism,* see my "Freud's Moses and the Ethics of Nomotropic Desire," *October* 88 (Spring 1999): 3–42.

ative to our thrownness—our *Geworfenheit*—pertains not simply to the fact that we can never fully grasp the reality into which we are born (we are forever deprived of the God's-eye view of it), but rather that reality is never fully identical with itself, *is fissured by lack.*[18]

This structure of temporality—or better, temporalization—is, of course, at the center of Benjamin's reflections in his *Theses.* The crucial argument there is that the past makes a claim on the present and future precisely insofar as that past is marked by a certain void or lack of being which persists into the present:

There is happiness—such as could arouse envy in us—only in the air we have breathed, among people we could have talked to, women who could have given themselves to us. In other words, the idea of happiness is indissolubly bound up with the idea of redemption. The same applies to our view of the past, which is the concern of history. That past carries with it a secret index by which it is referred to redemption. Doesn't a breath of the air that pervaded earlier days caress us as well? In the voices we hear, isn't there an echo of now silent ones? Don't the women we court have sisters they no longer recognize? If so, then there is a secret agreement between past generations and the present one. Then our coming was expected on earth. Then, like every generation that preceded us, we have been endowed with a *weak* messianic power, a power on which the past has a claim.[19]

In Benjamin's work, the registration of that claim takes the form of what he famously referred to as a "dialectical image." In the file of materials dealing with the method of the so-called *Arcades Project,* Benjamin included a series of variations of the formulations that would eventually be published as the *Theses.* One finds there Benjamin's idiosyncratic formulation of what Rosenzweig characterized as the fundamentally semiotic structure of miracle:

It is not that what is past casts its light on what is present, or what is present its light on what is past; rather, image is that wherein what has been comes together in a flash with the now to form a constellation. In other words: image is dialectics at a standstill. For while the relation of the present to the past is purely temporal, the relation of

18. Rosenzweig characterizes creation precisely as a lack of being: "Existence (*Dasein*) is in need, not merely of renewal of its existence, but also, as a whole of existence, in need of—Being. For what existence lacks is Being, unconditional and universal Being. In its universality, overflowing with all the phenomena of the instant, existence longs for Being in order to gain a stability and veracity which its own being cannot provide. . . . Its creatureliness presses under the wings of a Being such as would endow it with stability and veracity" (*Star,* 121).

19. Benjamin, "On the Concept of History," 389–90.

what-has-been to the now is dialectical: not temporal in nature but figural [*bildlich*]. Only dialectical images are genuinely historical—that is, not archaic—images. The image that is read—which is to say, the image in the now of its recognizability—bears to the highest degree the imprint of the perilous critical moment on which all reading is founded.[20]

Earlier in the same section of notes, Benjamin characterizes the "historical index" of an object or image as precisely its readability in a determinate historical situation or moment of crisis:

For the historical index of the images not only says that they belong to a particular time; it says, above all, that they attain to legibility only at a particular time. And, indeed, this acceding "to legibility" constitutes a specific critical point in the movement of their interior. Every present day is determined by the images that are synchronic with it: each "now" is the now of a particular recognizability. In it, truth is charged to the bursting point with time.[21]

It is precisely such an *eventful synchronicity* that constitutes what Benjamin portrays as an awakening to a new kind of answerability in ethical and political life. That such moments of awakening can and do occur, both Rosenzweig and Benjamin suggest, means that the experience of miracle persists into modernity. What this has to do with "materialism" we shall see in the following.

III

To get a better feel for this structure of temporalization and the ethical and political transformations it entails, I'd like to return to a work I discussed some years ago in a rather different context. There I suggested that Christa Wolf's important novel about coming of age during the Nazi period, *A Model Childhood*, was in large measure organized around the development of what we might call, with Benjamin, a weak messianic power on the part of the narrator as she comes to acquire a capacity to read the symptoms plaguing the members of her family (herself included).[22] What the narrator discovers is that such symptoms—head-

---

20. Walter Benjamin, *The Arcades Project*, trans. Howard Eiland and Kevin McLaughlin (Cambridge, MA: Harvard University Press, 1999), 463.

21. Ibid., 462–63.

22. I first discussed Wolf's novel in my *Stranded Objects: Mourning, Memory, and Film in Postwar Germany* (Ithaca, NY: Cornell University Press, 1990).

aches, anxiety attacks, a sudden pallor, fits of rage—form a sort of virtual archive. What is registered there are not so much forgotten deeds, but rather forgotten failures to act. In the course of the novel, Wolf suggests that such failures can, at least in part, be understood as failures to suspend the force of the social bond—call it the dominant ideology—inhibiting acts of solidarity with society's "others." In the novel, one of the central metaphors for such archives is a paleontological one:

Why, then, stir up settled, stabilized rock formations in order to hit on a possible encapsulated organism, a fossil. The delicately veined wings of a fly in a piece of amber. The fleeting track of a bird in once spongy sediments, hardened and immortalized by propitious stratification. To become a paleontologist. To learn to deal with petrified remains, to read from calcified imprints about the existence of early living forms which one can no longer observe.[23]

In the novel, these symptoms become legible—or as Benjamin puts it, readable in the now of their recognizability—as indices of missed opportunities to intervene on behalf of the oppressed during the Nazi regime, even missed opportunities for empathy with the victims.[24] The novel suggests that adaptation to the social reality of everyday life during the Nazi period involved forming pockets of congealed moral and social energies manifest as psychic perturbations, as a symptomatic torsion of one's being in the world, or what I have called signifying stress. Miracles happen when, upon registering their "historical truth," we are able to act, to intervene into these symptoms and enter the space of possibilities opened thereby.[25]

One way we might think about such acts is in relation to the problem of guilt and responsibility. Miracles happen when we find ourselves able to suspend a pattern—a *Kindheitsmuster*, as Wolf might say—whereby

23. Christa Wolf, *A Model Childhood*, trans. Ursule Molinaro and Hedwig Rappolt (New York: Farrar, Straus & Giroux, 1980), 151.

24. Benjamin defines one of his basic historical concepts this way: "Catastrophe: to have missed the opportunity" (*Arcades*, 474).

25. I think that this is what Slavoj Žižek had in mind in his own commentary on Benjamin's *Theses*: "The actual revolutionary situation is *not* a kind of 'return of the repressed'—rather, the returns of the repressed, the 'symptoms,' are the past failed revolutionary attempts, forgotten, excluded from the frame of the reigning historical tradition, whereas the actual revolutionary situation presents an attempt to 'unfold' the symptom, to 'redeem'—that is, realize in the Symbolic—these past failed attempts which 'will have been' only through their repetition, at which point they become retroactively what they already were" (*The Sublime Object of Ideology* [London: Verso, 1989], 141). I am suggesting that symptoms register not only past failed revolutionary attempts but also, more modestly, past failures to respond to calls for action or even for empathy on behalf of those whose suffering belongs to the form of life of which one is a part. They hold the place of something that is *there*, that *insists* in our life, though it has never achieved full ontological consistency.

one "culpabilizes" the Other or, in more Nietzschean terms, cultivates *ressentiment,* with respect to a fundamental dysfunction or crisis within social reality. As Slavoj Žižek has put it apropos of the *Kristallnacht* pogroms, one of the central points of reference in Wolf's novel, "the furious rage of such an outburst of violence makes it a symptom—the defense-formation covering up the void of the failure to intervene effectively in the social crisis."[26] In Wolf's novel, the narrator chronicles her own symptom-formation with respect to the *Kristallnacht* in rather more personal, though still closely related, terms:

Nelly couldn't help it: the charred building made her sad. But *she didn't know that she was feeling sad,* because she wasn't supposed to feel sad. She had long ago begun to cheat herself out of her true feelings. . . . Gone, forever gone, is the beautiful, free correlation between emotions and events. . . . It wouldn't have taken much for Nelly to have succumbed to an improper emotion: compassion. But healthy German common sense built a barrier against it: anxiety. (my emphasis)

And as the narrator quickly adds, "Perhaps there should be at least an intimation of the difficulties in matters of 'compassion,' also regarding compassion toward one's own person, the difficulties experienced by a person who was forced as a child to turn compassion for the weak and the losers into hate and anxiety."[27] The crucial thought in all of this is that such failures/defense-formations persist as a peculiar sort of stress in the individual and collective lives of those in some way linked to them. It is the signs/symptoms of such stress that await, as it were, the "miraculous" now of their recognizability.

IV

At this point I'd like to attend more closely to the nature of this stress that for Benjamin serves as the crucial historical index for any materialist engagement with history and that for Rosenzweig provides the basis for rethinking the fundamental monotheistic concepts: creation, revelation, and redemption. As I have suggested, Rosenzweig and Benjamin seem to agree that in modernity *miracles do happen* and that their happening must be understood as some sort of opening or unfolding of the semiotic energies condensed in such stress. What is, I think, misleading

26. Žižek, *Welcome to the Desert of the Real,* 23.
27. Wolf, *Patterns,* 161 (translation modified).

about some of Benjamin's formulations is that it can appear as if these semiotic energies merely stood in for a nameable, determinate possibility, in other words, one with a specifiable representational content, that was blocked from actualization. But this would result merely in a sort of negative historicism; instead of worrying about "*wie es eigentlich gewesen*," what objectively happened at some moment in the past, we would be concerned with, as it were, equally datable and objective nonhappenings inscribed in the virtual—yet nonetheless fully legible—archive of individual and collective symptoms.

The mistake would be to think of the signifying stress at issue here along the lines of Freud's original conception of the seduction theory. According to that first theory of the etiology of hysteria, symptoms are produced through the repression of a determinate and, as it were, datable experience of premature "sexualization" in childhood—the trauma of sexual abuse at the hands of an adult (and, thus, the trauma of one's own, if I might put it that way, overwhelming passivity). Freud would revise this theory to allow for the etiology of neurotic symptoms on the basis not simply of external events intruding upon an essentially passive subject but of *psychic* events connected to the birth of sexuality in the human child. These events pertain ultimately—and here I am reading Freud in light of Lacanian and post-Lacanian theory—to the encounter with the enigma of parental desire. The revised theory shares with the first the notion that what is traumatic is, ultimately, the overproximity to the mysterious desire of the other. The difference is that in the later theory such overproximity assumes a certain structural value and need not have been acted out in any egregious manner; the fundamentally disorienting encounter with the other's desire is now seen to be *constitutive* of what we understand as human subjectivity. This revision did not, of course, prevent Freud from attempting to locate *this* encounter in historical time, to date the psychic event—the *primal scene*—out of which the singular subjectivity of his various analysands emerged. Perhaps the most notable example of Freud's efforts in this direction is his attempt to reconstruct the scene of parental intercourse that the Wolf Man ostensibly witnessed as a child. Freud is still committed here to the importance of the original eyewitness in the birth of the expectation—in the form of symptoms—of the miracle of the analytic intervention and cure.

To return to a term I introduced earlier, according to this revised notion of seduction, the human child is *ex-cited* by enigmatic messages emanating from the parental other, messages indicating something profoundly amiss, something fundamentally lacking, in the other. As Lacan has put it,

A lack is encountered by the subject in the Other, in the very intimation that the Other makes to him by his discourse. In the intervals of the discourse of the Other, there emerges in the experience of the child something that is radically mappable, namely, *He is saying this to me, but what does he want?* . . . The desire of the Other is apprehended by the subject in that which does not work, in the lacks of the discourse of the Other, and all the child's *whys* reveal not so much an avidity for the reason of things, as a testing of the adult, a *Why are you telling me this?* ever-resuscitated from its base, which is the enigma of the adult's desire.[28]

According to this theory, the child works at translating this enigma into more or less determinate demands—demands one can comply with, reject, fail at fulfilling, feel guilty about, and so forth. As Jean Laplanche (the student of Lacan who has most systematically elaborated this notion of the enigmatic message) has written, the fundamental situation that gives rise to unconscious formations

is an encounter between an individual whose psycho-somatic structures are situated predominantly at the level of need, and signifiers emanating from an adult. Those signifiers pertain to the satisfaction of the child's needs, but they also convey the purely interrogative potential of other messages—and those other messages are sexual. These enigmatic messages set the child the difficult, or even impossible, task of mastery and symbolization, and the attempt to perform it inevitably leaves behind unconscious residues. . . . I refer to them as the source-objects of the drives.[29]

It is this never-ceasing work of symbolization and failure at symbolization, translation and failure at translation, that constitutes what I have referred to as signifying stress. We have here, then, something of a tragic cycle: my signifying stress is called forth—*ex-cited*—by my efforts to translate the signifying stress emanating from the other indicating, in its turn, the other's "addiction" to his/her own enigmas. Or, as Laplanche has put it: "Internal alien-ness maintained, held in place by external alien-ness; external alien-ness, in turn, held in place by the enigmatic relation of the other to his own internal alien."[30] In the view I have been outlining here, a "miracle" would represent the event of a genuine break in such a fateful enchainment of unconscious transmissions.

28. Lacan, *The Seminar of Jacques Lacan,* book 11: *The Four Fundamental Concepts of Psychoanalysis,* trans. Alan Sheridan (New York: W. W. Norton, 1981), 214.

29. Jean Laplanche, *New Foundations for Psychoanalysis,* trans. David Macey (Oxford: Basil Blackwell, 1989), 130.

30. Jean Laplanche, *Essays on Otherness,* ed. John Fletcher (London: Routledge, 1999), 80.

Perhaps the most vivid literary example of what it means to be caught up in the endless work of translation and failure, to live with—or perhaps better, simply to live—the pressures of signifying stress, is Kafka's great (unfinished) novel dealing with enigmatic address, *The Trial*. Beginning with the fateful morning of his arrest—apparently without his having done anything particular—the protagonist's entire existence becomes an attempt to discern the meaning of enigmatic communications emanating not from a parental other, but rather from the rather more ominous "big Other" of a complex bureaucratic entity, the law and its various visible and invisible institutions and agents. Indeed, one of the great achievements of Kafka's novel—and this no doubt contributes to Kafka's "canonicity"—is that it makes plausible that the familial scenario so central to psychoanalytic theory and practice is only one rather concentrated instance of a much more general dynamic pertaining to the subject's transferential relations to symbolic power and authority.[31] Joseph K. is forever trying to translate the inconsistencies of the legal bureaucracy into a set of demands that would allow for some sort of meaningful negotiation. Kafka's novel goes so far as to suggest that these inconsistencies are quite literally correlative to an obscene sexuality, that Joseph K.'s dilemma is indeed one of overproximity to the *desire* of the Other. One thinks here not only of the various sexually charged women who in some fashion "belong" to the court, but also of the scene of sadomasochistic punishment Joseph K. stumbles upon in a closet at his place of business, as well as K.'s discovery of pornographic materials among the books and legal documents at his initial hearing.

In his extended correspondence with Benjamin on the subject of Kafka, Gershom Scholem tried to capture what is canonical about the universe of Kafka's fiction by attending precisely to the nature of the signifying stress by which figures like Joseph K. are burdened. In a now famous letter of September 20, 1934, Scholem tries to clarify an earlier claim (letter of July 17, 1934) that Kafka's world is one of "revelation seen . . . from that perspective in which it is returned to its own nothingness"; in the September letter, he writes to his friend:

You ask what I understand by the "nothingness of revelation"? I understand by it a state in which revelation appears to be without meaning, in which it still asserts itself, in which it has *validity* but *no significance* [*in dem sie gilt, aber nicht bedeutet*]. A state

---

31. As Lacan has put it, "As soon as the subject who is supposed to know exists somewhere . . . there is transference" (Lacan, *Four Fundamental Concepts*, 232).

in which the wealth of meaning is lost and what is in the process of appearing (for revelation is such a process) still does not disappear, even though it is reduced to the zero
point of its own content, so to speak.[32]

In a beautiful reading of the Scholem-Benjamin correspondence on
Kafka, Robert Alter takes Scholem's essential point to be "that the world
in which we find ourselves has an ultimate, though also ultimately inscrutable, semantic power: something is always 'in the process of appearing' *from the ground of being* that imposes itself on us with the sheer
force of its validity, even if it finally has no safely construable significance." According to Scholem, that is, revelation "is not merely an idea
of Jewish tradition . . . but . . . an *underlying phenomenon of man's creaturely existence.*"[33] Clearly, such claims belong within the orbit of what
Rosenzweig called "the new thinking." The crucial difference introduced
by Rosenzweig is that the miracle of revelation is constituted not simply
by an inscrutable semantic power underlying the creaturely existence of
humans—by our signifying stress—but also by our capacity to "unfold"
this stress through *acts of neighbor-love,* something that perhaps lay beyond the boundaries of the Kafkan imagination.

V

The characterization of Scholem's claim as one pertaining to a semantic
power arising "from the ground of being" resonates not only with Lacan's thesis concerning unconscious mental activity which is, as he
notes, "ever-resuscitated from its base, which is the enigma of the adult's
desire"; it also nicely captures a fundamental structural feature of Rosenzweig's *Star of Redemption.* The entire first volume of the *Star* is entitled "The Elements or The Ever-Enduring Proto-Cosmos" [*Die Elemente
oder Die Immerwährende Vorwelt*] and provides a kind of logic of this "semantic power" as a dimension not only of human being but also of
worldly and divine being as well (the three fundamental "elements" or
regions of being). What Rosenzweig seems to mean here is that when we

32. Gershom Scholem, *The Correspondence of Walter Benjamin and Gershom Scholem, 1932–1940,*
trans. Gary Smith and Andre Lefevre (New York: Schocken, 1989), 142.

33. Robert Alter, *Necessary Angels: Tradition and Modernity in Kafka, Benjamin, and Scholem* (Cambridge, MA: Harvard University Press, 1991), 110, 109; my emphasis. These sentences also nicely capture why Rosenzweig both affirms and denies the "Jewishness" of *The Star of Redemption.* See his essay "The New Thinking."

attempt to think each element independently, to capture what each one is in abstraction from its relations to the other regions of being—in its pure tautological self-sameness (man is man, world is world, God is God)—what we encounter are not the elements in their ultimate reality, but rather, to use a Lacanian locution, the "Real" of each element, the specific way in which our access to knowledge is voided. In the first part of the *Star*, Rosenzweig tries to get us to brush up against that on account of which each element enjoys its irreducibility to anything else without thereby being knowable (*whatever* God might be, for example, we at least "know" that God is *not* simply a species of human or worldly being). It is in this sense that Rosenzweig was able to refer to his method in the *Star* as an "absolute empiricism," an attunement to the "'substances' of thinking, within the actual, nonobjective, and nonsubstantial experience."[34]

With respect to human being, Rosenzweig suggests that what is irreducible there pertains to a constitutive, rather than merely contingent, dimension of *trauma*. And it is clear from the first lines of the *Star* that this trauma that, paradoxically, makes us something *more* than just a piece of the world, *more* than a link in the "great chain of Being," is a function of our finitude, our subjection to death. For Rosenzweig, we acquire our singular density as human beings—Heidegger would say as *Dasein*—only by way of anxiety in the face of our own, ultimately unknowable, mortality (our death is not a natural fact to be known but a "facticity" to be borne). The absolute nullity that borders mortal life *intrudes* into our being as a strange sort of surplus vitality that has no proper place in the world, that can't be put to work, can't be fully absorbed by a project.

Rosenzweig develops this thought under the heading of what he re-

---

34. Rosenzweig, "The New Thinking,"138, 120. Earlier in the essay, Rosenzweig rehearses the various ways in which Western philosophy engaged in and failed at such projects of reduction (of one region of being to another): "As ever, the possibilities of the 'reduction' of each one to the other are untiringly permutated, [possibilities] that, seen in large, seem to characterize the three epochs of European philosophy—cosmological antiquity, the theological Middle Ages, [and] anthropological modernity" (115). Rosenzweig argues that each of these attempts at reduction is generated by the very form of the question at the heart of this philosophical tradition, the "what is it really?" question. Thus, in modernity, when subjectivity occupies the center stage, "philosophy takes reduction in general to be something so self-evident that if she takes the trouble to burn . . . a heretic, she accuses him only of a prohibited method of reduction, roasting him either as a 'crass materialist' who has said: everything is world, or as an 'ecstatic mystic' who has said: everything is God. That someone would not at all want to say: everything 'is' . . . does not enter into her mind. But, in the 'whatis?' question directed at everything, lies the entire error of the answers" (116). Ultimately, Rosenzweig claims, "Experience, no matter how deeply it may penetrate, discovers only the human in man, only worldliness in the world, only divinity in God. And only in God divinity, only in the world worldliness, and only in man the human" (116–17).

fers to as the *metaethical self,* which he distinguishes from the concept of the "personality." The personality signifies what is *generic* about a person, that is, everything about a person that can be subsumed under a concept, that can be subordinated to some sort of universal or genus. For Rosenzweig, the paradigm of this subsumption is sexual reproduction: "Natural birth was . . . the birth of individuality; in progeniture it died its way back into the genus" (70). In sexual reproduction, that is, our individuality is given over to the immortal life of the species that persists by way of the cycle of generation and corruption. Rosenzweig abbreviates this subsumption by the equation $B = A$, signifying the entrance of what is particular, individual, and distinctive [*das Besondere*] into the general or universal [*das Allgemeine*]: "Many predications are possible about personality, as many as about individuality. As individual predications they all follow the scheme $B = A$, the scheme in which *all the predications about the world and its parts* are conceptualized. Personality is always defined as an individual in its relation to other individuals and to a Universal" (69; my emphasis). But, as he quickly adds, "There are no derivative predications about the self, only the one, original $B = B$" (69).The self, that is, signifies *the part that is no part* (of a whole), a non-relational excess which is out-of-joint with respect to the generality of any classification or identification, any form of teleological absorption by a larger purpose.

Because the self pertains to that which, in some sense, persists beyond an individual's integration into the life of the genus, "we should," Rosenzweig writes, "be led to the inadequacy of the ideas of individuality and personality for comprehending human life" (*Star,* 70–71). Rosenzweig circumscribes what remains/insists beyond these ideas by means of the concepts of *character* and *defiance;* the self signifies nothing but the defiant persistence of one's character, its *demonic self-sameness.* This is what Rosenzweig tries to capture by the tautology, $B = B$: a distinctive insistence on pure distinctiveness.[35] This leads him to the thought

---

35. "True, ethos is content for this self and the self is the character. But it is not defined by this its content; it is not the self by virtue of the fact that it is this particular character. Rather it is already self by virtue of the fact that it has a character, any character, at all. Thus personality is personality by virtue of its firm interconnection with a definite individuality, but the self is self merely by its holding fast to its character at all. In other words, the self 'has' its character" (72). In his commentary on F. W. J. Schelling's *Weltalter,* the most important philosophical precursor to Rosenzweig's project, Žižek puts it this way: "That which, in me, resists the blissful submergence in the Good is . . . not my inert biological nature but the very kernel of my *spiritual* selfhood, the awareness that, beyond all particular physical and psychical features, I am 'me,' a unique *person,* an absolutely singular point of spiritual self-reference" (*The Indivisible Remainder: An Essay on Schelling and Related Matters* [London: Verso, 1996], 59).

of the second birth and second death as constitutive features of human existence:

Character, and therefore the self which bases itself on it, is not the talent which the celestials placed in the crib of the young citizen of the earth "already at birth" as his share of the commonweal of mankind [*am gemeinsamen Menschheitsgut*]. Quite the contrary: the day of the natural birth is the great day of destiny for individuality, because on it the fate of the distinctive [*das Schicksal des Besonderen*] is determined by the share in the universal [*den Anteil am Allgemeinen*]; for the self, this day is covered in darkness. The birthday of the self is not the same as the birthday of the personality. For the self, the character, too, has its birthday: one day it is there. It is not true that character "becomes," that it "forms." One day it assaults man like an armed man and takes possession of all the wealth of his property. . . . Until that day, man is a piece of the world even before his own consciousness. . . . The self breaks in and at one blow robs him of all the goods and chattel which he presumed to possess. He becomes quite poor, has only himself, knows only himself, is known to no one, for no one exists but he. The self is solitary man in the hardest sense of the word: the personality is the "political animal." (*Star,* 71)

Though this language might indicate a tendency similar to the one I noted in Freud, that is, a belief that the traumatic intrusion of selfhood into the human animal—our becoming *subject*—is a "datable" event in historical time, Rosenzweig for the most part exhibits no special preoccupation with "primal scenes." The paradox for both Freud and Rosenzweig is that something that has a *structural* status, something that is constitutive for being a human subject, also has the quality of an *event*—here contingency and necessity, eventfulness and essence, coincide. Indeed, the term "primal scene" may best be understood as naming just such a coincidence. Rosenzweig's language makes absolutely clear that his concern here is with what Freud characterized as the emergence of *Triebschicksal,* the drive destiny that *amplifies* the life of human beings, endows this life, to return to a term introduced earlier, with a *demonic* aspect:

Thus the self is born on a definite day. . . . It is the day on which the personality, the individual, dies the death of entering the genus [i.e., in progeniture]. . . . This speechless, sightless, introverted *daimon* assaults man first in the guise of *Eros,* and thence accompanies him through life until the moment when he removes his disguise and reveals himself as *Thanatos.* This is the second, and, if you will, the more secret birthday of the self, just as it is the second, and, if you will, the first patent day of death for individuality. . . . Whatever of the self becomes visible to us lies between these two births of the *daimon.* (*Star,* 71–72)

At one level Rosenzweig is simply noting here that the birth of human sexuality is fundamentally linked to intimations of mortality; in sexed reproduction we become most directly confronted with the fact that our death was "provided for," that our species-existence is correlative to our death, that our germ cells—or at least half of them—must split off from the mortal soma cells. But Rosenzweig is, I believe, also thinking about what we earlier characterized as a sort of "general seduction theory" (Laplanche's term) according to which the body/psyche of the child is from the start of life penetrated by enigmatic messages emanating from (the unconscious of) its caregivers and authority figures. Indeed, it is only on the basis of such enigmas that human sexuality proper gets off the ground. What is generally thought to be most animal-like about us— our sexuality—is, in this view, precisely where we are most out-of-joint with respect to any merely animal nature.[36] We might say that, whereas instincts *orient*, our drive destiny, which emerges on the basis of our seduction by enigmatic signifiers—our "second birthday"—*disorients*, leading us along utterly and often painfully eccentric paths and detours. We are "driven," we have "drive destinies," because we find ourselves, at some level of our being, addicted to an always idiosyncratic series of enigmatic signifiers pertaining to the desire of the "big Others" in our lives. This also means that the most intimate kernel of our being is also what is most tightly linked to Otherness, though this link gets laid down below the level of intentionality and intersubjectivity proper.[37] In Rosenzweig's view, it is precisely our drivenness that has a rightful claim to immortality. Thus, apropos of the hero of Attic tragedy who, in Rosenzweig's view, first gives visible shape and form to the metaethical self, Rosenzweig writes, "the tragic hero does not actually die after all. Death only cuts him off, as it were, from the temporal features of individuality. Character transmitted into heroic self is immortal" (*Star,* 79). And with immortality, Rosenzweig continues,

we touch on an ultimate yearning of the self. Personality does not demand immortality for itself, but the self does. Personality is satisfied with the eternity of the relations into which it enters and in which it is absorbed. *The self has no relations,* cannot enter into any, remains ever itself. Thus it is conscious of being eternal; *its immortality amounts to an inability to die.* All ancient doctrines of immortality come down to this

---

36. As Jonathan Lear has recently put it, "It is only a slight exaggeration to say that there is nothing about human life we hold less in common with animals than our sexuality. We can imagine a bird happening to make a nest out of a lady's shoe; we cannot imagine her getting excited about it" (*Therapeutic Action: An Earnest Plea for Irony* [New York: The Other Press, 2003], 150).

37. I am deeply grateful to Irad Kimhi for helping me to fully appreciate this paradox.

inability of the disengaged self to die. Theoretically, the only difficulty consists in finding a natural bearer of this inability to die, a "something" that cannot die. (*Star,* 79;
my emphasis)

Rosenzweig's "postmetaphysical" gesture is to refuse this preoccupation
with finding a natural bearer of the drive (say, a soul-substance), of this
quasi-semantic power emerging from "the ground of being," from what
Rosenzweig refers to as the *Vorwelt,* or protocosmos.

VI

Benjamin, who not only knew Rosenzweig's *Star* but also especially valued its first volume, evoked the notion of the *Vorwelt* in his important
essay on Kafka. There Benjamin refers to the "prehistoric forces [*vorwelt-
liche Gewalten*] that dominated Kafka's creativeness—forces which, to be
sure, may justifiably be regarded as belonging to our world as well."[38] As
I've noted, Kafka's protagonists are forever trying to get clear about a
message in which an enigmatic and unnerving surplus of validity beyond meaning persists as a chronic signifying stress "curving" the space
in which they move. Their inability to interpret or translate the enigma,
to stabilize its meaning in a legible call with which to identify, in a demand one can comply with or refuse, is what ultimately serves to draw
them all the more powerfully into the ban of the Law, Castle, and so
forth. (This thought will become more important in what follows: a certain hindrance to our institutional inscription/subjection serves as a
support of our affective attachment to this very subjection.) Later in
the same essay—and indeed just after a brief reference to Rosenzweig's
Star—Benjamin offers a reading of another series of Kafkan figures, figures whose being is distorted by a sort of cringe, as if the stress we have
been addressing had taken on direct, bodily form and density, endowing
these figures with their emphatic sense of creatureliness:

Odradek is the form which things assume in oblivion. They are distorted. The "cares
of a family man," which no one can identify, are distorted; the bug, which we know
all too well represents Gregor Samsa, is distorted; the big animal, half-lamb, half-
kitten, for which "the butcher's knife" might be "a release," is distorted. These Kafka

38. Walter Benjamin, "Franz Kafka: On the Tenth Anniversary of His Death," trans. Harry Zohn,
in *Selected Writings,* vol. 2, *1927–34,* ed. Michael W. Jennings, Howard Eiland, and Gary Smith (Cambridge, MA: Harvard University Press, 2001), 807.

figures are connected by a long series of figures with the prototype of distortion: a hunched back. Among the images in Kafka's stories, none is more frequent than that of the man who bows his head far down on his chest: the fatigue of the court officials, the noise affecting the doormen in the hotel, the low ceiling facing the visitors in the gallery. In the penal colony, those in power use an archaic apparatus which engraves letters with curlicues on the back of every guilty man.[39]

Suggesting that what is at stake in any miracle is precisely an intervention into the peculiar burdens of these uncanny "neighbors," Benjamin writes about the figure of the hunchback, that "he will disappear with the coming of the Messiah, who (a great rabbi once said) will not wish to change the world by force but will merely make a slight adjustment in it."[40]

Benjamin's evocation of the hunchback strongly resonates with Primo Levi's description of the so-called *Muselmann,* the figure who represents, for Levi, the paradox of the complete—and impossible—*witness* to the truth of the death camps: "They crowd my memory with their faceless presence, and if I could enclose all the evil of our time in one image, I would choose this image which is familiar to me: an emaciated man, with head dropped and shoulders curved, on whose face and in whose eyes not a trace of thought is to be seen."[41] The Muselmann is, it would seem, the figure whose being has been fully reduced to the substance of a "cringe," whose existence has been reduced to its pure, proto-cosmic being, who is *there,* yet no longer "in the world." What remains, that is, at this zero-degree of social existence, in this zone between symbolic and real death, is not pure biological (animal or vegetable) life, but rather something like the direct embodiment of signifying stress—the becoming flesh of the "state of emergency" of sociosymbolic meaning. Recalling Rosenzweig's use of the infinitesimal calculus in his construction of the protocosmos, we might say that the Muselmann is *the human in the neighborhood of zero.* But that also makes him the ultimate—and therewith impossible—embodiment of the *neighbor.*[42]

We are faced here with the topological paradox of a figure who is *included* within the sphere of political existence by virtue of his radical *exclusion,* whose *presence* within the order of the human is paid for by his deprivation of any symbolic *representation.* In his recent work, Giorgio

39. Ibid., 811.

40. Ibid.

41. Primo Levi, *Survival in Auschwitz: The Nazi Assault on Humanity,* trans. Stuart Wolf (New York: Touchstone, 1996), 90.

42. See Slavoj Žižek's remarks on the Muselmann in this volume.

Agamben has analyzed this paradoxical figure under the heading of the *homo sacer,* a term he appropriates from early Roman texts and which marks someone as being subject to murder without the prospect of punishment but who is nonetheless excluded from any form of ritual sacrifice. According to a text by Pompeius Festus, "it is not permitted to sacrifice this man, yet he who kills him will not be condemned for homicide. . . . This is why it is customary for a bad or impure man to be called sacred."[43] To return once more to Kafka, one might think here of Gregor Samsa, whose status as a *homo sacer* is supported by the etymological resonances of the words Kafka uses—*ungeheuere(s) Ungeziefer* ("monstrous vermin")—to introduce Gregor's transformation in the famous first sentence of the story. *Ungeheuer,* as Stanley Corngold has emphasized, "connotes the creature who has no place in the family; *Ungeziefer,* the unclean animal unsuited for sacrifice, the creature without a place in God's order."[44]

For Agamben, the crucial point is that the topological peculiarity that constitutes the figure of the *homo sacer* directly mirrors a comparable peculiarity at the heart of political sovereignty. At least according to one important tradition of political thought, the concept of sovereignty includes the dimension of the "state of exception," the sovereign's right to suspend the law in conditions that threaten the order of the state. That is to say that the sovereign, this embodiment of state law, has the *legal right to suspend law.* The sovereign is, then, in some peculiar sense, both inside and outside the law. According to Agamben, the *homo sacer* is the figure who stands in absolute intimacy with this dimension of sovereignty; he is utterly exposed to the state of exception/emergency immanent in the law, an exposure Agamben characterizes as a "ban": "He who has been banned is not, in fact, simply set outside the law and made indifferent to it, but rather *abandoned* by it, that is, exposed and threatened on the threshold in which life and law, outside and inside, become indistinguishable. It is literally not possible to say whether the one who has been banned is outside or inside the juridical order" (28–29). Interestingly, Agamben, too, suggests that there is a kind of *testimony* preserved in the figure of such exposure; the *homo sacer* is a kind of *impossible witness,* utterly consumed—"drowned," as Levi says—by the truth to which he testifies:

43. Cited in Giorgio Agamben, *Homo Sacer: Sovereign Power and Bare Life,* trans. Daniel Heller-Roazen (Stanford, CA: Stanford University Press, 1998), 71. Subsequent references are given in the text.

44. Stanley Corngold, introduction to *The Metamorphosis, By Franz Kafka* (New York: Bantam, 1986), xix.

Once brought back to his proper place beyond both penal law and sacrifice, *homo sacer* presents the originary figure of life taken into the sovereign ban and *preserves the memory* of the originary exclusion through which the political dimension was first constituted. . . . The sacredness of life, which is invoked today as an absolutely fundamental right in opposition to sovereign power, in fact originally expresses precisely both life's subjection to a power over death and life's irreparable exposure in the relation of abandonment. (83; my emphasis) [45]

To return to our initial problem—the problem of miracle—in the present context we might say that miracles happen when and where this impossible, mad "testimony" can be unfolded.

But this also suggests that the word *miracle,* for both Benjamin and Rosenzweig, means just the opposite of what the modern theorist of the state of exception, Carl Schmitt, posits as its meaning. In his book *Political Theology,* Schmitt suggests that the state of exception—the *Ausnahmezustand*—"has for jurisprudence an analogous meaning to that of miracle for theology." [46] And indeed, Schmitt argues that the notion of the state of exception suffered a parallel fate to the one we traced with regard to miracle, a fate that, for Schmitt, ultimately impoverishes the liberal theory of the state just as the disappearance of miracle impoverished liberal theology: "For the idea of the modern constitutional state [*Rechtsstaat*] attains predominance along with deism, with a theology and metaphysics, that is, that just as much banishes miracle from the world (along with any sort of interruption of natural laws—the exception that belongs to the very concept of miracle) as it does the direct intervention of the sovereign into the governing rule of law. The rationalism of the Enlightenment repudiates the state of exception in every form" (43). My argument here has been, however, that for both Ro-

45. In a brilliant essay on *The Tempest,* Julia Reinhard Lupton has argued that one needs to understand the figure of Caliban within the framework of bare/creaturely life we have been elaborating here, i.e., as a figure embodying radical exposure to the operations of the sovereign exception. As she puts it, "the Creature represents the flip side of the political theology of absolute sovereignty." Such exposure generates a peculiar coincidence of oppositional determinations: "From one point of view the Creature suffers from *too much body,* collecting in its leaden limbs the earthliness and passionate intensity of mere life uninspired by form. From another the Creature suffers from *too much soul,* taking flight in 'speculation,' as reason soaring beyond its own self-regulating parameters toward a second-order materiality of signifiers unfixed to signifieds." What I have referred to as the "matter" of the neighbor is just this strange overlapping of two seemingly opposite forms of "too muchness." Lupton also notes that it is melancholy, the affect that Benjamin most intimately links to creaturely life, that "identifies the psychosomatic foundations of this creaturely consciousness, its violent yoking of an excessive, even symptomatic mental production to the dejected gravity of an unredeemed body" ("Creature Caliban," *Shakespeare Quarterly* 51, no. 1 [Spring 2000]: 5).

46. Carl Schmitt, *Politische Theologie. Vier Kapitel zur Lehre von der Souveränität* (Berlin: Duncker & Humblot, 1993), 43; my translation.

senzweig and Benjamin a miracle signifies not the state of exception, but rather its suspension, an intervention into this peculiar topological knot—the outlaw dimension internal to law—that serves to sustain the symbolic function of sovereignty. Rosenzweig's and Benjamin's thinking about miracle must, thus, be seen as critiques of political theology, but as critiques which gain their force from the resources of theology (understood as a form of "new thinking").[47] But what might such a suspension look like? What does it mean to suspend what is, ultimately, itself a sort of suspension (of law by way of the state of exception)?

VII

The first thing to notice is that Agamben's characterization of the sovereign exception and its effects closely resembles the psychoanalytic understanding of the (punitive) superego, a psychic agency that does not so much represent the "rule of law" internalized by a subject as a set of impossible demands holding the place of a void, of the missing foundations of such rule. The superego, in this view, represents not the psychic agency of interpellation that endows us with a symbolic mandate in the world but the signifying stress left over from such an operation. Here we might recall Louis Althusser's famous allegory of ideological interpellation. According to Althusser, ideology takes hold of a subject—successfully interpellates an individual into a subject—at the moment when this individual recognizes himself in a "master's" call, much as when a man turns toward a police officer who has hailed him on the street. "Assuming the theoretical scene I have imagined takes place in the street," Althusser writes, "the hailed individual will turn round. By this mere one-hundred-and-eighty-degree physical conversion, he becomes a *subject*. Why? Because he has recognized that the hail was 'really' addressed to him, and that 'it was *really him* who was hailed' (and not someone else). . . . The existence of ideology and the hailing or interpellating of individuals as subjects are one and the same thing."[48] If

47. I am ultimately in agreement with Jan Assmann that the concern to separate *Herrschaft* and *Heil*, political rule and salvation, i.e., the critique of political theology as understood by Schmitt, belongs within a more broadly conceived domain of politicotheological reflection. See his *Herrschaft und Heil. Politische Theologie in Altägypten, Israel und Europa* (Munich: Hanser, 2000). The "new thinking" represents a powerful intervention into and transformation of political theology rather than a mere passage beyond it. Put somewhat differently, the new thinking might be understood as a "deconstruction" of political theology.

48. Louis Althusser, "Ideology and Ideological State Apparatuses," in *Lenin and Philosophy,* trans. Ben Brewster (New York: Monthly Review Press, 1971), 174–75. We find a now classical literary ver-

we let Rosenzweig's formula for the predications about the world and its parts, $B = A$, stand for any instance of successful interpellation—the individual recognizes himself as being a part within the totality in the name of which he has been hailed—then $B = B$ will signify what in the individual "contracts" from the interpellation and the identification established through it. $B = B$ registers, we might say, not so much the master's call as the impact of his *voice,* that which in the act of hailing occupies the uncanny zone between corporeal event and event of meaning (the voice is always *more* than the body from which it emanates and *less* than the meaning it materially supports).[49] The self, in Rosenzweig's sense, is born when this "vocal object" finds an initial organization in fantasy, when the uncanny *externality* of the Other's voice congeals as an *intimate* locus of persistent solicitation or ex-citation.[50] This "extimate" bit of fantasy out of which the agency of the superego is constructed, this *congealed excitation,* is, I am suggesting, the *matter* or *materiality* at the heart of the neighbor, the excess that makes the neighbor irreducible to the "political animal." The paradox, however, is that it is for the most

---

sion of the scene of interpellation at the end of *The Trial,* when Josef K. hears himself addressed by the chaplain in the cathedral: "K. hesitated and stared at the floor in front of him. For the time being he was still free, he could still walk on and get out through one of the small dark wooden doors that stood close before him. To do so would simply mean that he hadn't understood or that he indeed had understood but for that very reason paid no heed to it. Should he turn around, however, he would be caught, for then he would have confessed that he had well understood, that he really was the one who was called and that he would follow" (Franz Kafka, *Der Process* [Fischer: Frankfurt a.M., 1998], 221–22; my translation).

49. Here I am deeply indebted to the work of Mladen Dolar.

50. In an essay on Freud's Rat Man case, Jonathan Lear has offered the following scenario for understanding the birth of that patient's metaethical self around the formation of a punishing—and binding—superegoic voice, a process that yields another exemplar of *das bucklicht Männlein,* or hunchback: "Melanie Klein has argued that the earliest internalizations occur via phantasies of physical incorporation. In good-enough circumstances, the comfort, reassurance, and satisfaction which the child receives at the breast is taken in with the mother's milk. That is, the milk itself becomes a concrete vehicle of meaning. Goodness is the meaning of the milk. . . . Similarly, the child may begin to form a superego around a prohibitive utterance: for the Rat Child, it may have been the voice of the father saying, 'Don't do that!' The utterance is itself the physical movement of meaning. The father's tongue has set the air around it vibrating, and a prohibitive meaning informs that vibrating air. That meaning reaches the Rat Child's ear via its concrete vehicle and triggers a chain of neurological reactions. One outcome is that the Rat Child can hear his father; another is that he can hear the prohibitive voice over and over 'inside his head.' The Rat Child experiences his own rage as tremendously powerful; and one way to deal with the anxiety it arouses is, in phantasy, to move it over to invest the father's voice. This isn't a thought or a judgment; it is the nonrational, phantastic movement of content. However, though the phantasy-movement of content is not itself rational, it may acquire a dynamic, intrapsychic function. Rage gains some expression, phantastically expressed over there, in the voice of the father, and it is used intrapsychically to inhibit outbursts of rage. And so the movement of meaning in phantasy helps to shape intrapsychic structure. The Rat Child begins to live a life which is to be understood in significant part as *an extended cringe* before the voice of the Rat Dad" (*Open Minded: Working Out the Logic of the Soul* [Cambridge, MA: Harvard University Press, 1998], 99; my emphasis).

part this very dimension that seals our fate *as* political animals, that keeps us affectively—we might say, superegoically—*attached* to the constrained space of a determinate social formation. A "miracle" would thus signal the intervention into and suspension of this dimension of superego attachment. As Žižek has put it apropos of the notion of *homo sacer:*

> The distinction between those who are included in the legal order and *Homo sacer* is not simply horizontal, a distinction between two groups of people, but more and more also the "vertical" distinction between two (superimposed) ways of how the *same* people can be treated—briefly: on the level of Law, we are treated as citizens, legal subjects, while on the level of its obscene superego supplement, of this empty unconditional law, we are treated as *Homo sacer.* Perhaps, then, the best motto for today's analysis of ideology is the line quoted by Freud at the beginning of his *Interpretation of Dreams: Archeronta movebo*—if you cannot change the explicit set of ideological rules, you can try to change the underlying set of obscene unwritten rules [i.e., dimension of superego demands].[51]

And as Žižek illustrates in a telling example, such an act can indeed display the quality of a miracle. Speaking of the group of Israeli reservists who refused to serve in the occupied territories in the winter of 2002, Žižek writes:

> The point is not the cruel arbitrary treatment as such, but, rather, that Palestinians in the occupied territories are reduced to the status of *Homo sacer,* the object of disciplinary measures and/or even humanitarian help, but not full citizens. And what the *refuseniks* accomplished is the passage from *Homo sacer* to "neighbor": they treat the Palestinians not as "equal full citizens" but as *neighbors* in the strict Judeo-Christian sense.

For Žižek, this passage represents the ethical moment/act at its purest:

> It is here, in such acts, that—as Saint Paul would have put it—there actually are no longer Jews or Palestinians, full members of the polity and *Homo sacer.* . . . We should be unashamedly Platonic here: this "No!" designates the miraculous moment in which eternal Justice momentarily appears in the temporal sphere of empirical reality.[52]

It should be clear that we are here at the furthest possible remove from the Schmittian notion of the sovereign exception. Or rather, we are at a

---

51. Žižek, *Welcome to the Desert of the Real,* 32.
52. Ibid., 116.

point of the most profound proximity, but it is the proximity of disease and cure.

VIII

Fidelity to what opens at such moments, the labor of sustaining such a break *within* the order of the everyday, of going on with what interrupts our ordinary goings on—this is what it means to remain true to the trajectory of what Rosenzweig calls the "star of redemption." In light of Rosenzweig's work, we would nonetheless want to modify the claim regarding the Pauline dimension of this labor identified by Žižek. The first modification would be to exchange "Israelis" for "Jews" in the above passage. The second, more properly Rosenzweigian claim, would be that the possibility of such a "Pauline" suspension is itself held open by the Jewish insistence on always already *anticipating* this eternal realm of Justice. For Rosenzweig, this insistence takes shape in the liturgical time established in and through the rituals and practices of Jewish life, which together serve to sustain a gap between the flow of historical time—the time of the "nations"—and that of the "remnant of Israel." We might say that it is precisely in this gap that the gesture of the *refuseniks* transpires.

The difficulty of grasping Rozenzweig's peculiar understanding of the Jewish community as one oriented by a fundamental gap has led one Rosenzweig scholar to what I take to be a potentially serious misunderstanding of Rosenzweig's originality.[53] In his otherwise compelling comparative reading of Rosenzweig and Heidegger, Peter Gordon argues that the recent trend in Rosenzweig scholarship to read Rosenzweig in light of Emmanuel Levinas's ethics of radical alterity—a reading suggested, in part, by Levinas's own expressed debt to his predecessor's work—misses the point of Rosenzweig's "holism." What Gordon means is that for Rosenzweig the Jewish people represent an "irreducible unit of redemptive meaning" whose internal uniformity does not leave room for alterity at all:

Ethics for Rosenzweig is forged from structures of familiarity rather than alterity. Here Rosenzweig's ideas concerning the priority of holistic, communal bonds sets him dra-

---

53. I also hope that the following will help to clarify a bit more what is at stake in Žižek's discussion, in this volume, of "the relationship between Judaism as a formal, 'spiritual' structure and Jews as its empirical bearers" (p. 154) along with the corollary matter of Jewish election.

matically at odds with new developments in contemporary Jewish ethics, especially those of Levinas. Indeed, it seems misleading to call Rosenzweig's ideas "ethical" in the customary sense. . . . For Rosenzweig, the community is a unified and organic structure, not a collective of discrete individuals. Beginning with religiously dissociated selves cut off from the social and historical world, *The Star* develops a holistic theory of human groups but for this same reason prohibits any sustained understanding of truly "public" life.

Gordon goes on to compare Rosenzweig's "holism" to that of Heidegger for whom "to live in an intelligible world at all requires that we live within hermeneutical horizons, those shared forms of life that comprise the fundamentally social phenomena of language, history, and people."[54]

What Gordon misses here is that, as I've already noted, even for Heidegger, to find ourselves always already in the midst of life does not simply mean that we always find ourselves in the midst of a social formation and space of meaning that we did not choose (our language, our family, our society, our class, our gender, etc.); it means, more importantly, that this social formation in which we find ourselves immersed is *itself* permeated by inconsistency and incompleteness, is itself punctuated by a lack by which we are, in some peculiar way, addressed, "ex-cited," and for which we are in some fashion *responsible*. In Levinas's terms, this responsibility is what becomes manifest—*revealed*—in the face of the other who *thereby becomes my neighbor*. To put it simply, for Gordon, belonging to a community is a matter of a part-whole logic in which an item finds its meaning only within the context of a historically determined matrix of relations, against the backdrop of a "hermeneutical horizon." But Rozenzweig's "new thinking" is not simply a species of hermeneutic holism, which would, ultimately, remain within the logic of the $B = A$. His more radical claim pertaining to Judaism is that it opens the possibility of community on the basis of a shared orientation with respect to a nonrelational remainder/excess, to the signifying stress that every "normal" community attempts to gentrify by way of some sort of simulated "holism." Rosenzweig's point is not that the Jews are the only people to achieve a proper holism (or even one just like that of other people qua national, cultural, or ethnic formation), but rather that they are "the one people" to have structured a form of life around precisely what disrupts the life of "the nations." Historicity, for Rosenzweig, per-

54. Peter Gordon, *Rosenzweig and Heidegger: Between Judaism and German Philosophy* (Berkeley: University of California Press, 2003), 199, 201, 202.

tains not to the succession of one space of social meaning by another—
the merely "natural history" of the rise and fall of nations and empires—
but rather to moments of uncoupling—of *exodus*—from the fantasmatic
"holism" of epochal or cultural totalities. And as we have seen, this uncoupling pertains to the possibility of the passage from *homo sacer* to
neighbor. Indeed, this is precisely what makes the gesture of the *refuseniks*
so radical. It recalls Jews to remember the distinction between any possible "holism" of the Israeli nation and the logic of community of the
Jewish "nation." To put it in a formula, *holism and holiness never simply
overlap.* In Rosenzweig's view, the Jews as a people persevere not simply on one side or the other of this distinction, but rather within this
noncoincidence, this nonoverlapping. If there is a unity to the Jewish
people, it is a strange one, owing to this unique topology, one that is, I
am suggesting, structured in *response* to the topological peculiarities of
the couple: sovereign exception—*homo sacer.*[55]

How, then, are we to understand the passages from the *Star* cited by
Gordon, which suggest a certain righteousness and even violence in the
self-understanding of all communities and *above all* those that understand themselves as bearers of redemptive energies?[56] The passages in

55. Rosenzweig attempts to articulate this singular topology in a number of ways. In one passage, for example, we read: "The very difference of an individual people from other peoples establishes its connection with them. There are two sides to every boundary. By setting separating borders
for ourselves, we border on something else. By being an individual people, a nation becomes a
people among others. To close oneself off is to come close to another. *But this does not hold when a
people refuses to be merely an individual people and wants to be 'the one people.'* Under these circumstances it must not close itself off within borders, but include within itself such borders as would,
through their double function, tend to make it one individual people among others. And the same
is true of its God, man, and world. These three must likewise not be distinguished from those of others; their distinction must be included within its own borders" (*Star,* 305–6; my emphasis).

56. In his book *Moses the Egyptian: The Memory of Egypt in Western Monotheism* (Cambridge, MA:
Harvard University Press, 1997), Jan Assmann argues that it is only with monotheism that we encounter the phenomenon of a "counterreligion," that is, a religious formation that posits a distinction between *true* and *false* religion. Before that, the boundaries between polytheistic—or as Assmann prefers, *cosmotheistic*—cults were in principle open, the names of gods *translatable* from cult
to cult because of a shared evidentiary base in nature, i.e., in cosmic phenomena. Translatability is,
in such a universe, grounded in and guaranteed by ultimate reference to *nature.* Monotheism, by
contrast, because grounded in (revealed) *scripture,* tends to erect a rigid boundary between true religion and everything else, now rejected as "paganism": "Whereas polytheism, or rather 'cosmothe-
ism,' rendered different cultures mutually transparent and compatible, the new counterreligion
blocked intercultural translatability. *False gods cannot be translated*" (3; my emphasis). According to
Assmann, this rupture in patterns and possibilities of cultural translation and, thus, of a genuine cultural pluralism—a rupture that has been codified in the West as the *Mosaic* distinction between Israel in truth and Egypt in error—must be understood as a profound historical trauma and indeed as
one that continues to haunt the West in the guise of violence against racial and cultural "others."
Assmann has returned to this material in a new book in which he insists, even more emphatically,
on the potential for violence opened by what he refers to as the "Mosaic distinction" (see Assmann,
Die Mosaische Unterscheidung. Oder der Preis des Monotheismus [Munich: Hanser, 2003]). What I think

question pertain to the status of the first-person plural pronoun, the "We," in Rosenzweig's discussion of redemption in the third section of the second volume of the *Star*. There, Rosenzweig writes of the necessity of a judgment or verdict to be enunciated by the community "charged" with redemptive energies against all the others, a verdict of a We against a You.

In these sections, Rosenzweig is concerned with the discursive dimension of the constitution of community/solidarity and posits the polyphonic choral chant of congregational thanksgiving—a thanksgiving that is fundamentally *anticipatory*—as its crucial linguistic/performative locus. Choral singing is posited here as a model of what it means to anticipate *now* the becoming-neighbor of the other, who thereby comes to represent all the world for me. "Where . . . someone or something has become neighbor to a soul, there a piece of the world has become something which it was not previously: soul" (*Star*, 235). And later: "The effect of the love of 'neighbor' is that 'Anyone' and 'all the world' . . . belong together. . . . whoever be momentarily my neighbor represents all the world for me in full validity" (*Star*, 236). In the chant of the chorus, we are all, as it were, brought into the circle of this ensouling proximity, a proximity that does not, however, depend on any positive features of its "members"; being-neighbor in this sense does not imply resemblance, familiarity, or likeness, but rather a kind of shared resoluteness sustained, in large measure, by certain kinds of linguistic and social practices (rather than merely individual intentions or states of mind). The We is not simply an aggregation of individuals, nor is it some sort of group identity or tolerant universalism (posited as being higher or more encompassing than our individual/cultural/ethnic/sexual differences). It is, rather, a form of *militant fidelity* with respect to the testimony borne by the *homo sacer*.

This testimony does not pertain, however, to what is "most human" in all of us once we subtract all our social predicates, to our "sacred" humanity beyond individual and cultural differences; if that were the case, then the work of redemption would be nothing but a kind of charitable, humanitarian assistance program. As we have seen, the testimony immanent to the locus of the *homo sacer* pertains to the signifying stress produced by way of the "exceptional" operations of sovereignty. It is

---

Assmann continues to miss in his otherwise lucid and compelling account of the Mosaic innovation and its implications for ethical and political life is that this innovation was not only a trauma; it was, paradoxically, the trauma that has the potential to open us to the force of trauma in the lives of others, *who thereby become our neighbors.*

against this background, I am arguing, that we need to understand the meaning of the judgment that is born of the We. As Rosenzweig puts it, "The We encompasses everything it can grasp and reach or at least sight. But what it can no longer reach nor sight, that it must eject from its bright, melodious circle into the dread cold of the Nought: for the sake of its own exclusive-inclusive unity, it must say to it: Ye" (237). And as Rosenzweig adds, "Yes, the Ye is dreadful. It is the judgment." But the crucial point here is that this judgment does not pertain to any positive content of this Ye; it is not that what belongs to the We is in any way endowed with special attributes or talents. What is at issue here is more a *subjective stance* (with respect to the operations of sovereignty), a stance that must itself, however, be sustained by practices that thereby delimit a paradoxical boundary of those who remain faithful: "The We cannot avoid this sitting in judgment, for only with this judgment does it give a definite content to the totality of its We. This content nevertheless is not distinctive; it subtracts nothing from the totality of the We. For the judgment does not distinguish a distinct content as against the We, no other content, that is, than the Nought" (237).[57]

IX

The delimitation of the We is produced not out of the fabric of a distinct content allowing for group identification in the usual sense, but rather on the basis of what Alain Badiou has called "ethical consistency." Badiou develops this notion in conjunction with a larger argument about the ways in which human subjects undergo tears in the fabric of their lives, tears that, in principle, allow not simply for new choices of objects of desire, but rather for the radical restructuring of the coordinates of desire, for genuine changes of direction in life. Ethical consistency will mean something like the creation of new fabric *out of a tear*. Al-

57. Zupancic has correlated the logic of ethical consistency with the Nietzschean concept of forgetting, in which "the point is not simply that the capacity to forget, or the 'ahistorical condition,' is the condition of 'great deeds' or 'events.' On the contrary: it is the pure surplus of passion or love (for something) that brings about this closure of memory, this 'ahistorical condition.' In other words, it is not that we have first to close ourselves within a defined horizon in order then to be able to accomplish something. The closure takes place with the very . . . opening toward something. . . . Nietzsche's point is that if this surplus passion engages us 'in the midst of life,' instead of mortifying us, it does so via its inducement of forgetting" (*Shortest Shadow*, 59). Zupancic's larger point is that, in the absence of such a passion, we become subject to the absolute closure of the reality principle and the concomitant disappearance of the space of creativity, which together define modern nihilism (as the ethics of the "last man").

though Badiou's primary examples come from the domains of art, science, love, and politics, the theological background of this theory of "truth-processes"—his name for such sudden tears or ruptures and the processes of their elaboration—is clear throughout and made explicit in his work on St. Paul, whose letters produced, for Badiou, a formal model of the temporality of the truth-event. Indeed, we might say that for the three contemporary thinkers I have been in dialogue with throughout this essay—Žižek, Agamben, and now Badiou—the wizened dwarf beneath the chess table in Benjamin's allegory is none other than Paul (I will return to Paul's "contemporaneity" in the following).

Badiou's thought is related to the Heideggerian notion of "authenticity," according to which, our immersion in the practices and opinions of the social world we inhabit—in what Heidegger calls *"das Man"*—is structurally susceptible to a disruption that "compels us to decide a new way of being."[58] Such disruptions effectuate a transformation of the *animal* that I was into the *subject* I am to become:

If there is no ethics "in general," that is because there is no abstract Subject, who would adopt it as his shield. There is only a particular kind of animal, convoked by certain circumstances to *become* a subject—or rather, to enter into the composing of a subject. That is to say that at a given moment, everything he is—his body, his abilities—is called upon to enable the passing of a truth along its path. This is when the human animal is convoked [*requis*] to be the immortal that he was not yet. (40)

Badiou goes on to give examples from the domains of politics, love, science, and art to indicate what can count as such "truth-events": "the French Revolution of 1792, the meeting of Heloise and Abelard, Galileo's creation of physics, Haydn's invention of the classical musical style" (41). Each such event generates within our animal inertia or mere perseverance in being a "vital disorganization" that can become the source of a radically new kind of subjective stance in the world or, at the very least, within the spheres at issue:

Every pursuit of an interest has success as its only source of legitimacy. On the other hand, if I "fall in love" (the word "fall" indicates disorganization in the walk of life), or if I am seized by the sleepless fury of a thought, or if some radical political engagement proves incompatible with every immediate principle of interest—then I find myself compelled to measure life, my life as a socialized human animal, against some-

58. Alain Badiou, *Ethics: An Essay on the Understanding of Evil*, trans. Peter Hallward (London: Verso, 2001), 41. Subsequent references are given in the text.

thing other than itself. And this above all when, beyond the joyful or enthusiastic clarity of the seizing, it becomes a matter of finding out if, and how, I am to continue along the path of vital disorganization, thereby granting to this primordial disorganization a secondary and paradoxical organization, that very organization which we have called "ethical consistency." (60)

The paradox Badiou invokes here is even more complex than may at first appear, indeed, more complex than he himself at times allows. For the "vital disorganization" inaugurated by a "truth-event" happens not simply to an animal pursuing its predatory interests but to one whose animal life has already been amplified—one might even say disrupted, disorganized—by what Freud referred to as *Triebschicksal*, or "drive destiny." What Badiou seems to lose sight of here is nothing less than the difference between animal instinct and human drive. As I put it earlier, there is nothing that differentiates us more from animal life than that dimension that has traditionally been characterized as the locus of our animality—our drives. To put it in the terms laid out by Rosenzweig, the human drive for "self-preservation," to which Badiou refers, ultimately pertains neither simply to animal life nor to the personality (Badiou collapses these into the formulation "socialized human animal"; this is precisely what Rosenzweig abbreviates by the equation $B = A$), but rather to the *metaethical* self ($B = B$). The new "ethical consistency" that emerges by way of a truth-event has as its ground not simply this socialized human animal—in other words, a mere perseverance in being, a predatory pursuit of interests—but the metaethical "substance" that already exceeds such life (from within). Man is, in short, the creature whose creatureliness has been *amplified* by a death-driven singularity that makes him more than creature or, rather, *more creaturely* than any other part of creation.

Badiou's theory does, however, have a place for this intermediate area between perseverance in being, on the one hand, and truth-events, on the other. Though Badiou is for the most part much more concerned with the problem of fidelity (the work that is done to *sustain* the break with the norms of a historical situation), he does indicate that a break emerges only insofar as such norms are themselves articulated around a void: "You might then ask what it is that makes the connection between the event and that 'for which' it is an event. This connection is the void of the earlier situation. What does this mean? It means that at the heart of every situation, as the foundation of its being, there is a 'situated' void [*vide*], around which is organized the plenitude (or the stable multiples) of the situation in question" (68).

In his *Ethics,* Badiou gives two examples of such a "situated void," one from the realm of art and one from politics: "Thus at the heart of the baroque style at its virtuoso saturation lay the absence [*vide*] (as decisive as it was unnoticed) of a genuine conception of musical architectonics. The Haydn-event occurs as a kind of musical 'naming' of this absence [*vide*]" (68). And further: "Marx is an event for political thought because he designates, under the name 'proletariat,' the central void of early bourgeois societies. For the proletariat—being entirely dispossessed, and absent from the political stage—is *that around which is organized* the complacent plenitude established by the rule of those who possess capital" (69; my emphasis).

As Badiou sums up: "the fundamental ontological characteristic of an event is to inscribe, to name, the situated void of that for which it is an event" (69). And as he emphasizes elsewhere, what he refers to here as a "situated void" has the status of what we have more generally come to understand as a *symptom.*[59] Our "thrownness," to use the Heideggerian term again, generates anxiety not so much because we can never master the wealth of meanings in which we always already find ourselves, in other words, because we are not the authors of the social roles we are compelled to assume, but rather because these roles are in turn never fully identical with themselves, are inconsistent/incomplete, haunted by a void. What this means, of course, is that what Badiou refers to as our life as a socialized human animal is already sustained, in its very animal normality, by the singular way in which each of us comes to be "excited" by such voids and defends against knowing anything about it (this is what I earlier referred to as "signifying stress"). We are thereby back at Laplanche's concise formulation of the situation of the child with respect to its caregivers and authority figures: "Internal alien-ness maintained, held in place by external alien-ness; external alien-ness, in

---

59. Badiou speaks of the "symptomal torsion of being" (cited in Žižek, *The Ticklish Subject: The Absent Centre of Political Ontology* [London: Verso, 1999]), 131). Žižek nicely summarizes the symptomal reading of the "situated void": "The texture of Knowledge is, by definition, always total—that is, for Knowledge of Being, there is no excess; excess and lack of a situation are visible only from the standpoint of the Event, not from the standpoint of the knowing servants of the State. From within this standpoint, of course, one sees 'problems,' but they are automatically reduced to 'local,' marginal difficulties, to contingent errors—what Truth does is to reveal that (what Knowledge misperceives as) marginal malfunctionings and points of failure are a structural necessity. Crucial for the Event is thus the elevation of an empirical obstacle into a transcendental limitation. With regard to the *ancien régime,* what the Truth-Event reveals is how injustices are not marginal malfunctionings but pertain to the very structure of the system which is in its essence, as such, 'corrupt.' Such an entity—which, misperceived by the system as a local 'abnormality,' effectively condenses the global 'abnormality' of the system as such, in its entirety—is what, in the Freudo-Marxist tradition, is called the *symptom*" (131).

turn, held in place by the enigmatic relation of the other to his own internal alien."[60] The socialized human animal that we are is, so to speak, always already bent over, locked into some sort of cringe. What Badiou refers to as the "vital disorganization" generated by a truth-event thus signifies a disruption of this symptomatic cringe already constraining/intensifying our life. If we think of a symptom as being a locus of some sort of disorganization, then the "vital disorganization" at issue in a truth-event must be understood in this reflexive sense as a disorganization of a disorganization already at the heart of our animal—or rather, our "creaturely life."

X

Certainly one of the most striking examples of what it means to be seized by a truth-event and to organize one's life in fidelity to it was provided by Rosenzweig himself, who gave up a promising career as an academic in order to sustain, in his work as a teacher, organizer, translator, and community leader, the break he experienced in an especially concentrated fashion during a Yom Kippur service in a Berlin synagogue in 1913. This was the moment he definitively decided to give up plans for conversion and to remain a Jew. In a now famous letter written to his mentor, Friedrich Meinecke, seven years later, in which he turned down the latter's offer of an assistantship in Berlin, Rosenzweig explained his decision as the result of his new commitment to Judaism. As Rosenzweig tells it, this commitment emerged in the context of a breakdown: "In 1913 something happened to me for which *collapse* [*Zusammenbruch*] is the only fitting name. I suddenly found myself on a heap of wreckage, or rather I realized that the road I was then pursuing was flanked by unrealities."[61] Of the academic road he had been traveling—Badiou would call this the life of the socialized human animal—Rosenzweig writes that it "was the very road defined for me by my talent, and my talent only. I began to sense how meaningless such a subjection to the rule of one's talent was and what abject servitude of the self it involved." Rosenzweig's collapse and recovery in 1913 transpired, as he puts it, in relation to a force—a "dark drive"—that allowed him to suspend such subjection: "The one thing I wish to make clear is that scholarship [*Wissen-*

---

60. Laplanche, *Otherness*, 80.

61. Cited in Nahum Glatzer, ed., *Franz Rosenzweig: His Life and Thought* (Indianapolis: Hackett, 1998), 95.

schaft] no longer holds the center of my attention, and that my life has fallen under the rule of a 'dark drive' which I'm aware that I merely *name* by calling it 'my Judaism.'" One of the effects of this "rule" was, as Rosenzweig puts it, that he was now "more firmly rooted in the earth" than he had been when he wrote his dissertation, *Hegel and the State,* under Meinecke's supervision. One aspect of this new rootedness—Badiou would speak of one's "seizure by a truth-process"—was an enhanced capacity to find value in the mundane details of everyday life, details that were now linked to a truth-process: "The small—at times exceedingly small—thing called [by Goethe] 'demand of the day' [*Forderung des Tages*] which is made upon me in my position at Frankfurt, I mean the nerve-wracking, picayune, and at the same time very necessary struggles with people and conditions, have now become the real core of my existence—and I love this form of existence despite the inevitable annoyance that goes with it." [62] Finally, Rosenzweig links this transformation to one pertaining to the very substance of his attentiveness to and curiosity—his capacity for *Aufmerksamkeit*—about the world; his language furthermore suggests that it was made possible by, or, perhaps more accurately, was coterminus with, a passage through a domain of fantasy:

Cognition is autonomous; it refuses to have any *answers* foisted on it from the outside. Yet it suffers without protest having certain *questions* prescribed to it from the outside (and it is here that my heresy regarding the unwritten law of the university originates). Not every question seems to me worth asking. Scientific curiosity and omnivorous aesthetic appetite mean equally little to me today, though I was once under the spell of both, particularly the latter. Now I only inquire when I find myself *inquired of.* Inquired of, that is, by *men* [*Menschen*] rather than by scholars. There is a man in each scholar, a man who inquires and stands in need of answers. I am anxious to answer the scholar *qua* man but not the representative of a certain discipline, that insatiable, ever inquisitive phantom which *like a vampire* drains him whom it possesses of his humanity. I hate that phantom as I do all phantoms. Its questions are meaningless to me.[63]

Rosenzweig's words concord with the claim made above, namely, that our life as a socialized human animal is, at its heart, sustained by a peculiar sort of hauntedness, by a congealed excitation that we might call, following Rosenzweig's lead here, a phantomlike *undeadness.* Seizure by a truth-event thus implies, among other things, a suspension, a de-

---

62. Ibid., 95, 96. In Badiou's terms, Rosenzweig is describing what it means to adhere to the ethic of a truth: "Do all that you can to persevere in that which exceeds your perseverance. Persevere in the interruption" (Badiou, *Ethics,* 47).

63. Glatzer, *Franz Rosenzweig,* 96–97; my emphasis.

animation of, this undeadness, its being rendered, if only momentarily, inoperative.[64]

XI

Badiou offers a quite compelling presentation of this dynamic of "de-animation" in his book on Saint Paul.[65] Badiou positions his reflections on Paul as a challenge to the multiculturalist consensus of contemporary thought and culture, a consensus that he sees as being an integral part of the neoliberal understanding of the "progress" associated with processes of globalization. Badiou sees the tendency toward ever more subtle modes of identifying individuals and groups—a tendency often linked with grievances and claims to victim status (black, lesbian, single-parent, etc.)—in much the same way that Michel Foucault understood the proliferation of sexualities: as an expansion of the field by which power is able to invest human life with certain kinds of meaning, knowledge, and value. The "deterritorialization" of populations into diverse minority identities is seen here as the means by which capital spreads its logic of general equivalence throughout the globe, configuring the world precisely as world-market: "Capital demands a permanent creation of subjective and territorial identities in order for its principle of movement to homogenize its space of action; identities, moreover, that never demand anything but the right to be exposed in the same way as others to the uniform prerogatives of the market. The capitalist logic of the general equivalent and the identitarian and cultural logic of communities and minorities form an articulated whole" (10–11).

In Rosenzweigian terms, multiculturalist politics and market capital-

---

64. One must not conflate such a "deanimation" with the narcoticization of the will that Nietzsche associated with a form of nihilism. The point here is precisely to break out of the oscillation between an active and passive nihilism—between undeadness and narcoticization—that together compose the full picture of modern nihilism. Zupancic has lucidly summarized this oscillation in the following terms: "There is, on the one hand, the imperative or the need for excitement, the need to be in touch with the 'Real,' to 'feel life' as vividly as possible, to feel awake—the imperative or need in which Nietzsche recognizes the core of the ascetic ideal. This imperative, precisely as an imperative, holds us in a kind of mortifying grip, a paralysis that can very well take the form of some intense activity while still remaining that: a paralysis. On the other hand (and in response to this), there is passive nihilism as a defense that operates by mortifying this excitement itself. In other words, one kind of mortification (the one that takes the path of surplus excitement) is regulated or moderated by another kind. The 'will to Nothingness' is combined with the 'narcoticization' of the will—exciting stimulant combines with sedating tranquilizer" (*Shortest Shadow*, 67).

65. Alain Badiou, *Saint Paul: The Foundation of Universalism*, trans. Ray Brassier (Stanford, CA: Stanford University Press, 2003). Subsequent references will be made in the text.

ism conspire to articulate a global system in which every B can enter into the sphere of general equivalence, A. This would represent a triumph of what Rosenzweig characterizes as "the world in the form of the third person," in which all "singularity" is ultimately identifiable and marketable by means of its predicates.[66] Against this background, Badiou proposes Paul as a radical alternative, as the militant proponent of a uniquely subjective—and yet somehow materialist—rupture with this world system that exhibits the formal features of the closed cosmos of antiquity (as readers of the *Star* know, Greek antiquity formed the paradigm for Rosenzweig's understanding of the world in the form of the third person). About the Pauline break with that world, Badiou writes that "'the world' that Paul declares has been crucified with Jesus is the Greek cosmos, the reassuring totality that allots places and orders thought to consent to those places, and that it is consequently a question of letting in the vital rights of the infinite and the untotalizable event" (71). Paul's great achievement, in Badiou's eyes, was to have articulated the procedures for and virtues appropriate to the composition of a subjectivity correlative to "that uncountable infinity constituted by a singular human life" (10), a subjectivity thereby in excess of the predicative particularity of any sort of cultural identity.

At the heart of Badiou's understanding of Paul is the thought that Paul introduced into the world of late antiquity a distinct form of discourse that positioned and engaged the human subject in a radically different way than the reigning discursive links of that world. In contrast to the discourse of the *wise man* (the Greek discourse concerning man's proper place in the order of the natural totality of the cosmos) and that of the *prophet* (the Jewish discourse concerning the decipherment of exceptional signs and the fulfillment of providential miracles), Paul's discourse was that of the *apostle*. What distinguishes the apostle from both wise man and prophet is, according to Badiou, a refusal of the ambition to mastery proper to the other subjective figures, "whether it be through direct mastery of the totality (Greek wisdom), or through mastery of a literal tradition and the deciphering of signs (Jewish ritualism and prophetism)" (42). Paul's project, Badiou argues,

is to show that a universal logic of salvation cannot be reconciled with any law, be it one that ties thought to the cosmos, or one that fixes the effects of an exceptional election. It is impossible that the starting point be the Whole, but just as impossible

66. Rosenzweig, "'Urzelle' to the Star of Redemption," in *Philosophical and Theological Writings*, 60.

that it be an exception to the Whole. Neither totality nor sign will do. One must proceed from the event as such, which is a-cosmic and illegal, refusing integration into any totality and signaling nothing. (42)

For Badiou this amounts to the claim that both Greek and Jewish discourses are discourses of the Father, whereas the new discourse is that of the son, "equidistant from Jewish prophecy and the Greek logos" (43). Indeed, the new discourse is one that "can only be accomplished through a sort of decline of the figure of the Master" or Father (43), a decline captured in such passages as the famous statement of 1 Corinthians 4:13: "We have become, and are now, as the refuse of the world, the offscouring of all things."[67] It is, according to this view, only at the site of such predicative disqualification, such utter phallic ruination, testifying to the vanity of every identification and symbolic investiture (every $B = A$) that the possibility of a genuinely new beginning—the life of the *son*—becomes realizable. The Christ-event—which for Paul has little to do with any sort of moral teaching (the figure of Jesus is almost entirely absent from Paul's letters) but is concentrated, rather, in the gift of new life signaled in the declaration "Christ is resurrected"—is, as Badiou claims, "heterogeneous to the law, pure excess over every prescription, grace without concept or appropriate rite. . . . The pure event can be reconciled neither with the natural Whole nor with the imperative of the letter" (57).

It should be clear that what is at stake in this version of Paul is nothing other than the pure possibility of a life uncoupled from the figure of law, whether it be the law of cosmic totality or that delimiting the exceptional ethical sphere and substance of a community. The formula for such an uncoupling is the "not . . . but" of Romans 6:14, "for you are not under law, but under grace": "For the 'not' is the potential dissolution of closed particularities (whose name is 'law'), while the 'but' indicates the task, the faithful labor, in which the subjects of the process opened by the event (whose name is 'grace') are the coworkers" (64). The very emptiness or formalism of this gesture/gift of what he refers to as "evental grace" allows Badiou to place the Pauline notion of the son in proximity to the Nietzschean thought of the Overman as a figure of pure affirmation of life beyond any guilty attachment to law. This formalism notwithstanding, it is crucial that the *site* of such grace be grasped in its spe-

67. References from Paul's letters are taken from *The Writings of St. Paul,* ed. Wayne A. Meeks (New York: W. W. Norton, 1972). Such a decline is, Badiou suggests, correlative to the subjective destitution Lacan associated with the position of the analyst as the key to the working through of the transference (the positing of the analyst as Master, as subject supposed to know).

cial sort of material density. This density is provided, in Paul's writings, by the thought of death understood as the obstacle to such an affirmation.

Perhaps Badiou's most important achievement in his essay on Paul is to emphasize that, for Paul, death does not so much signify a biological terminus as a certain subjective stance or path, a way of dying to life within life—in a word, a form of nihilism. Indeed, what Paul understands by death, which he links to the way of the flesh and of sin, would seem to correspond quite closely to what I have referred to as *undeadness*.[68] "Resurrection" thereby designates precisely the possibility of some sort of deanimation of this peculiar sort of death-in-life that both intensifies and constrains human existence. The crucial point for Badiou is that it is exactly from this point, that is, from this uncanny site of undeadness, that the upsurge of life signified by the Christ-event first becomes possible. That is the meaning of the claim that "death is the construction of the eventai site" (70).

We might note at this point another important parallel between this understanding of Paul and Rosenzweig's project. In volume two of the *Star*, in a section forming the transition between book 1 and book 2 (the former addressing "Creation or the Ever-Enduring Base of Things," the latter "Revelation or the Ever-Renewed Birth of the Soul") and entitled "The Prophecy of Miracle," Rosenzweig offers a commentary on Genesis 1: 31. Rosenzweig notes—and here he joins a larger tradition of Rabbinic exegesis—that it is only at this point in the biblical narration of beginnings, that is, after the creation of man, that God uses for the first time the comparative form by proclaiming creation to be *"very* good":

Within the general Yea of creation, bearing everything individual on its broad back, an area is set apart which is affirmed differently, which is "very" affirmed. Unlike anything else in creation, it thus points beyond creation. This "very" heralds a supercreation [*eine Überschöpfung*] within creation itself, something more than worldly within the worldly, something other than life which yet belongs to life and only to life, which was created with life as its ultimate, and which yet first lets life surmise a fulfillment beyond life: this "very" is death. The created death of the creature portends the revelation of a life which is above the creaturely level. For each created thing, death is *the very consummator of its entire materiality*. (*Star*, 155; my emphasis)

For both Paul and Rosenzweig, creaturely materiality enjoys its supreme density in the death-driven singularity of human being that provides the

---

68. Rosenzweig speaks of "tragically immobile vitality" [*tragisch starre Lebendigkeit*] (*Star*, 230) and Benjamin of "immobilized restlessness" [*erstarrte Unruhe*] (*Arcades Project*, J55 a, 4).

very *matter of the neighbor,* that is, the very thing—we should perhaps write, Thing—to which the love that emerges in and through the messianic gift is addressed.[69] We should say, then, that the socialized human animal becomes susceptible to the force of truth only because his or her animality or creatureliness has been heightened by the impact of an anxiety-filled encounter with a void.

As Badiou emphasizes, in Paul's writings, the key name of death is the Law. The most famous and difficult passage in Paul's letters linking death and law is no doubt Romans 7, from which I will quote at length:

Likewise, my brethren, you have died to the law through the body of Christ, so that you may belong to another, to him who has been raised from the dead in order that we may bear fruit for God. While we were living in the flesh, our sinful passions, aroused by the law, were at work in our members to bear fruit for death. But now we are discharged from the law, dead to that which held us captive, so that we serve not under the old written code but in the new life of the Spirit.

Paul continues along this path of paradoxical formulations by claiming, in effect, that death first comes alive through the law:

What then shall we say? That the law is sin? By no means! Yet, if it had not been for the law, I should not have known sin. I should not have known what it is to covet if the law had not said "You shall not covet." But sin, finding opportunity in the commandment, wrought in me all kinds of covetousness. Apart from the law sin lies dead. I was once alive apart from the law, but when the commandment came, sin revived and I died; the very commandment which promised life proved to be death to me. For sin, finding opportunity in the commandment, deceived me and by it killed me. . . . Did that which is good, then, bring death to me? By no means! It was sin, working death in me through what is good, in order that sin might be shown to be sin, and through the commandment might become sinful beyond measure.

Finally, Paul seems to offer a solution to this set of paradoxes by suggesting that one differentiate between different registers, levels, or di-

---

69. I am alluding here, of course, to Freud's remark in his *Project for a Scientific Psychology* concerning the thingness of the neighbor, a remark taken up by Lacan to great profit. Speaking of the perceptual experience of another human being—"ein *Nebenmensch,*" the human being next to me, my neighbor—Freud writes: "And so the complex of the neighbor divides into two constituent parts, the first of which *impresses* [*imponiert;* my emphasis] through the constancy of its composition [*durch konstantes Gefüge*], its persistence as a *Thing* [*Ding*], while the other is *understood* by means of memory-work" (*Gesammelte Werke, Nachtragsband: Texte aus den Jahren 1885–1938* [Frankfurt a.M.: Fischer, 1987], 426–27; my translation).

mensions of law: the law articulated in commandment and what he calls the "law in my members":

I do not understand my own actions. For I do not do what I want, but I do the very thing I hate. Now if I do what I do not want, I agree that the law is good. So then it is no longer I that do it, but sin which dwells within me. For I know that nothing good dwells within me, that is, in my flesh. I can will what is right, but I cannot do it. For I do not do the good I want but the evil I do not want is what I do. Now if I do what I do not want, it is no longer I that do it, but the sin which dwells within me. So I find it to be a law that when I want to do right, evil lies close at hand. For I delight in the law of God, in my inmost self, but I see in my members another law at war with the law of my mind and making me captive to the law of sin which dwells in my members.

As Badiou rightly notes apropos of these passages, we are offered here nothing short of a theory of unconscious mental activity (the laws of which dwell "in my members") as generated by the seductions of law: "Paul's fundamental thesis is that the law, and only the law, endows desire with an autonomy sufficient for the subject of this desire, from the perspective of that autonomy, to come to occupy the place of the dead" (79). Badiou underlines here the exact same admixture of uncanny animation and constriction that we have been attending to under a variety of headings throughout this essay: "The law is what *gives life* to desire. But in so doing, it *constrains* the subject so that he wants to follow only the path of death" (79; my emphasis). We are back, in other words, at the Freudian notion of the *drive destiny* that both intensifies and constrains life:

What is sin exactly? It is not desire as such, for if it were one would not understand its link to the law and death. *Sin is the life of desire as autonomy, as automatism.* The law is required in order to unleash the automatic life of desire, the automatism of repetition. For only the law *fixes* the object of desire, binding desire to it regardless of the subject's "will." It is this objectal automatism of desire, inconceivable without the law, that assigns the subject to the carnal path of death. (79)

It is, in other words, the fixity of drive destiny manifest in the compulsion to repeat that is at issue in Paul's understanding of the "flesh," "sin," and "death." The glad tidings of the Christ-event are just this: it is possible, thanks to grace, to unplug from this destiny, to change direction and destination in a radical way.

XII

Against the background of such an understanding, the strict separation of the discourse of the prophet and that of the apostle can no longer be rigorously sustained. That, at least, is the wager of Rosenzweig's effort to restore, on the basis of the "new thinking," the relevance of the concept of miracle that, according to Badiou, strictly speaking belongs to the discourse of prophecy alone. Rosenzweig's whole point is, of course, that under conditions of modernity the semiotic structure of miracle would have to be reconceived along the very lines that Badiou presents as the essential features of the discourse of the apostle. That is to say, what can now occupy the place of prophecy is the construction of the evental site understood as our "protocosmic being," the drive destiny framing/fixing our possibilities of desire, the way in which one is, at the level of one's character, (dis)oriented in the world. Once again, the signs that are at issue in the semiotic structure of miracle are *symptoms*, which are, in turn, the ways in which the subject registers/represses—"cringes" around— the voids in the historical situation into which he is thrown. (The "cringe" is thus a kind of *virtual archive* of a void.) Badiou's claim that death is the construction of the evental site means just that our death-driven singularity is the very point at which the possibility of new possibilities can emerge. As Badiou writes, "resurrection . . . comes forth *out from* the power of death, not through its negation" (73). In the *Star*, Rosenzweig puts it this way:

> What then was the *daimon*, the character as distinct from the personality? Personality was an innate disposition, character something which suddenly overcame a man. Character, then, was no disposition: vis-à-vis the broad diversity of dispositions it was, rather, a dividing line or, better, a direction [*Richtung*]. Once man is possessed by his *daimon*, he has received "direction" for his whole life. His will is now destined to run in this direction which directs him once and for all. By receiving direction he is in truth already corrected [*gerichtet*]. For that which is subject to correction in man [*dem Gericht unterliegt*], his essential will, is already fixed once and for all in its direction. (*Star*, 213)

This translation only vaguely captures the series of puns at work in the cluster of terms: direction, correction, to direct. In German, the word *gerichtet*, translated here as "corrected," also means "judged" and even resonates with the word for execution (*Hinrichtung*). Direction and law, destiny and judgment, are obviously deeply intertwined here; this entanglement forms, of course, the central target of Paul's polemic against the Law. To put it somewhat differently, *drive destiny* and *superego* belong together. But Rosenzweig quickly adds to this passage concerning the fixity of our fundamental world-orientation the following: "Fixed, that is, unless there occur the one thing that can interrupt this once-and-for-all again, and invalidate the correction [*Gericht*] along with the direction [*Richtung*]: the inner conversion [*die innere Umkehr*]" (*Star*, 213).[70]

What is crucial for both Paul and Rosenzweig—for the discourse of the apostle and the "new thinking"—is that the construction of the evental site in no way automatically produces the miracle of awakening to new life. As Badiou puts it, "death is an operation that immanentizes the evental site, while resurrection is the event as such. . . . Resurrection is neither a sublation, nor an overcoming of death. They are two distinct functions, whose articulation contains no necessity. For the event's sudden emergence never follows from the existence of an evental site. Although it requires conditions of immanence, that sudden emergence nevertheless remains of the order of grace" (71). The emergence of new life, the possibility of new possibilities, is not a dialectical outcome of the material itself, in other words, of the dense materiality of undeadness. To put it in psychoanalytic terms, symptoms do not dissolve simply by way of construction and interpretation. Even more to the point, there is really no such thing as self-analysis; one cannot give to oneself the possibility of new possibilities. Something must *happen,* something beyond one's own control, calculations, and labor, something that comes from the locus of the Other. To recall Rosenzweig's account of the "new thinking," it is not just that theology requires philosophy, now understood as the construction of the evental site; philosophy needs theology, understood as the insistence on the nondialectical place of the grace-event. To put it again in psychoanalytic terms, the mapping of unconscious

---

70. In a new book, Jonathan Lear has addressed precisely this possibility of *Umkehr* in conjunction with the notion of the transference and its working through. Apropos of a case presentation involving a woman whose fundamental direction in life was organized around disappointment—who had been, as it were, sentenced to a life of disappointment—he indicates what successful therapeutic action would involve. It would require, he writes, "a moment in which the world itself shifts: there is, as it were, a possibility for new possibilities. This 'possibility for new possibilities' is not an ordinary possibility, like all the others, only new. The fact that Ms. C. inhabited a world meant that she lived amidst what for her were all the possibilities there were. For her, there simply was no possibility of experiencing, say, a promotion as a success rather than as a disappointment. One cannot simply add that possibility to Ms. C.'s world piecemeal, as though everything else about her can remain the same, only now it is possible for her to experience promotion as a success. Rather, the order of possibilities itself has to shift so that now success becomes an intelligible and welcome aspect of life. The possibility for new possibilities is not an addition of a special possibility to the world; it is an alteration in the world of possibilities" (*Therapeutic Action*, 204).

mental activity—think of Freud's "self-analysis" in the *Interpretation of Dreams*—does not in and of itself generate the cure.

In Rosenzweig's understanding, the event of "inner conversion" transpires under the impact of divine love, a love directed precisely at that bit of demonic self-sameness that Rosenzweig called the metaethical self ($B = B$). It is not enough to separate out the self from the personality, to isolate, as it were, the workings of the automatism of desire—what I have been calling "drive destiny"—as the key to the "symptomal torsion" within the sphere of one's multiple identifications ($B = A$); this separating *out*—this is the work of "materialist" analysis—can only become a separating *from* by way of the supplement of divine love. What Rosenzweig means here is, I would suggest, that divine love is the singular force that first allows us *to uncouple the drive from its destiny,* from its *Richtung/Gerichtetsein.* And if I understand Badiou correctly, this is precisely what he takes Paul to have proposed under the sign of "resurrection." To return to Rosenzweig's discussion of the tragic self, we might say that *eternity* opens for human existence precisely where the *immortality* of drive destiny is interrupted.

For both Paul and Rosenzweig, then, divine love must be clearly distinguished from any sort of oblatory love, a love understood as selfless devotion and surrender. For Rosenzweig, such love is ultimately love in the third person, love understood as the giving of one's individuality over to a higher unity, cause, ideal, or totality, love as immersion of self into some sort of greater, more beautiful whole or universal (for Rosenzweig, Goethe was the modern master of such love as a principle of artistic activity and form of life). "Against such love," Rosenzweig writes,

stands the other that rises out of the event, that is out of the most particular (thing) there is [*dem Allerbesondersten was es gibt*]. This particular goes step by step from one particular to the next particular, from one neighbor to the next neighbor, and denies love to the furthest until it can be love of neighbor. The concept of order of this world is thus not the universal [*das Allgemeine*], neither the *arche* nor the *telos,* neither the natural nor the historical unity, but rather the singular, the event, *not beginning or end, but center of the world.*[71]

71. Rosenzweig, "*Urzelle,*" 56–57. For Rosenzweig and, later, for Levinas, it is just such "centrality" that is at issue in the biblical notion of "election." As Levinas puts it apropos of this notion, Israel "knows itself at the center of the world and for it the world is not homogeneous: for I am always alone in being able to answer the call, I am irreplaceable in my assumption of responsibility" (Emmanuel Levinas, *Difficult Freedom: Essays on Judaism,* trans. Sean Hand [Baltimore: Johns Hopkins University Press, 1990], 177–76).

For Badiou, such love is the only true basis of universality, one based not on predicates, on cultural identities forming closed particularities, but on "that uncountable infinity constituted by a singular human life" (10). In Rosenzweig's terms, such universality is nothing but the infinite dissemination of the capacity for neighbor-love. Only because the loving word of God has gone out to the metaethical self, "only that leads $B = B$ beyond itself, and only in this *event* that has occurred to it can it think another $B = B$, to which the same has occurred, a neighbor, that is like You. It discovers the other, not from its own *essence* and its heart's pure regions, but rather from the *occurrence* that has occurred to him and from his heart's deafness."[72]

Apropos of Romans 13, where Paul famously reduces all the biblical commandments to the single one "You shall love your neighbor as yourself," Badiou argues that such a reduction of the multiplicity of commandments to a "single, affirmative, and nonobjectal maxim" is required in order that "the infinity of desire through the transgression of the prohibition" (89) not be released anew. Everything I have been saying here suggests that the commandment to love the neighbor is perhaps the most "objectal" maxim there is, for it directs our minds, indeed our entire being, toward that which is most objectlike, most thinglike about the other, the dense and resistant materiality of his or her drive destiny. Indeed, it is Badiou's tendency to lose sight of this peculiar materiality of the neighbor that allows him to conclude his otherwise compelling commentary on Paul with a universalism of sameness:

Thought becomes universal only by addressing itself to all others, and it effectuates itself as power through this address. But the moment all, including the solitary militant, are counted according to the universal, it follows that what takes place is the subsumption of the Other by the Same. Paul demonstrates in detail how a universal thought, proceeding on the basis of the worldly proliferation of alterities (the Jew, the Greek, women, men, slaves, free men, and so on), *produces* a Sameness and an Equality. . . . The production of equality and the casting off, in thought, of differences are the material signs of the universal. (109)

XIII

It is precisely this conception of universalism that is the object of Giorgio Agamben's critique in his own recent study of Saint Paul. In the pres-

---

72. Rosenzweig, "*Urzelle*," 63.

ent context, what is especially interesting about Agamben's work is his insistence on the link between Paul's conception of the Christ-event and Benjamin's messianism as elaborated, above all, in the theses "On the Concept of History." The idea that the dwarf-theologian in Benjamin's famous allegory is none other than Saint Paul becomes fully explicit here. In a seminar on Paul held shortly before his death, Jacob Taubes had already argued that Benjamin's early text "Theologisch-Politisches Fragment" was to be understood as a commentary on Romans 8 and 13. Following Taubes's lead, Agamben proposes an even tighter conceptual and philological connection between the *Theses* and Paul.[73]

Agamben notes the various ways in which Benjamin directly appropriates Paul's terminology (by way of the Luther translation) and suggests that in the *Theses* Benjamin engaged in the practice of unmarked citation he had proposed as the methodological principle of his *Arcades Project*. Thus, Benjamin's famous invocation of a "weak messianic force" [*eine schwache messianische Kraft*] which I cited earlier, is read as an allusion to 2 Corinthians 12: 9–10, where Paul speaks of the messianic power finding its fulfillment in weakness. (Luther's translation reads: *denn meine Kraft ist in den Schwachen mächtig.*) More importantly, Agamben compellingly argues that Benjamin's otherwise enigmatic conception of *image*, of *Bild*, as it is deployed in the *Theses* as well as in the *Arcades Project*, finds its original source in Paul's understanding of typological relations which represent, in turn, a version of the semiotic structure of miracle I have been elaborating throughout this essay. In each case, a moment of the past is recognized as the *typos* of the messianic present. Indeed, this very instance and instant of recognition is what constitutes the present *as* messianic. As Agamben puts it, "the messianic *kairos* is precisely nothing but this very [typological] relation" (221). The crucial difference between the "old thinking" and the "new thinking" concerning such typological relations (or rather, the difference between such typological relations and the construction of dialectical images) is that in the new thinking the element of the past that is at issue has the structural status of *trauma*, a past that in some sense never fully took place and so continues to insist in the present precisely as drive destiny, the symptomal torsion of one's being in the world, one's relation to and capacity to use the object-world. As Rosenzweig has argued, under conditions of modernity, the first element of the semiotic structure of mira-

---

73. See Jacob Taubes, *Die Politische Theologie des Paulus*, ed. Aleida Assmann and Jan Assmann (Munich: Wilhelm Fink, 1995). The following discussion of Agamben is based on the French translation of his book on Paul, *Le temps qui reste*, trans. Judith Revel (Paris: Bibliothèque Rivages, 2000). Subsequent references are given in the text.

cle is played not by an eyewitness to an event in the past (registered in and cultivated by scriptural tradition), but rather by the peculiar sort of testimony borne by the symptom.[74]

It is only against this background that one can understand Benjamin's critique of Max Horkheimer's claim regarding the "completeness" of history. In a letter to Benjamin from 1937, Horkheimer wrote that "the determination of incompleteness is idealistic if completeness is not comprised within it. Past injustice has occurred and is completed. The slain are really slain. . . . If one takes the lack of closure entirely seriously, one must believe in the Last Judgment." Benjamin's response to this view reads as follows: "The corrective to this line of thinking may be found in the consideration that history is not simply a science but also and not least a form of remembrance [*Eingedenken*]. What science has 'determined,' remembrance can modify. Such mindfulness can make the incomplete (happiness) into something complete, and the complete (suffering) into something incomplete." Benjamin then adds the following remark that returns us to the allegory of the chess player and the role of theology in the "new thinking" more generally: "That is theology; but in remembrance we have an experience that forbids us to conceive of history as fundamentally atheological, little as it may be granted to write it with immediately theological concepts."[75] Regarding this understanding of remembrance which, according to Agamben goes back to some early reflections shared by Scholem with his friend on the verb forms of Hebrew (where one finds the aspects of accomplished versus unaccomplished rather than the tenses of past and future), Agamben writes that it perfectly captures the essence of the typological relation in Paul: "it is a field of tension in which the two times enter into a constellation which the apostle calls *ho nun kairos,* where the past (the complete) again finds its actuality and becomes incomplete, while the present (the incomplete) acquires a sort of completeness or fulfillment" (124).

It is also, Agamben argues, Saint Paul who stands behind Benjamin's idiosyncratic use of the term "now-time" [*Jetztzeit*]. Noting the negative connotations this term carries in, among other places, Heidegger's *Being and Time,* where "now-time" signifies the flattening out of lived temporality into the empty, homogeneous clock-time of modern experience,

---

74. In *Moses and Monotheism,* Freud collapses, in a sense, the old and new thinking by arguing that, in and through the scriptural tradition maintained in liturgical practices, the Jews transmit a testimony of trauma with regard to their own ethnogenesis. For a discussion of Freud's views, see my "Freud's Moses and the Ethics of Nomotropic Desire." Freud's method here suggests, perhaps, that the "new thinking" can never be a simple overcoming of the "old thinking."

75. Benjamin, *Arcades Project,* 471 [N 8, 1].

Agamben suggests that Benjamin's inversion of such connotations is performed under the auspices of Paul's notion of *ho nun kairos,* the now of messianic time in which a certain *recapitulation* of the past serves to suspend the *repetition* compulsion that had so painfully narrowed the possibilities of the present.[76]

Perhaps most significant for our purposes, however, is another set of philological reflections Agamben introduces apropos of Benjamin and Paul. In one of the methodological notes he made concerning the *Arcades Project,* Benjamin used a phrase the sources of which scholars have been unable to trace. Speaking of the way in which a properly dialectical treatment of historical material reorganizes temporal structure, Benjamin writes that "the historical evidence polarizes into fore- and after-history always anew, never in the same way. And it does so at a distance from its own existence, in the present instant itself—like a line which, divided according to the Apollonian section, experiences its partition from outside itself."[77] Agamben, who has worked on the Italian edition of Benjamin's works, argues that "Apollonian section," which has no source in Greek mythology, ought to read, instead, "Apelles' section," referring to the fourth-century BC painter who, in a contest, divided a narrow line by one yet narrower and of a different color.[78] Agamben makes creative use of this notion to get at Paul's understanding of the way in which the messianic advent enters into and transforms the closed particularities of cultural, ethnic, social, and sexual identity, in other words, all differences that are legible at the level of $B = A$ (Jew/Greek, male/female, master/slave). Rather than, as Badiou had argued, producing an element of sameness that would serve as the basis of a genuine universality, Agamben argues that the effect of the Apelles' section or cut is to produce, instead, a unique kind of *remainder* or *remnant.* The most concise formulation of this claim can be found on the dust jacket of Agamben's book, which also makes the eminently Benjaminian gesture of suggesting that Paul has only now found his true moment of legibility/recognizability ("there is a kind of secret link . . . between Paul's letters and our epoch"):

Paul is no longer the founder of a new religion, but the most demanding representative of Jewish messianism; no longer the inventor of universality, but the one who surpassed the division of peoples with a new division [i.e., an Apelles' cut] and who in-

76. Agamben is thinking here, above all, of the parallels between Benjamin's eighteenth thesis and Ephesians 1:10.

77. Benjamin, *Arcades Project,* 570 [N7a, 1].

78. See the editors' notes to the *Arcades Project,* 990 n. 21.

troduced it as a remainder; no longer the proclamation of a new identity and of a new vocation, but the revoking of every identity and every vocation; no longer the simple critique of the Law, but its opening toward a use beyond every system of law.

What Agamben means here is that Paul does not simply revoke the division Jew/Greek by appealing to some positive feature we might discover beneath or beyond such divisions (some sort of sameness); Agamben's claim is, rather, that Paul divides both sides of the identitarian division such that neither side can any longer enjoy stable self-coincidence. The divisions become nonexhaustive, "not-all"; they leave a *remainder:* "This means that the messianic division introduces into the large division of the nations according to the law a remainder and that the Jews and the non-Jews are, in a constitutive sense, 'not-all'" (85). Agamben adds that this "remainder" is "not something that resembles a numerical portion or a substantial positive residue." It represents, instead, a cut into the bipolar partition between Jews and non-Jews that allows for the passage to an entirely new sort of logic of being-with, one that no longer operates on the basis of membership in bounded sets or totalities set off against exceptions. For Agamben, the figure that holds the place of this logic (of the noncoincidence of every identity with itself) is that of the "non non-Jew," the figure who is *not not-in-the-law.*

Although he never mentions Lacan, Agamben's understanding of this logic of "not-all" clearly recalls Lacan's elaboration of feminine jouissance as distinct from masculine, phallic jouissance. As Suzanne Bernard has put it in her reading of seminar 20, where Lacan elaborates this distinction,

the feminine structure . . . is produced in relation to a "set" that *does not* exist on the basis of an external, constitutive exception. . . . However, this does not mean, in turn, that the non-whole of feminine structure is simply outside of or indifferent to the order of masculine structure. Rather, she is in the phallic function *altogether* or, in Lacan's words, "She is *not* not at all there. She is there in full." . . . By being in the symbolic "without exception" then, the feminine subject has a relation to the Other that produces another "unlimited" form of *jouissance.*[79]

In the essays published in this volume, both Reinhard and Žižek attempt to translate this "not-all" logic into the very terms of ethical responsibility that have been at the center of my discussion. The position of true

---

79. Suzanne Bernard, "Tongues of Angels," in *Reading Seminar XX,* ed. Suzanne Bernard and Bruce Fink (Albany: State University of New York Press, 2002), 178.

moral autonomy, in this view, is not "I am not responsible for every-thing," but rather "there is nothing for which I am not responsible," the counterpart of which is "I am not responsible for All": precisely because I cannot have an overview over All, there is nothing for which I can ex-empt myself from responsibility.[80] This "not-all" logic represents a sharp alternative to that of the relation of *part* to *whole* as well as to that of *ex-ception* to *norm*. As I already noted apropos of the Schmittian conception of the state of exception, one only arrives at the logic of the remainder—the Apelles' cut into every part-whole relation, every $B = A$—by working through, by traversing the fantasy of the exception, a fantasy that is, in turn, "condensed" within and as one's characterological *daimon, B = B*. As I have argued here, a "successful" interpellation, one culminating in an act of identification—a "yes, that is me"—always produces a "vocal object" that finds an initial organization in fantasy, that persists as an intimate locus of solicitation or ex-citation congealing as the *matter* or *materiality* at the heart of the neighbor. Though this "extimate" bit of fantasy makes us irreducible to the "socialized human animal," it is also what for the most part seals our fate *as* such animals, that keeps us affectively, superegoically, *attached* to the constrained space of the determinate social formation—the world in the form of the third per-son—we happen to find ourselves in. In more Pauline terms, the closed particularities of cultural sets are sustained by an automatism of trans-gressive desire (the path of the flesh, sin, and death) solicited by the very law that established the boundaries of those sets. But such desires are, at bottom, nothing but fantasies of exception. What allows Paul to speak both about the nullification of the law as well as its fulfillment is the fact that what he is ultimately interested in is the suspension not of the law but of the element of fantasy that *undeadens* us. It is, in a word, precisely this bit of fantasy that is the object of the Apelles' cut. The Apelles' cut is thus not so much the division of the subject into personality and (metaethical) self as it is a cut into the metaethical self itself, one that momentarily—we might just as easily say, for an eternity—uncouples the *drive* from its *destiny*. To refer to the psychoanalytic clinic, the work that, ideally, takes place in a successful analysis is, according to this view, nothing but the (always renewed) shift from a logic of exception, from a structure of fantasy whereby at some level of my being I imagine that I can *except* myself from the midst of life (and the answerability proper to

---

80. See Žižek's "Neighbors and Other Monsters," n. 21. Reinhard's essay culminates in the claim that the concept of neighbor-love as developed by thinkers such as Rosenzweig and Levinas can be properly understood only by means of a logic of the "not-all."

it), to one where I am, without restraint, exposed to the proximity of the *neighbor*. We might even say that the neighbor as such only truly becomes manifest—only becomes *revealed*—by means of such a shift.[81] Žižek has, in effect, made the same point apropos of two different ways of conceiving the "state of emergency":

It is therefore crucial to distinguish between the Jewish-Pauline "state of emergency," the suspension of the "normal" immersion in life, and the standard Bakhtinian carnivalesque "state of exception" when everyday moral norms and hierarchies are suspended, and one is encouraged to indulge in transgressions: the two are opposed—that is to say, what the Pauline emergency suspends is not so much the explicit Law regulating our daily life, but, precisely, its obscene unwritten underside: when, in his series of *as if* prescriptions, Paul basically says: "obey the law as if you are not obeying it," this means precisely that *we should suspend the obscene libidinal investment in the Law, the investment on account of which the Law generates/solicits its own transgression.*[82]

What we find in Paul is, in other words, "an engaged position of struggle, an uncanny 'interpellation' beyond ideological interpellation, an interpellation which suspends the performative force of the 'normal' ideological interpellation that compels us to accept our determinate place within the sociosymbolic edifice."[83] The Apelles' cut intervenes into our ego-life, the cluster of closed particularities that endow us with an authoritative identity and cultural intelligibility, by producing a *remnant* out of the "state of exception" that had served to keep that very ego-life going, if only in a condition of moribund inflexibility. As I have put it elsewhere, "revelation converts the 'surplus cause' of our . . . passionate attachments to ideological formations—our various forms of *idolatry*—into a 'remnant' of them."[84] In more Rosenzweigian terms, if the response elicited by ideological interpellation is a "that's me," what becomes possible by way of the "uncanny 'interpellation' beyond ideological interpellation" is the "Here I am" modeled forth in Abraham's response to God's address (Genesis 22:1). For Rosenzweig, the core content of such an interpellation, which signifies, for him, the "truth-event" of revelation, will ultimately be the imperative to love—to love God and to

---

81. One will recall, in this context, that Rosenzweig's project in the *Star* is, ultimately, to reconstruct a systematic understanding of the relations between worldly, human, and divine being without recourse to a concept/fantasy of a closed *All*.

82. Slavoj Žižek, *The Puppet and the Dwarf: The Perverse Core of Christianity* (Cambridge, MA: MIT Press, 2003), 113.

83. Ibid., 112.

84. See my *On the Psychotheology of Everyday Life*, 116.

manifest this love as love of neighbor. It is, Rosenzweig suggests, only such love and the language informed by it that can exceed the representational thinking that produces only further instances of "that's me." And as I have been emphasizing throughout this essay, the transition from "that's me" to "Here I am" can take place only by way of a different level or register of "that's me," that is, by way of a "recognition" of oneself not in the identification proposed/mandated by way of ideological interpellation, but rather in its "objectal" leftover that persists in the formations of fantasy.

XIV

I would like to sum up where I think these reflections lead and leave us. The first thing to say is that we seem to have reached the conclusion that Saint Paul was the first great German-Jewish thinker, equal in stature to Rosenzweig, Freud, and Benjamin! That is, of course, to say that if indeed, as Agamben claims, there is a secret link between Paul's letters and our own epoch, if Paul's letters in some sense become legible only now, it is only because of the work done by the great German-Jewish thinkers I have been discussing here. In a sense, each one of these figures arrived, by radically divergent pathways, at the same conclusion, namely, that to even conceive of radical shifts of direction in life—of a genuine *exodus* from deep individual and social patterns of servitude—human beings, both individually and collectively, require the notion of an interpellation beyond (ideological) interpellation. Freud, of course, thought that the psychoanalytic clinic, the position or, as Lacan put it, the discourse, of the analyst, could provide the locus of such an uncanny calling that would not only not reproduce a discourse of mastery but serve to unplug the analysand from the multiple forms of servitude dwelling in his or her "members." Benjamin, who spent the better part of his energies constructing the "evental site" of such an address—the notes for the *Arcades Project* provide the basis of what was to become his grandest version of such a construction—no doubt believed that only a revolutionary politics could be the source of such a calling, the force of which he characterized, however, by terms such as "divine violence" or "weak messianic force." Rosenzweig, for his part, concluded that the very fact that we arrive at such an impossible notion—an interpellation beyond interpellation—in the first place, testifies to the ongoing necessity of theological thinking, that the pressure, as it were, arising from within thought to reach for such a notion, is already a mode of registering the region of being we call God and a kind of love that exceeds any sort of mere "object cathexis," in other words, a love that is no longer tied to a representation. What makes this thinking new is that it works at showing how this necessity emerges out of the immanent impasses of secular thought. In Rosenzweig's work, the central paradox is that it is really *secular* thought that is most deeply invested in fantasies of exception, in other words, of being "excepted" from the lot—and love—of finite human existence and that monotheism is actually a form of therapy that allows for a genuine return to the midst of life with our neighbor.[85] We don't, in a word, need God for the sake of divine things but for the sake of proper attentiveness to secular things. We might even say that all that Rosenzweig wanted to show was that truly inhabiting the midst of life—being answerable to our neighbor and the demands of the day, *die Forderung des Tages*—was actually a remarkable, even miraculous, achievement that required some form of divine support—ultimately, a form of *love*—kept alive, in turn, by a certain form of life. My own sense is that it is not a matter of choosing one of these options over the others—say, the Freudian over the Rosenzweigian or Benjaminian—but rather of thinking them together and trying to appreciate the ways in which each one provides a resource for deepening our grasp of the others. Rather than a form of religious thinking, I'd like to consider this to be a first, tentative step along a path of what we might more modestly call *postsecular* thinking.[86]

85. It is in this sense that Rosenzweig referred to monotheism as an antireligion directed against the "religionitis" of humans. See Rosenzweig, *Der Mensch und sein Werk. Gesammelte Schriften,* ed. Reinhold Mayer and Annemarie Mayer (Dordrecht: Martinus Nijhoff, 1984), 1:2:770–71.

86. Here I would like to cite the final lines of Lupton's essay on "Creature Caliban," where she also proposes that it is precisely the creaturely dimension we have been elaborating here—the "matter of the neighbor"—that offers us the eventual site for the elaboration of new forms of solidarity/community/universality. She writes that Shakespeare's "decisive crystallization of a certain material moment within the theology of the Creature might help us to find a postsecular solution to the predicament of modern humanity, trapped in the increasingly catastrophic choice between the false universalism of global capitalism on the one hand and the crippling particularisms of apartheid, separatism, and segregation on the other" (23).

SLAVOJ ŽIŽEK

Neighbors and Other Monsters: A Plea for Ethical Violence

Critique of Ethical Violence?

In one of his stories about Herr Keuner, Bertolt Brecht ruthlessly asserted the Platonic core of ethical violence: "Herr K.
was asked: 'What do you do when you love another man?'
'I make myself a sketch of him,' said Herr K., 'and I take care
about the likeness.' 'Of the sketch?' 'No,' said Herr K., 'of
the man.'"[1] This radical stance is more than ever needed
today, in our era of oversensitivity for "harassment" by the
Other, when every ethical pressure is experienced as a false
front of the violence of power. This "tolerant" attitude fails
to perceive how contemporary power no longer primarily
relies on censorship, but on unconstrained permissiveness,
or, as Alain Badiou put it in thesis 14 of his "Fifteen Theses on Contemporary Art": "Since it is sure of its ability to
control the entire domain of the visible and the audible via
the laws governing commercial circulation and democratic
communication, Empire no longer censures anything. All
art, and all thought, is ruined when we accept this permission to consume, to communicate and to enjoy. We should
become pitiless censors of ourselves."[2]

1. Bertolt Brecht, *Prosa 3* (Frankfurt: Suhrkamp, 1995), 24.
2. Alain Badiou, "Fifteen Theses on Contemporary Art," *Lacanian Ink* 23
(Spring 2004): 100–119.

Today, we seem effectively to be at the opposite point from the ideology of 1960s: the mottos of spontaneity, creative self-expression, and so on, are taken over by the System; in other words, the old logic of the system reproducing itself through repressing and rigidly channeling the subject's spontaneous impetuses is left behind. Nonalienated spontaneity, self-expression, self-realization, they all directly serve the system, which is why pitiless self-censorship is a *sine qua non* of emancipatory politics. Especially in the domain of poetic art, this means that one should totally reject any attitude of self-expression, of displaying one's innermost emotional turmoil, desires, and dreams. True art has *nothing whatsoever* to do with disgusting emotional exhibitionism—insofar as the standard notion of "poetic spirit" is the ability to display one's intimate turmoil, what Vladimir Mayakovski said about himself with regard to his turn from personal poetry to political propaganda in verses ("I had to step on the throat of my Muse") is the constitutive gesture of a true poet. If there is a thing that provokes disgust in a true poet, it is the scene of a close friend opening up his heart, spilling out all the dirt of his inner life. Consequently, one should totally reject the standard opposition of "objective" science focused on reality and "subjective" art focused on emotional reaction to it and self-expression: if anything, true art is *more* asubjective than science. In science, I remain a person with my pathological features, I just assert objectivity *outside* it, while in true art, the artist has to undergo a radical *self*-objectivization, he has to die *in and for himself,* turn into a kind of living dead.[3]

Can one imagine a stronger contrast to today's all-pervasive complaints about "ethical violence," in other words, to the tendency to submit to criticism ethical injunctions that "terrorize" us with the brutal imposition of their universality. The (not so) secret model of this critique is an "ethics without violence," freely (re)negotiated—the highest Cultural Critique meets here unexpectedly the lowest of pop psychology. John Gray, the author of *Men Are from Mars, Women Are from Venus,* deployed in a series of Oprah Winfrey shows a vulgarized version of the narrativist-deconstructionist psychoanalysis: since we ultimately "are" the stories we are telling ourselves about ourselves, the solution to a psychic deadlock resides in a creative "positive" rewriting of the narrative of our past. What he had in mind is not only the standard cognitive therapy of changing negative "false beliefs" about oneself into a more posi-

---

3. This, of course, in no way implies that art has nothing to do with the "inner Thing" that haunts and drives the artist; the point is, rather, that this "inner Thing" emerges only through a "pitiless censorship" of one's imaginary "inner life."

tive attitude of the assurance that one is loved by others and capable of creative achievements, but a more "radical," pseudo-Freudian notion of regressing back to the scene of the primordial traumatic wound. That is to say, Gray accepts the psychoanalytic notion of a hard kernel of some early childhood traumatic experience that forever marked the subject's further development, giving it a pathological spin. What he proposes is that, after regressing to his primal traumatic scene and thus directly confronting it, the subject should, under the therapist's guidance, "rewrite" this scene, this ultimate fantasmatic framework of his subjectivity, in a more "positive," benign, and productive narrative. Say, if your primordial traumatic scene that insisted in your Unconscious, deforming and inhibiting your creative attitude, was that of your father shouting at you, "You are worthless! I despise you! Nothing will come out of you!" you should rewrite it into the new scene with a benevolent father kindly smiling at you and telling you, "You're OK! I trust you fully!" (In one of the Oprah Winfrey shows, Gray directly enacted this rewriting-the-past experience with a woman who, at the end, gratefully embraced him, crying from happiness that she was no longer haunted by her father's despising attitude toward her.) To play this game to the end, when the Wolf Man "regressed" to the traumatic scene that determined his further psychic development—witnessing the parental *coitus a tergo*—the solution would be to rewrite this scene, so that what the Wolf Man effectively saw was merely his parents lying on the bed, father reading a newspaper and mother a sentimental novel? Ridiculous as this procedure may appear, let us not forget that it also has its politically correct version, that of the ethnic, sexual, and so on minorities rewriting their past in a more positive, self-asserting vein (African-Americans claiming that long before European modernity, ancient African empires already had highly developed science and technology, etc.). Along the same lines, one can even imagine a rewriting of the Decalogue itself: is some command too severe? Let us regress to the scene on Mount Sinai and rewrite it: adultery—yes, if it is sincere and serves the goal of your profound self-realization. . . . What disappears in this total availability of the past to its subsequent retroactive rewriting are not primarily the "hard facts," but the Real of a traumatic encounter whose structuring role in the subject's psychic economy forever resists its symbolic rewriting.

The ultimate irony is that this "critique of ethical violence" is sometimes even linked to the Nietzschean motif of moral norms as imposed by the weak on the strong, thwarting their life-assertiveness: moral sensitivity, bad conscience, and guilt feeling are internalized resistances to the heroic assertion of Life. For Nietzsche, such "moral sensitivity" culminates in the contemporary Last Man who fears excessive intensity of life as something that may disturb his search for "happiness" without stress, and who, for this very reason, rejects "cruel" imposed moral norms as a threat to his fragile balance. No wonder, then, that the latest version of the critique of ethical violence was proposed by Judith Butler, whose last book,[4] although it does not mention Badiou, is *de facto* a kind of anti-Badiou manifesto: hers is an ethics of finitude, of making a virtue out of our very weakness, in other words, of elevating into the highest ethical value the respect for our very inability to act with full responsibility. The question one should ask concerns the limits of this operation.

Butler's elementary move is the standard Derridean turn from condition of impossibility to condition of possibility: the fact that a human subject is constrained in its autonomy, thrown into a pregiven complex situation which remains impenetrable to him and for which he is not fully accountable, is simultaneously the condition of possibility of moral activity, what makes moral activity meaningful, since we can be responsible for others only insofar as they (and we) are constrained and thrown into an impenetrable situation. (The paradox is that Butler, who is generally anti-Lacanian, reproaching Lacan for not allowing for change, is here asserting the inertia of human existence—against Lacan, who allows for a much stronger subjective intervention.) Butler describes how, in every narrative account of myself, I have to submit myself to the foreign temporality of my language tradition and thus have to accept my radical decenterment. The irony of this description is that Butler, the sharp critic of Lacan, renders here (a somewhat simplified version of) what Lacan calls "symbolic castration," the subject's constitutive alienation in the decentered symbolic order. Is, then, the subject totally determined by the signifying structure, or does it dispose of a margin of freedom? In order to account for this resistance to the rule of symbolic norms, Butler turns to Foucault: norms rule only insofar as they are practiced by subjects, and the subject disposes here of a minimum of freedom to arrange itself with these norms, to subvert them, to (re)inscribe them in different modes, and so on. Lacan, on the contrary, allows for a much stronger subjective autonomy: insofar as the subject occupies the place of the lack in the Other (symbolic order), it can perform separation (the operation which is the opposite of alienation), and suspend the reign of the big Other, in other words, separate itself from it.

The impossibility of fully accounting for oneself is conditioned by the irreducible intersubjective context of every narrative reconstitution:

4. See Judith Butler, *Kritik der ethischen Gewalt* (Frankfurt: Suhrkamp, 2003), quoted as *KEG*.

when I reconstruct my life in a narrative, I always do it within a certain intersubjective context, answering the Other's call-injunction, addressing the Other in a certain way. This background, including the (unconscious) motivations and libidinal investments of my narrative, cannot ever be rendered fully transparent within the narrative. To fully account for oneself in a symbolic narrative is a priori impossible; the Socratic injunction, "know thyself," is impossible to fulfill for a priori structural reasons. My very status as a subject depends on its links to the substantial Other: not only the regulative-symbolic Other of the tradition in which I am embedded, but also the bodily-desiring substance of the Other, the fact that, in the core of my being, I am irreducibly vulnerable, exposed to the Other(s). And far from limiting my ethical status (autonomy), this primordial vulnerability due to my constitutive exposure to the Other *grounds* it: what makes an individual *human* and thus something for which we are responsible, toward whom we have a duty to help, is his/her very finitude and vulnerability. Far from undermining ethics (in the sense of rendering me ultimately nonresponsible: "I am not a master of myself, what I do is conditioned by forces that overwhelm me."), this primordial exposure/dependency opens up the properly ethical relation of individuals who accept and respect each other's vulnerability and limitation. Crucial here is the link between the impenetrability of the Other and my own impenetrability to myself: they are linked because my own being is grounded in the primordial exposure to the Other. Confronted with the Other, I never can fully account for myself. And when Butler emphasizes how one should not close oneself off to this exposure to the Other, how one should not try to transpose the unwilled into something willed (*KEG*, 100), is she not thereby opposing the very core of Nietzsche's thought, the stance of willing the eternal return of the Same, which involves precisely the transposition of everything unwilled, everything we are thrown into as given, into something Willed?

The first ethical gesture is thus to abandon the position of absolute self-positing subjectivity and to acknowledge one's exposure/thrownness, being overwhelmed by Other(ness): far from limiting our humanity, this limitation is its positive condition. This awareness of limitation implies a stance of fundamental forgiveness and a tolerant "live and let live" attitude: I will never be able to account for myself in front of the Other, because I am already nontransparent to myself, and I will never get from the Other a full answer to "who are you?" because the Other is a mystery also for him/herself. To recognize the Other is thus not primarily or ultimately to recognize the Other in a certain well-defined capacity ("I recognize you as . . . rational, good, lovable"), but to recognize you in the abyss of your very impenetrability and opacity. This mutual recognition of limitation thus opens up a space of sociality that is the solidarity of the vulnerable.

Butler's central "Hegelian" reflexive turn here is that it is not only that the subject has to adopt a stance toward the norms that regulate his activity—these norms in their turn determine who and what is or is not recognized as subject. Relying on Foucault, Butler thus formulates the basic feature of critical tradition: when one criticizes and judges phenomena on behalf of norms, one should in the same gesture question the status of these norms. Say, when one holds something to be (un)true, one should at the same time question the criteria of "holding something to be true," which are never abstract and ahistorical, but always part of a concrete context into which we are thrown. This move, of course, is the elementary Hegelian move formulated in the introduction to the *Phenomenology:* testing is always minimally self-relating and reflexive, in other words, when I am testing the truth of a statement or an act, I am always also testing the standard of testing, so that if the test fails, the standard of success or failure should also be problematized.

This reference to Hegel is mediated by Adorno's critique of Hegel's idealism, a critique which Butler submits to critical reading.[5] When Adorno claims that "the true injustice is always located at the place from which one blindly posits oneself as just and the other as unjust" (*KEG*, 251), does he thereby not basically repeat Hegel's old argument about the Beautiful Soul: "The true Evil is the very gaze which sees evil all around itself"? Recall the arrogance of many West Germans in 1990, when they condemned the majority of East Germans as moral weaklings corrupted by the Communist police regime—this very gaze which saw in East Germans moral corruption was corruption itself. (Symptomatically, although many DDR files were opened to the public, the ones that remained secret are the files recording contact between East German and West German politicians—too much West sycophancy would be revealed here.)

---

5. There is a double paradox in Butler's establishing the link between Adorno's critique of the ethical violence of the abstract universality imposed from outside upon a concrete life-world and Hegel's critique of revolutionary terror as the supreme reign of the abstract universality (*KEG*, 17). First, one should bear in mind that Hegel here relies on the standard conservative motif (elaborated before him by Edmund Burke) of organic traditional ties which a revolution violently disrupts and that Hegel's rejection of universal democracy is part of the same line of thought. So we have here Butler praising the "conservative" Hegel! Furthermore, Hegel is not simply rejecting revolutionary terror. He is in the same gesture asserting its necessity: we do not have a choice between the abstract universality of terror and the traditional organic unity—the choice is here forced, the first gesture is necessarily that of asserting abstract universality.

The limit of such a reference to the impenetrable background into which we are thrown and on account of which we cannot be taken as fully accountable and responsible for our acts is the negativity of freedom: even when the entire positive content of my psyche is ultimately impenetrable, the margin of my freedom is that I can say No! to any positive element that I encounter. This negativity of freedom provides the zero-level from which every positive content can be questioned. Lacan's position is thus that being exposed/overwhelmed, caught in a cobweb of preexisting conditions, is *not* incompatible with radical autonomy. Of course, I cannot undo the substantial weight of the context into which I am thrown; of course, I cannot penetrate the opaque background of my being; but what I can do is, in an act of negativity, "cleanse the plate," draw a line, exempt myself, step out of the symbolic in a "suicidal" gesture of a radical act—what Freud called "death drive" and what German Idealism called "radical negativity."

What gets lost in this "critique of ethical violence" is precisely the most precious and revolutionary aspect of the Jewish legacy. Let us not forget that, in the Jewish tradition, the divine Mosaic Law is experienced as something externally, violently imposed, contingent and traumatic— in short, as an impossible/real Thing that "makes the law." What is arguably the ultimate scene of religious-ideological interpellation—the pronouncement of the Decalogue on Mount Sinai—is the very opposite of something that emerges "organically" as the outcome of the path of self-knowing and self-realization: the pronouncement of the Decalogue is *ethical violence at its purest.* The Judeo-Christian tradition is thus to be strictly opposed to the New Age Gnostic problematic of self-realization or self-fulfillment, and the cause of this need for a violent imposition of the Law is that *the very terrain covered by the Law is that of an even more fundamental violence, that of encountering a neighbor:* far from brutally disturbing a preceding harmonious social interaction, the imposition of the Law endeavors to introduce a minimum of regulation onto a stressful "impossible" relationship. When the Old Testament enjoins you to love and respect your neighbor, this does not refer to your imaginary *semblable*/double, but to the neighbor qua traumatic Thing. In contrast to the New Age attitude which ultimately reduces my Other/Neighbor to my mirror-image or to the means in the path of my self-realization (like the Jungian psychology in which other persons around me are ultimately reduced to the externalizations-projections of the different disavowed aspects of my personality), Judaism opens up a tradition in which an alien traumatic kernel forever persists in my Neighbor—the Neighbor remains an inert, impenetrable, enigmatic presence that hystericizes me. The core of this presence, of course, is the Other's desire, an enigma not only for us, but also for the Other itself.[6] For this reason, the Lacanian *"Che vuoi?"* is not simply an inquiry into "What do you want?" but more an inquiry into "What's bugging you? What is it in you that makes you so unbearable, not only for us but also for yourself, that you yourself obviously do not master?"—in Serb, there is a vulgar expression which perfectly renders this meaning: when somebody is getting on one's nerves, one asks him, "What for a prick is fucking you? [*Koji kurac te jebe?*]"

It is against this background that one should approach the topic of iconoclasm. The Jewish commandment which prohibits images of God is the obverse of the statement that relating to one's neighbor is the *only* terrain of religious practice, of where the divine dimension is present in our lives—"no images of God" does not point toward a Gnostic experience of the divine beyond our reality, a divine which is beyond any image; on the contrary, it designates a kind of ethical *hic Rhodus, hic salta:* you want to be religious? OK, prove it *here,* in the "works of love," in the way you relate to your neighbors. Levinas was therefore right to emphasize how "nothing is more opposed to a relation with the face than 'contact' with the Irrational and mystery."[7] Judaism is anti-Gnosticism par excellence. We have here a nice case of the Hegelian reversal of reflexive determination into determinate reflection: instead of saying "God is love," we should say "love is divine" (and, of course, the point is not to conceive of this reversal as the standard humanist platitude). It is for this precise reason that Christianity, far from standing for a regression toward an image of God, only draws the consequence of the Jewish iconoclasm through asserting the identity of God and man—or, as it is said in John 4:12: "No man has ever seen God; if we love one another, God abides in us and his love is perfected in us." The radical conclusion to be drawn from this is that one should renounce striving for one's own (spiritual) salvation as the highest form of egotism. According to Leon Brunschvicg, therein resides the most elementary ethical lesson of the West against Eastern spirituality: "The preoccupation with our salvation is a remnant of self-love, a trace of natural egocentrism from which we must be torn by the religious life. As long as you think only salvation, you turn your back on God. God is God, only for the person who over-

6. This notion of neighbor is elaborated in detail in Ken Reinhard's contribution to the present volume. The present text is much more indebted to the work of Eric Santner and Ken Reinhard than a couple of footnote references can indicate—it is part of an ongoing dialogue.

7. Levinas, *Difficult Freedom: Essays on Judaism,* trans. Sean Hand (Baltimore: Johns Hopkins University Press, 1990), 9; cited as *DF.*

comes the temptation to degrade Him and use Him for his own ends."[8] This is, in theological terms, the extreme of "pitiless censorship" Badiou talks about, and it is only through such a censorship that the dimension of what one is tempted to call *ethical transcendence* opens itself up.

Smashing the Neighbor's Face

How does subjectivity relate to transcendence? There seem to be two basic modes exemplified by the names of Jean-Paul Sartre and Levinas. (1) The "transcendence of the ego" (Sartre), in other words, the notion of subject as the force of negativity, self-transcending, never a positive entity identical to itself. (2) The existence of the subject as grounded in its openness to an irreducible-unfathomable-transcendent Otherness— there is a subject only insofar as it is not absolute and self-grounded but remains in a tension with an impenetrable Other; there is freedom only through the reference to a gap which makes the Other unfathomable (according to Manfred Frank and others, this is what Hölderlin, Novalis, Schelling, etc., knew in their critique of idealism[9]). As expected, Hegel offers a kind of "mediation" between these two extremes, asserting their ultimate identity. It is not only that the core of subjectivity is inaccessible to the subject, that the subject is decentered with regard to itself, that it cannot assume the abyss in its very center; it is also not that the first mode is the "truth" of the second (in a reflexive twist, the subject has to acknowledge that the transcendent power which resists it is really its own, the power of subject itself), or vice versa (the subject emerges only as confronted with the abyss of the Other). This seems to be the lesson of Hegel's intersubjectivity—I am a free subject only through encountering another free subject—and the usual counterargument is here that, for Hegel, this dependence on the Other is just a mediating step/detour on the way toward full recognition of the subject in its Other, the full appropriation of the Other. But are things so simple? What if the Hegelian "recognition" means that I have to recognize in the impenetrable Other which appears as the obstacle to my freedom its positive-enabling ground and condition? What if it is *only* in this sense is that the Other is "sublated"?

8. Quoted from *DF,* 48. So what about the Buddhist figure of bodhisattva who, out of love for the not-yet-enlightened suffering humanity, postpones his own salvation to help others on the way toward it? Does bodhisattva not stand for the highest contradiction: is not the implication of his gesture that love is higher than salvation? So why still call salvation salvation?

9. See, for example, Manfred Frank, *Der unendliche Mangel an Sein* (Munich: Fink, 1992).

The topic of the "other" is to be submitted to a kind of spectral analysis that renders visible its imaginary, symbolic, and real aspects—it provides perhaps the ultimate case of the Lacanian notion of the "Borromean knot" that unites these three dimensions. First, there is the imaginary other—other people "like me," my fellow human beings with whom I am engaged in the mirrorlike relationships of competition, mutual recognition, and so forth. Then, there is the symbolic "big Other"—the "substance" of our social existence, the impersonal set of rules that coordinate our coexistence. Finally, there is the Other qua Real, the impossible Thing, the "inhuman partner," the Other with whom no symmetrical dialogue, mediated by the symbolic Order, is possible. And it is crucial to perceive how these three dimensions are hooked up. The neighbor (*Nebenmensch*) as the Thing means that, beneath the neighbor as my *semblant,* my mirror image, there always lurks the unfathomable abyss of radical Otherness, of a monstrous Thing that cannot be "gentrified." In his seminar 3, Lacan already indicates this dimension:

And why "the Other" with a capital *O?* For a no doubt mad reason, in the same way as it is madness every time we are obliged to bring in signs supplementary to those given by language. Here the mad reason is the following. You are my wife—after all, what do you know about it? You are my master—in reality, are you so sure of that? What creates the founding value of those words is that what is aimed at in the message, as well as what is manifest in the pretence, is that the other is there qua absolute Other. Absolute, that is to say he is recognized, but is not known. In the same way, what constitutes pretence is that, in the end, you don't know whether it's a pretence or not. Essentially it is this unknown element in the alterity of the other which characterizes the speech relation on the level on which it is spoken to the other.[10]

Lacan's notion, from the early 1950s, of the "founding word," of the statement which confers on you a symbolic title and thus makes you what you are (wife, master), is usually perceived as an echo of the theory of performative speech acts (the link between Lacan and J. L. Austin, the author of the notion of the performative, was Emile Benveniste). However, it is clear from the above quote that Lacan aims at something more: we need the recourse to performativity, to the symbolic engagement, precisely and only insofar as the other whom we encounter is not only the imaginary *semblant,* but also the elusive absolute Other of the Real Thing with whom no reciprocal exchange is possible. In order to render our coexistence with the Thing minimally bearable, the symbolic order

10. Jacques Lacan, *Le séminaire, livre 3: Les psychoses* (Paris: Seuil, 1981), 48.

qua Third, the pacifying mediator, has to intervene: the "gentrification" of the Other-Thing into a "normal human fellow" cannot occur through our direct interaction, but presupposes the third agency to which we both submit ourselves—there is no intersubjectivity (no symmetrical, shared, relation between humans) without the impersonal symbolic Order. So no axis between the two terms can subsist without the third one: if the functioning of the big Other is suspended, the friendly neighbor coincides with the monstrous Thing (Antigone); if there is no neighbor to whom I can relate as a human partner, the symbolic Order itself turns into the monstrous Thing which directly parasitizes upon me (like Daniel Paul Schreber's God who directly controls me, penetrating me with the rays of jouissance). If there is no Thing to underpin our everyday symbolically regulated exchange with others, we find ourselves in a Habermasian "flat," aseptic universe in which subjects are deprived of their hubris of excessive passion, reduced to lifeless pawns in the regulated game of communication.

More precisely, one can distinguish three stages in Levinas's account of the emergence of the Ethical. The subject emerges as an ego by way of appropriating alterity through labor and possession, thereby creating a realm of familiarity in which he can dwell—such a domesticated Other with whom I can share a home is for Levinas the "feminine Other" (one can, of course, raise here the question of what happens with the non-familiar, properly uncanny, dimension of femininity). After this first "alienation" in an established particular life-form comes the *separation* from my familiar world: when I am addressed by the absolutely Other beyond my world, I am shattered from the complacency of my life-world, and, in answering this address, I have to renounce my egotism and the safety of my Home (of what Peter Sloterdijk calls my "Sphere"[11]). This call is not an empirical spatiotemporal event, but rather a kind of ethical transcendental a priori—it does not happen to (a preexisting) me, it makes me into a subject, and, as such, it always-already happens, in a past which never was present: "This summons, as always having taken place no matter what actual response I make, is without limit, infinite, and so summons me to infinite responsibility for the Other. Such a summons can only come from 'an absolutely heteronomous call,' one which *commands* me, and so comes from a *height,* and before which I am *absolutely* responsible, unable to be replaced by anyone else."[12]

---

11. See Peter Sloterdijk, *Sphären I* (Frankfurt a.M.: Suhrkamp, 1998).
12. Michael Weston, *Kierkegaard and Modern Continental Philosophy* (London: Routledge 1994), 163.

My elementary situation is thus that of an eternal struggle against myself: I am forever split between egotistic rootedness in a particular familiar world around which my life gravitates and the unconditional call of responsibility for the Other: "The I which arises in enjoyment as a separated being, and has in itself the center around which its existence gravitates, is only confirmed in its singularity when it purges itself of this gravitation; and since the I's roots in separation are ineradicable, this process of purging is interminable."[13] (Would this version of what Badiou calls "pitiless censorship of oneself" not make the heart of every Stalinist lover of purges beat with joy?) The entire domain of laws and universality is grounded in this responsibility to and for the nonfamiliar Other: I enter the domain of justice and universal laws when I renounce my small world and its possessions and offer to see things from the standpoint of the Other. Concepts and their universality are thus grounded in my responsibility to the Other—ethics preexists and grounds ontology. In this domain of justice and laws, we are always dealing with a "third party," the multitude of empirical others, which raises the problem of justice, of rules of how to treat them, and thus compels us to "compare the incomparable": "The notions through which that prior structure has been articulated become through the command to justice the more familiar concepts of the structure of rationality: the infinite responsibility of the I for the Other becomes co-existence concretized as responsibilities in an historical world."[14]

The difference between this Levinasian account and Kierkegaard is crucial; it is not only that Levinas's account remains a philosophical one, a "transcendental" turn toward what is *always*-already here as the condition of possibility of ethics (the ethical call which precedes all empirical encounters of others), while Kierkegaard is dealing with decisions, "leaps of faith" into a New. More radically, perhaps, for Levinas, the Other who addresses me with the unconditional call and thus constitutes me as an ethical subject is—in spite of the fact that this is an absolutely heteronomous call which *commands* me and so comes from a *height*—the *human* other, the *face*, the transcendental form of neighbor as radical Other, while, for Kierkegaard, God does not mediate between me and my neighbors. *God is the primordial Other itself,* so that *all neighbors,* all "empirical" others with whom I interact, *are primordially figures of the third,* a "third party." It is for this reason that there is no place, in Levinas's edifice, for the Kierkegaardian theological suspension of the ethical. The paradox is that it is precisely because Levinas asserts the re-lation to my neighbor, my unconditional responsibility for him, as the true terrain of ethical activity that he still has to cling to an "impersonal" God (God is for him, ultimately, the name for the Law itself that enjoins me to love my neighbor), while Kierkegaard, because he asserts the *gap* between my direct responsibility to God and my love for (human) neigh-bors (the gap which becomes palpable in the case of Abraham and Isaac), has to endorse the Christian dogma of Incarnation, of positing God Himself as identical to a man like others (Christ). And it is from here that one should approach the key Levinasian notion of encountering the other's face as the epiphany, as the event that precedes Truth itself: "To seek truth, I have already established a relationship with a face which can guarantee itself, whose epiphany itself is somehow a word of honor. Every language as an exchange of verbal signs refers already to this pri-mordial word of honor. . . . deceit and veracity already presuppose the absolute authenticity of the face." [15]

One should read these lines against the background of the circu-lar, self-referential, character of the Lacanian "big Other," the symbolic "substance" of our being, which is perhaps best rendered by Donald Da-vidson's "holistic" claim that "our only evidence for a belief is other be-liefs. . . . And since no belief is self-certifying, none can supply a certain basis for the rest." [16] Far from functioning as the "fatal flaw" of the sym-bolic order, this circularity is the very condition of its effective func-tioning. So when Levinas claims that a face "can guarantee itself," this means that it serves as the nonlinguistic point of reference that also en-ables us to break the vicious circularity of the symbolic order, providing it with the ultimate foundation, the "absolute authenticity." The face is thus the ultimate *fetish,* the object which fills in (obfuscates) the big Other's "castration" (inconsistency, lack), the abyss of its circularity. At a different level, this fetishization—or, rather, fetishist disavowal—is dis-cernible also in our daily relating to another person's face. This dis-avowal does not primarily concern the raw reality of flesh ("I know very well that beneath the face there is just the Real of the raw flesh, bones, and blood, but I nonetheless act as if the face is a window into the mys-terious interiority on the soul"), but rather, at a more radical level, the abyss/void of the Other: the human face "gentrifies" the terrifying Thing that is the ultimate reality of our neighbor. And insofar as the void called "the subject of the signifier" ($) is strictly correlative to this inconsis-

---

15. Levinas, *Totality and Infinity,* 202.
16. Quoted from *Truth and Interpretation,* ed. Ernest Lepore (Oxford: Blackwell, 1986), 331.

tency (lack) of the Other, subject and face are to be opposed: the Event of encountering the other's face is not the experience of the abyss of the other's subjectivity—the only way to arrive at this experience is through defacement in all its dimensions, from a simple tic or grimace that disfigures the face (in this sense, Lacan claims that the Real is "the grimace of reality") up to the monstrosity of the total loss of face. Perhaps the key moment in Jerry Lewis's films occurs when the idiot he plays is compelled to become aware of the havoc his behavior has caused: at this moment, when he is stared at by all the people around him, unable to sustain their gaze, he engages in his unique mode of making faces, of ridiculously disfiguring his facial expression, combined with twisting his hands and rolling his eyes. This desperate attempt of the ashamed subject to efface his presence, to erase himself from others' view, combined with the endeavor to assume a new face more acceptable to the environs, is subjectivization at its purest.

So what is shame, this experience of "losing one's face"? In the standard Sartrean version, the subject, in his "For-Itself," is ashamed of the "In-Itself," of the stupid Real of his bodily identity: am I really *that,* this bad smelling body, these nails, these excrements? In short, "shame" designates the fact that "spirit" is directly linked to the inert vulgar bodily reality—which is why it is shameful to defecate in public. However, Lacan's counterargument is here that shame by definition concerns fantasy. Shame is not simply passivity, but an *actively assumed passivity:* if I am raped, I have nothing to be ashamed of; but if I enjoy being raped, then I deserve to feel ashamed. Actively assuming passivity thus means, in Lacanian terms, finding jouissance in the passive situation in which one is caught. And since the coordinates of jouissance are ultimately those of the fundamental fantasy, which is the fantasy of (finding jouissance in) being put in the passive position (like the Freudian "My father is beating me"), what exposes the subject to shame is not the disclosure of how he is put in the passive position, treated only as the body. Shame emerges only when such a passive position in social reality touches upon the (disavowed intimate) fantasy. Let us take two women, the first, liberated and assertive, active; the other, secretly daydreaming about being brutally handled by her partner, even raped. The crucial point is that, if both of them are raped, the rape will be much more traumatic for the second one, on account of the fact that it will realize in "external" social reality the "stuff of her dreams." Why? There is a gap which forever separates the fantasmatic kernel of the subject's being from the more "superficial" modes of his or her symbolic and/or imaginary identifications—it is never possible for me to fully assume (in the sense of symbolic integration) the fantasmatic kernel of my being. When I approach it too closely, what occurs is the *aphanisis* of the subject: the subject loses his or her symbolic consistency, it disintegrates. And the forced actualization in social reality itself of the fantasmatic kernel of my being is, perhaps, the worst, most humiliating kind of violence, a violence which undermines the very basis of my identity (of my "self-image") by exposing me to an unbearable shame.

We can clearly see, now, how far psychoanalysis is from any defense of the dignity of the human face. Is the psychoanalytic treatment not the experience of rendering public (to the analyst, who stands for the big Other) one's most intimate fantasies and thus the experience of losing one's face in the most radical sense of the term? This is already the lesson of the very material *dispositif* of the psychoanalytic treatment: *no* face-to-face between the subject-patient and the analyst; instead, the subject lying and the analyst sitting behind him, both staring into the same void in front of them. There is no "intersubjectivity" here, only the two without face-to-face, the First and the Third.

How, then, do the law, courts, judgments, institutions, and so on enter? Levinas's answer is: by way of the presence of the *third*. When face to face with the other, I am infinitely responsible to him. This is the original ethical constellation. There is always a third one, however, and from that moment new questions arise: How does my neighbor whom I face relate to this Third? Is he the Third's friend or his foe or even his victim? Who, of the two, is my true neighbor in the first place? All this compels me to compare the infinites that cannot be compared, to limit the absolute priority of the other, to start to calculate the incalculable. However, what is important for Levinas is that this kind of legal relationship, necessary as it is, remains grounded in the primordial ethical relationship to the other.[17] The responsibility for the other—the subject as the response to the infinite call embodied in the other's face, a face that is simultaneously helpless, vulnerable, and issuing an unconditional command—is, for Levinas, asymmetrical and nonreciprocal: I am responsible for the other without having any right to claim that the other should display the same responsibility for me. Levinas likes to quote Fyodor Dostoyevsky here: "We are all responsible for everything and guilty in front of everyone, but I am that more than all others." The ethical asymmetry between me and the other addressing me with the infi-

---

17. At the end of this road of the celebration of irreducible Otherness, of the rejection of closure, there is, of course, as its effective spiritual movens, the ineluctable political conclusion: "Political totalitarianism rests on an ontological totalitarianism" (*DF*, 206).

nite call is the primordial fact, and "I" should never lose my grounding in this irreducibly first-person relationship to the other, which should go to extremes, if necessary. I should be ready to take responsibility for the other up to taking his place, up to becoming a hostage for him: "Subjectivity as such is primordially a hostage, responsible to the extent that it becomes the sacrifice for others" (*DF*, 98). This is how Levinas defines the "reconciliatory sacrifice": a gesture by means of which the Same as the hostage take the place of (replaces) the Other. Is this gesture of "reconciliatory sacrifice," however, not Christ's gesture par excellence? Was He not the hostage who took the place of all of us and, therefore, exemplarily human ("ecce homo")?

Far from preaching an easy grounding of politics in the ethics of the respect and responsibility for the Other, Levinas instead insists on their absolute incompatibility, on the gap separating the two dimensions: ethics involves an asymmetric relationship in which I am always-already responsible for the Other, while politics is the domain of symmetrical equality and distributive justice. However, is this solution not all too neat? That is to say, is such a notion of politics not already "postpolitical," excluding the properly political dimension (on account of which, for Hannah Arendt, tyranny is politics at its purest), in short, excluding precisely the dimension of what Carl Schmitt called political theology? One is tempted to say that, far from being reducible to the symmetric domain of equality and distributive justice, politics is the very "impossible" link between this domain and that of (theological) ethics, the way ethics cuts across the symmetry of equal relations, distorting and displacing them.

In his *Ethics and Infinity*, Levinas emphasizes how what appears as the most natural should become the most questionable—like Spinoza's notion that every entity naturally strives for its self-perseverance, for the full assertion of its being and its immanent powers: Do I have (the right) to be? By insisting on being, do I deprive others of their place, do I ultimately kill them? [18] (Although Levinas dismisses Freud as irrelevant for his radical ethical problematic, was Freud also in his own way not aware of it? Is "death drive" at its most elementary not the sabotaging of one's own striving to be, to actualize one's powers and potentials? And for that very reason, is not death drive the last support of ethics?) What one should fully acknowledge and endorse is that this stance of Levinas is radically *antibiopolitical*. Levinasian ethics is the absolute opposite of to-

18. See Emmanuel Levinas, *Ethics and Infinity: Conversations with Phillip Nemo* (Pittsburgh: Duquesne University Press, 1985).

day's biopolitics, with its emphasis on regulating life and deploying its potentials. For Levinas, ethics is not about life, but about something *more* than life. It is at this level that Levinas locates the gap that separates Judaism and Christianity—Judaism's fundamental ethical task is that of how "to be without being a murderer":

If Judaism is attached to the here below, it is not because it does not have the imagination to conceive of a supernatural order, or because matter represents some sort of absolute for it; but because the first light of conscience is lit for it on the path that leads from man to his neighbor. What is an individual, a solitary individual, if not a tree that grows without regard for everything it suppresses and breaks, grabbing all the nourishment, air and sun, a being that is fully justified in its nature and its being? What is an individual, if not a usurper? What is signified by the advent of conscience, and even the first spark of spirit, if not the discovery of corpses beside me and my horror of existing by assassination? Attention to others and, consequently, the possibility of counting myself among them, of judging myself—conscience is justice. (*DF,* 100)

In contrast to this admission of terrestrial life as the very terrain of our ethical activity, Christianity simultaneously goes too far and not far enough: it believes that it is possible to overcome this horizon of finitude, to enter collectively a blessed state, to "move mountains by faith" and realize a utopia; *and* it immediately transposes the place of this blessed state into an Elsewhere, which then propels it to declare our terrestrial life of ultimately secondary importance and to reach a compromise with the masters of this world, giving to Caesar what belongs to Caesar. The link between spiritual salvation and worldly justice is cut short.

Along these Levinasian lines, Jean-Claude Milner recently elaborated the notion of "Jews" in the European ideological imaginary as the obstacle that prevents unification and peace, that has to be annihilated for Europe to unite, which is why Jews are always a "problem/question" demanding a "solution"—Hitler is merely the most radical point of this tradition.[19] No wonder that the European Union is getting more and more anti-Semitic in its blatantly biased criticism of Israel. The very concept of Europe is tainted with anti-Semitism, which is why the first duty of Jews is to "get rid of Europe," not by ignoring it (only the United States can afford to do that), but by bringing to light the dark underside of European Enlightenment and democracy. The truly problematic part of

---

19. See Jean-Claude Milner, *Les penchants criminels de l'Europe democratique* (Paris: Editions Verdier, 2003).

Milner's argument concerns his "Lacanian" grounding of this notion of anti-Semitism inscribed into the very European identity: the European dream is that of *parousia* (Greek and Christian), of a full jouissance beyond Law, unencumbered by any obstacles or prohibitions. Modernity itself is propelled by a desire to move beyond Laws to a self-regulated, transparent social body; the last installment of this saga, today's postmodern, neopagan Gnosticism, perceives reality as fully malleable, enabling humans to transform themselves into a migrating entity floating between a multitude of realities, sustained only by infinite Love. Against this tradition, Jews, in a radically antimillenarian way, persist in their fidelity to the Law. They insist on the insurmountable finitude of humans and, consequently, on the need for a minimum of "alienation," which is why they are perceived as an obstacle by everyone bent on a "final solution." The weakness of Milner's argument is obvious: Is one of the key roots of European modernity not the tradition of secularized Judaism? Is arguably the ultimate formulation of a "full jouissance beyond Law" not found in Spinoza, in his notion of the third, highest, level of knowing? Is the idea of modern, "total" political revolution not rooted in Jewish messianism, as Walter Benjamin, among others, made it clear? Furthermore, is all we find beyond the Law really only the dream of a full jouissance? Is not the fundamental insight of the late Lacan precisely that there is an inherent obstacle to full jouissance operative already in the drive which functions beyond the Law? The inherent "obstacle" on account of which a drive involves a curved space, gets caught in a repetitive movement around its object, is not yet "symbolic castration." For the late Lacan, on the contrary, Prohibition, far from standing for a traumatic cut, enters precisely in order to pacify the situation, to rid us of the inherent impossibility inscribed in the functioning of a drive.

Blut ohne Boden, Boden ohne Blut

The determination of Judaism as the religion of the Law is to be taken literally: it is the Law at its purest, deprived of its obscene superego supplement. Recall the traditional obscene figure of the father who officially prohibits his son casual sex, while the message between the lines is to solicit him to engage in sexual conquests—prohibition is here uttered in order to provoke its transgression. And, with regard to this point, Paul was wrong in his description of the Law as that which solicits its own violation—wrong insofar as he attributed this notion of the Law to Jews: the miracle of the Jewish prohibition is that it effectively *is* just a prohi-

bition, with no obscene message between the lines. It is precisely because of this that Jews can look for the ways to get what they want while
literally obeying the prohibition. Far from displaying their casuistry and
externally manipulative relationship to the Law, this procedure rather
bears witness to the direct and literal attachment to the Law. And it is in
this sense that the position of the analyst is grounded in Judaism. Recall
Henry James's "The Lesson of the Master," in which Paul Overt, a young
novelist, meets Henry St. George, his great literary master, who advises
him to stay single, since a wife is not an inspiration but a hindrance.
When Paul asks St. George if there are no women who would "really understand—who can take part in a sacrifice," the answer he gets is: "How
can they take part? They themselves are the sacrifice. They're the idol
and the altar and the flame." Paul follows St. George's advice and re-
nounces the young Marian, whom he passionately loves. However, after
returning to London from a trip to Europe, Paul learns that, after the
sudden death of his wife, St. George himself is about to marry Marian.
After Paul accuses St. George of shameful conduct, the older man says
that his advice was right: he will not write again, but Paul will achieve
greatness. Far from displaying cynical wisdom, St. George acts as a true
analyst, as the one who is not afraid to profit from his ethical choices, in
other words, as the one who is able to break the vicious cycle of ethics
and sacrifice.

It is possible to break this vicious cycle precisely insofar as one escapes
the hold of the superego injunction to enjoy. Traditionally, psychoanalysis was expected to allow the patient to overcome the obstacles
which prevented him or her the access to "normal" sexual enjoyment.
Today, however, when we are bombarded from all sides by the different
versions of the superego injunction "Enjoy!"—from direct enjoyment in
sexual performance to enjoyment in professional achievement or in
spiritual awakening—one should move to a more radical level: psychoanalysis is today the only discourse in which you are allowed *not* to
enjoy (as opposed to "not allowed to enjoy"). (And, from this vantage
point, it becomes retroactively clear how the traditional prohibition to
enjoy was sustained by the implicit opposite injunction.) This notion of
a Law that is not sustained by a superego supplement involves a radically
new notion of society—a society no longer grounded in shared common roots:

Every word is an uprooting. The constitution of a real society is an uprooting—the end
of an existence in which the "being-at-home" is absolute, and everything comes from
within. Paganism is putting down roots. . . . The advent of the scriptures is not the sub-

ordination of the spirit to a letter, but the substitution of the letter to the soil. The spirit is free within the letter, and it is enslaved within the root. It is on the arid soil of the desert, where nothing is fixed, that the true spirit descended into a text in order to be universally fulfilled.

Paganism is the local spirit: nationalism in terms of its cruelty and pitilessness. . . . A humanity with roots that possesses God inwardly, with the sap rising from the earth, is a forest or prehuman humanity. . . .

A history in which the idea of a universal God must only be fulfilled requires a beginning. It requires an elite. It is not through pride that Israel feels it has been chosen. It has not obtained this through grace. Each time the peoples are judged, Israel is judged. . . . It is because the universality of the Divine exists only in the form in which it is fulfilled in the relations between men, and because it must be fulfillment and expansion, that the category of a privileged civilization exists in the economy of Creation. This civilization is defined in terms not of prerogatives, but of responsibilities. Every person, as a person—that is to say, one conscious of his freedom—is chosen. If being chosen takes on a national appearance, it is because only in this form can a civilization be constituted, be maintained, be transmitted, and endure. (*DF,* 137–38)

We are so used to the syntagm *Blut und Boden* that we tend to forget the split signaled by the *und,* in other words, the fact that the relationship between the two is that of what Gilles Deleuze called "disjunctive synthesis"—what better proof than Jews themselves, who are precisely the people of *Blut ohne Boden,* supplementing the lack of land with the excessive investment into blood relations? It is as if the first and foremost effect of migration is to foreground even more the blood relations, thus violating the basic territorial definition of a modern state. The member of a state is defined not by his or her "blood" (ethnic identity) but by being fully acknowledged as residing in the state's territory. And the state's unity was historically established by the violent erasure of local blood links. In this sense, the modern state is the outcome of an "inner migration," of the transubstantiation of one's identity: even if, physically, one does not change one's dwelling, one is deprived of a particular identity with its local color—or, to put it again in Deleuze's terms, a state's territory is by definition that of a reterritorialized deterritorialization. And, perhaps, as was made clear in Fascism, violence explodes precisely when one tries to deny the gap and bring together the two dimensions of blood *and* soil into a harmonious unity. This bringing-together accounts for the "innocent" tautological formulas of today's neoracists: le Pen's entire program can be summed up in "France to the French!" (and this allows us to generate further formulas: "Germany to Germans!" etc.)—"We do not want anything foreign. We want only

153

what is ours!" (to put it in more pathetic terms, the ultimate counter-argument of a nationalist is the disarming question "Is it a crime to love one's country?").

Jews are constituted by the lack of land, of territory—however, this lack is reinscribed into an absolute longing ("Next year in Jerusalem!"). What about an unconditional uprooting, renunciation of territory? In other words, does the Jewish identity not involve the paradox of the being-uprooted itself functioning as the foundation of ethnic roots and identity?[20] Is there not, consequently, the next step to be accomplished, namely, that of forming a collective which no longer relies on an ethnic identity, but is in its very core the collective of a struggling universality? Levinas is right in locating Jewish universalism in their very nonprose-lyte stance: Jews do not try to convert all others to Judaism, to impose their particular religious form onto all others; they just stubbornly cling to this form. The true universalism is thus, paradoxically, this very refusal to impose one's message on all others—in such a way, the wealth of the particular content in which the universal consists is asserted, while all others are left to be in their particular ways of life. However, this stance nonetheless involves its own limitation: it reserves for itself a privileged position of a singularity with a direct access to the universal. All people participate in the universality, but Jews are "more universal than others": *"The Jewish faith involves tolerance because, from the beginning, it bears the entire weight of all other men"* (*DF*, 173). The Jewish man's burden. . . . In other words, insofar as Jews are absolutely responsible, responsible for all of us, at a meta or reflexive level, are we not all doubly responsible to the Jews? Or, in an inverted way, if they are responsible for all of us, isn't the way to get rid of our responsibility to annihilate them (those who condense our responsibility)?[21] What is still missing here is the notion (and practice) of antagonistic universality, of the universality as struggle which cuts across the entire social body, of universality as a partial, engaged position.

The relationship between Judaism as a formal, "spiritual" structure and Jews as its empirical bearers is difficult to conceptualize. The prob-

---

20. Which is why, when it comes to collective relations between Jews and other ethnic groups, Levinas cannot but accept the necessity of war. When he writes, "my Muslim friend, my unhated enemy of the Six-Day-War" (*DF*, 17), he thereby endorses the necessity to fight the war. In a move recalling the old Buddhist warrior ethic, what his position amounts to is that we have to fight the enemy without hatred.

21. The paradox of responsibility perfectly fits the Lacanian logic of not-all: if I am responsible for everything, there has to be some exception that makes me non-responsible; and, on the other side, if I am not responsible for all and everything, there is nothing for which I can say that I am simply not responsible.

lem is how to avoid the deadlock of the dilemma: either Jews are privileged as an empirical group (which means their spirituality, inaccessible to others, is also ultimately of no relevance to them), or Jews are a contingent bearer of a universal structure. In this second case, the dangerous conclusion is at hand that, precisely in order to isolate and assert this formal structure, the "principle" of Jewishness, one has to eliminate, erase, the "empirical" Jews. Furthermore, the problem with those who emphasize how Jews are not simply a nation or an ethnic group like others and side by side with others is that, in this very claim, they define Jews in contrast to other "normal" groups, as their constitutive exception.

The standard humanist-humanitarian answer to Levinas's ethic of radical responsibility would have been that one can truly love others only if one loves oneself. However, at a more radical level, is there not something inherently *false* in such a link between the responsibility for/ to the other and questioning one's own right to exist? Although Levinas asserts this asymmetry as universal (*every one* of us is in the position of primordial responsibility toward others), does this asymmetry not effectively end up in privileging *one* particular group that assumes responsibility for all others, that embodies in a privileged way this responsibility, directly stands for it—in this case, of course, Jews, so that, again, one is ironically tempted to speak of the "Jewish man's (ethical) burden": "The idea of a chosen people must not be taken as a sign of pride. It does not involve being aware of exceptional rights, but of exceptional duties. It is the prerogative of a moral consciousness itself. It knows itself at the centre of the world and for it the world is not homogeneous: for I am always alone in being able to answer the call, I am irreplaceable in my assumption of responsibility" (*DF,* 176–77).

In other words, do we not get here—in a homology with Marx's forms of the expression of value—a necessary passage from simple and developed form (I am responsible for you, for all of you) to the general equivalent and then its reversal (I am the privileged site of responsibility for all of you, which is why you are all effectively responsible to me.)? And is this not the "truth" of such an ethical stance, thereby confirming the old Hegelian suspicion that every self-denigration secretly asserts its contrary? Self-questioning is always by definition the obverse of self-privileging; there is always something false about respect for others which is based on questioning of one's own right to exist.

A Spinozistic answer to Levinas would have been that our existence is not at the expense of others, but a part of the network of reality. For Spinoza there is no Hobbesian "Self" as extracted from and opposed to reality. Spinoza's ontology is one of full immanence to the world; in other words, I "am" just the network of my relations with the world, I am totally "externalized" in it. My *conatus,* my tendency to assert myself, is thus not my assertion at the expense of the world, but my full acceptance of being part of the world, my assertion of the wider reality only within which I can thrive. The opposition of egotism and altruism is thus overcome: I fully am, not as an isolated Self, but in the thriving reality, part of which I am. When Levinas writes that "enjoyment is the singularization of an ego. . . . it is the very work of egoism" and when he concludes from it that "giving has meaning only as a tearing from oneself despite oneself. . . . Only a subject that eats can be for-the-Other,"[22] he therefore secretly imputes to Spinoza an egotistic "subjectivist" notion of (my) existence. His anti-Spinozistic questioning of my right to exist is inverted arrogance, as if I am the center whose existence threatens all others.

So the answer should not be an assertion of my right to exist in harmony with and tolerance of others, but a more radical claim: Do I exist in the first place? Am I not, rather, a *hole in the order of being?* This brings us to the ultimate paradox on account of which Levinas's answer is not sufficient: I am a threat to the entire order of being not insofar as I positively exist as part of this order, but precisely insofar as I am a hole in the order of being. As such, as nothing, I "am" a striving to reach out and appropriate all (only a Nothing can desire to become Everything). Friedrich Schelling already defined the subject as the endless striving of the Nothing to become Everything. On the contrary, a positive living being occupying a determinate space in reality, rooted in it, is by definition a moment of its circulation and reproduction.

Recall the similar paradox that structures the politically correct landscape: people far from the Western world are allowed to fully assert their particular ethnic identity without being proclaimed essentialist racist identitarians (native Americans, blacks, etc.). The closer one gets to the notorious white heterosexual males, the more problematic this assertion is: Asians are still OK; Italians and Irish maybe; with Germans and Scandinavians, it is already problematic. However, such a prohibition of asserting the particular identity of White Men (as the model of oppression of others), although it presents itself as the admission of their guilt, nonetheless confers on them a central position: this very prohibition to assert their particular identity makes them into the universal-neutral medium, the place from which the truth about the others' oppression is accessible.

22. Emmanuel Levinas, *Otherwise than Being* (The Hague: Martinus Nijhoff, 1981), 73, 74.

The figure of Benny Morris, this symptom of the falsity of the liberal-benevolent-peacenik Israelis,[23] is to be conceived as the concealed obscene supplement to Levinasian ethics. After bringing to the light the "dark" side of the emergence of the State of Israel (the aim of David Ben-Gurion and the first generation of Israeli leaders in the 1949 war was to provoke the Arab population to leave Palestine, and in order to achieve this goal, they resorted to an albeit limited amount of terror, including raping and killing innocent civilians), for which he was shunned by the Israeli academic establishment, Morris surprised everyone by the position he adopted toward his own discoveries: he stated that these "dark" acts were necessary for the constitution and survival of the State of Israel. And his logic is convincing in its ruthless sincerity: if Arabs were not a clear minority in Israel, Israel would never function as a state; Ben-Gurion's mistake was that he did not complete the ethnic cleaning, including expelling Arabs from the West Bank—in this case, there would have been peace today in the Middle East. The merit of this reasoning is that it thoroughly avoids the standard liberal hypocrisy: if you want the State of Israel, you have to accept the price of ethnic cleansing; there was *never* any third way of living peacefully side by side with the Palestinians in a Jewish or even secular democratic state. All the liberal complaints about the unfair harshness in the treatment of Palestinians, all their condemnation of the terror of the West Bank occupation, avoid the key issue by sustaining the illusion that a little bit more tolerance and withdrawal will bring peace. Of course, Morris is full of the usual racist clichés (the clash of civilizations with the barbarian Arabs, etc.), but these clichés are not the gist, the essential part, of his argument, which is that the State of Israel was possible only through the ethnic cleansing of the majority of people living there prior to the Jewish resettlement. One should effectively read Morris as anti-Levinas par excellence, as the truth of Levinas's hope that the State of Israel will be a unique state directly grounded in the messianic promise of Justice; to retain his vision of Israel, Levinas has to deny what Morris ruthlessly admits. Morris's attitude, his cold acceptance of the fact that we have to kill others in order to survive, is the truth of the Levinasian questioning of one's own right to exist.[24]

23. See his interview reprinted in English as "On Ethnic Cleansing," *New Left Review* 26 (March/April 2004).

24. The same ruthlessness, the same rejection of the easy (third) way out, should be practiced in all domains today. For example, it is not enough to oppose the U.S. military presence in Iraq—one should condone the taking and killing of Western civilian hostages.

Odradek as a Political Category

The limitation of Levinas is not simply that of a Eurocentrist who relies on a too narrow definition of what is human, a definition that secretly excludes non-Europeans as "not fully human."[25] What Levinas fails to include into the scope of "human" is, rather, the *inhuman* itself, a dimension which eludes the face-to-face relationship of humans. In a first approach, Butler may seem to be more sensitive to this aspect—say, when she provides a subtle description of Adorno's ambiguity with regard to the "inhuman" (*KEG*, 109–10): while Adorno is well aware of the violence involved in the predominant definition of what counts as "human" (the implied exclusion of whole dimensions as "nonhuman"), he nonetheless basically conceives "inhuman" as the depository of "alienated" humanity—ultimately, for Adorno, "inhuman" is the power of barbarism we have to fight. What he misses here is the paradox that every normative determination of the "human" is only possible against an impenetrable ground of "inhuman," of something which remains opaque and resists inclusion into any narrative reconstitution of what counts as "human." In other words, although Adorno recognizes that being-human is constitutively finite, nontotalized, that the very attempt to posit the Human as "absolute subject" dehumanizes it, he does not deploy how this self-limitation of the Human defines "being-human": Is being-human just the limitation of human, or is there a positive notion of this limitation which constitutes being-human?

The same paradox is at work in the core of the "dialectic of Enlightenment": although Adorno (and Horkheimer) conceive the catastrophes and barbarisms of the twentieth century as inherent to the project of enlightenment, not as a result of some remainder of preceding barbarism to be abolished by way of bringing "enlightenment as an unfinished project" to its completion, they insist on fighting this excess-consequence of enlightenment by the means of enlightenment itself. So, again, if enlightenment brought to the end equals regression into barbarism, does this mean that the only concept of enlightenment that we possess is the one which should be constrained, rendered aware of its limitation, or is there another positive notion of enlightenment which already includes this limitation? There are two basic answers to this in-

25. One may formulate the reproach also at this level, however. Today, in our politically correct anti-Eurocentric times, one is tempted to admire Levinas's readiness to openly admit his being perplexed by the African-Asian other who is too alien to be a neighbor: our time is marked, he says, by "the arrival on the historical scene of those underdeveloped Afro-Asiatic masses who are strangers to the Sacred History that forms the heart of the Judaic-Christian world" (*DF*, 160).

consistency of Adorno's critical project: Jürgen Habermas or Lacan. With Habermas, one breaks the deadlock by formulating a positive normative frame of reference. Through Lacan, one reconceptualizes the "humanity" of the deadlock/limitation as such; in other words, one provides a definition of the "human" which, beyond and above (or, rather, beneath) the previous infinite universal, accentuates the limitation as such: being-human is a specific attitude of finitude, of passivity, of vulnerable exposure.

Therein resides, for Butler, the basic paradox: while we should, of course, condemn as "inhuman" all those situations in which our will is violated, thwarted, or under the pressure of an external violence, we should not simply conclude that a positive definition of humanity is the autonomy of will, because there is a kind of passive exposure to an overwhelming Otherness which is the very basis of being-human. How, then, are we to distinguish the "bad" inhumanity, the violence which crushes our will, from the passivity constitutive of humanity? At this point, Butler compromises her position, introducing a naive distinction which recalls Herbert Marcuse's old distinction between "necessary" repression and "surplus" repression: "of course we can and must invent norms which decide between different forms of being-overwhelmed, by way of drawing a line of distinction between the unavoidable and unsurpassable aspect here and the changeable conditions there" (*KEG*, 110).

What Butler (as well as Adorno) fails to render thematic is the changed status of the "inhuman" in Kant's transcendental turn. Kant introduced a key distinction between negative and indefinite judgment: the positive judgment "the soul is mortal" can be negated in two ways, when a predicate is denied to the subject ("the soul is not mortal") and when a nonpredicate is affirmed ("the soul is nonmortal"). The difference is exactly the same as the one, known to every reader of Stephen King, between "he is not dead" and "he is undead." The indefinite judgment opens up a third domain which undermines the underlying distinction: the "undead" are neither alive nor dead; they are the monstrous "living dead."[26] The same goes for *inhuman*. "He is not human" is not the same as "he is inhuman." "He is not human" means simply that he is external to humanity, animal or divine, while "he is inhuman" means something thoroughly different, namely, that he is neither simply human nor simply inhuman, but marked by a terrifying excess

26. For a closer elaboration of this distinction, see chapter 3 of Slavoj Žižek, *Tarrying with the Negative* (Durham, NC: Duke University Press, 1993). The Lacanian *objet petit a* also follows the logic of indefinite judgment: one should not say that it isn't an object, but rather that it *is* a nonobject, an object that from within undermines/negates objectivity.

which, although it negates what we understand as "humanity," is inherent to being-human. And perhaps I should risk the hypothesis that this is what changes with the Kantian revolution: in the pre-Kantian universe, humans were simply humans, beings of reason, fighting the excesses of animal lusts and divine madness, but since Kant and German Idealism, the excess to be fought is absolutely immanent, the very core of subjectivity itself (which is why, with German Idealism, the metaphor for the core of subjectivity is Night, "Night of the World," in contrast to the Enlightenment notion of the Light of Reason fighting the surrounding darkness). So when, in the pre-Kantian universe, a hero goes mad, it means he is deprived of his humanity, in other words, the animal passions or divine madness took over, while with Kant, madness signals the unconstrained explosion of the very core of a human being.

This dimension is missing also in Levinas. In a properly dialectical paradox, what Levinas (with all his celebration of Otherness) fails to take into account is not some underlying Sameness of all humans but the radical, "inhuman" Otherness itself: the Otherness of a human being reduced to inhumanity, the Otherness exemplified by the terrifying figure of the *Muselmann,* the "living dead" in the concentration camps. This is why, although Levinas is often perceived as the thinker who endeavored to articulate the experience of the *Shoah,* one thing is self-evident apropos his questioning of one's own right to be and his emphasis on one's unconditional asymmetrical responsibility: this is not how a survivor of the *Shoah,* one who effectively experienced the ethical abyss of *Shoah,* thinks and writes. This is how those think who feel guilty for observing the catastrophe from a minimal safe distance.[27]

Agamben posits the Muselmann as a kind of absolute/impossible witness: he is the only one who fully witnessed the horror of the concentration camp and, for that very reason, is not able to bear witness to it. It is as if he was "burned by the black sun" of the horror he saw. "Authentic" witnessing can thus be defined as involving the mediation of an invisible Third embodied in the Muselmann: in it, it is never just me and the event I am witnessing; my relationship to this event is always mediated by someone who fully witnessed it and is, for that very reason, no

27. At a different level, the same goes for Stalinist Communism. In the standard Stalinist narrative, even the concentration camps were a place for fighting against Fascism, where imprisoned Communists were organizing networks of heroic resistance. In such a universe, of course, there is no place for the limit-experience of the Muselmann, of the living dead deprived of the capacity for human engagement. No wonder that Stalinist Communists were so eager to "normalize" the camps into just another site of the anti-Fascist struggle, dismissing the Muselmann as simply representing those who were too weak to endure the struggle.

longer able to report on it. That is to say, insofar as, in his description of the ethical call, Levinas reproduces the basic coordinates of ideological interpellation (I become an ethical subject when I respond with "Here I am!" to the infinite call emanating from the vulnerable face of the other), one could say that the Muselmann is precisely the one who is no longer able to say "Here I am!" (and in front of whom I can no longer say "Here I am!").[28] Recall the big gesture of identification with the exemplary victim: "We are all citizens of Sarajevo!" and such; the problem with the Muselmann is that this gesture is no longer possible. It would be obscene to proclaim pathetically, "We are all *Muselmänner!*" Agamben should also be supplemented here by transposing the same gap into the counterpart of the witness, the receiver of its testimony, the big Other whose full acceptance of my testimony would permit me to exorcise my inner demons. In an exactly symmetric way, I never encounter a "true" receiver who would fully authenticate my witnessing: my words of witnessing are always received by finite others who fail to authenticate them. Is this structure not that of the so-called *L* scheme of communication from the Lacan of the early 1950s, in which the "true communication" (the diagonal *S-A*) is cut across by the diagonal *a-a'* of the imaginary relationship? *S* would be here the Muselmann, the ideal-impossible witness; *A* his ideal-impossible receiver authenticating his words; *a* the survivors as imperfect witnesses; and *a'* the imperfect receivers of their words. The tragedy of witnessing is thus not only that the ideal witness (the Muselmann who would himself bear witness, report on what he went through) is impossible, but also that there is no ideal receiver, such that, when we are aware that our testimony is safely deposited there, we get rid of our demons—*there is no big Other.*

Consequently, is the paradox of the Muselmann not that this figure is simultaneously a zero-level, a total reduction to life, *and* a name for the pure excess as such, excess deprived of its "normal" base? This is why the figure of the Muselmann signals the limitation of Levinas: when describing it, Primo Levi repeatedly uses the predicate *faceless,* and this term should be given here its entire Levinasian weight. When confronted with a Muselmann, one cannot discern in his face the trace of the abyss of the Other in his/her vulnerability, addressing us with the infinite call of our responsibility. What one gets instead is a kind of blind wall, a lack of depth. Maybe the Muselmann is thus the zero-level neigh-

28. See Giorgio Agamben, *What Remains of Auschwitz: The Witness and the Archive,* trans. Daniel Heller-Roazen (Stanford, CA: Stanford University Press, 2002).

bor, the neighbor with whom no empathetic relationship is possible.[29] However, at this point, we again confront the key dilemma: what if it is precisely in the guise of the "faceless" face of a Muselmann that we encounter the Other's call at its purest and most radical? What if, facing a Muselmann, one hits upon one's responsibility toward the Other at its most traumatic? In short, what about bringing together Levinas's face and the topic of the "neighbor" in its strict Freudo-Lacanian sense, as the monstrous, impenetrable Thing that is the *Nebenmensch,* the Thing that hystericizes and provokes me? What if the neighbor's face stands neither for my imaginary double/*semblant* nor for the purely symbolic abstract "partner in communication," but for the Other in his or her dimension of the Real? What if, along these lines, we restore to the Levinasian "face" all its monstrosity: face is not a harmonious Whole of the dazzling epiphany of a "human face," face is something the glimpse of which we get when we stumble upon a grotesquely distorted face, a face in the grip of a disgusting tic or grimace, a face which, precisely, confronts us when the neighbor "loses his face"? To recall a case from popular culture, "face" is what, in Gaston Leroux's *The Phantom of the Opera,* the heroine gets a glimpse of when she sees for the first time the Phantom without his mask (and, as a reaction to the horror that confronts her, immediately loses her consciousness and falls to the ground).

The problem with this solution, acceptable in itself, is that it undermines the ethical edifice Levinas is trying to build upon it: far from standing for absolute authenticity, such a monstrous face is, rather, the ambiguity of the Real embodied, the extreme/impossible point at which opposites coincide, at which the innocence of the Other's vulnerable nakedness overlaps with pure evil. That is to say, what one should focus on here is the precise meaning of the term *neighbor:* is the "neighbor" in the Judeo-Freudian sense, the neighbor as the bearer of a monstrous Otherness, this properly *inhuman* neighbor, the same as the neighbor that we encounter in the Levinasian experience of the Other's face? Is there not, in the very heart of the Judeo-Freudian inhuman neighbor, a monstrous dimension which is already minimally "gentrified," domesticated, once it is conceived in the Levinasian sense? What if the Levinasian face is yet another defense against this monstrous dimension of subjectivity? And what if the Jewish Law is to be conceived as strictly correlative to this inhuman neighbor? In other words, what if the ultimate function of the Law is not to enable us not to forget the neighbor, to re-

29. For a more detailed elaboration of this notion of the Muselmann as the zero-level neighbor, see Eric Santner's contribution to the present volume.

tain our proximity to the neighbor, but, on the contrary, to keep the neighbor at a proper distance, to serve as a kind of protective wall against the monstrosity of the neighbor? In short, *the* temptation to be resisted here is the ethical "gentrification" of the neighbor, the reduction of the radically ambiguous monstrosity of the Neighbor-Thing into an Other as the abyssal point from which the call of ethical responsibility emanates.

This topic agitates the very heart of Kafka's universe. Reading Kafka demands a great effort of abstraction—not of learning more (the proper interpretive horizon to understand his works), but of unlearning the standard interpretive references, so that one becomes able to open up to the raw force of Kafka's writing. There are three such interpretive frames: theological (modern man's anxious search for the absent God); socio-critical (Kafka's staging of the nightmarish world of modern alienated bureaucracy); and psychoanalytic (Kafka's "unresolved Oedipus complex," which prevented him from engaging in a "normal" sexual relationship). All this has to be erased. A kind of childish naïveté has to be regained for a reader to be able to feel the raw force of Kafka's universe. This is why, in Kafka's case, the first (naive) reading is often the most adequate one, and the second reading is the one which tries to "sublate" the first reading's raw impact by way of forcing the text into the frame of a given interpretation. This is how one should approach "Odradek," one of Kafka's key achievements:

Some say the word *Odradek* is of Slavonic origin, and try to account for it on that basis. Others again believe it to be of German origin, only influenced by Slavonic. The uncertainty of both interpretations allows one to assume with justice that neither is accurate, especially as neither of them provides an intelligent meaning of the word.

No one, of course, would occupy himself with such studies if there were not a creature called Odradek. At first glance it looks like a flat star-shaped spool for thread, and indeed it does seem to have thread wound upon it; to be sure, they are only old, broken-off bits of thread, knotted and tangled together, of the most varied sorts and colors. But it is not only a spool, for a small wooden crossbar sticks out of the middle of the star, and another small rod is joined to that at a right angle. By means of this latter rod on one side and one of the points of the star on the other, the whole thing can stand upright as if on two legs.

One is tempted to believe that the creature once had some sort of intelligible shape and is now only a broken-down remnant. Yet this does not seem to be the case; at least there is no sign of it; nowhere is there an unfinished or unbroken surface to suggest anything of the kind; the whole thing looks senseless enough, but in its own way perfectly finished. In any case, closer scrutiny is impossible, since Odradek is extraordinarily nimble and can never be laid hold of.

He lurks by turns in the garret, the stairway, the lobbies, the entrance hall. Often for months on end he is not to be seen; then he has presumably moved into other houses; but he always comes faithfully back to our house again. Many a time when you go out of the door and he happens just to be leaning directly beneath you against the banisters you feel inclined to speak to him. Of course, you put no difficult questions to him, you treat him—he is so diminutive that you cannot help it—rather like a child. "Well, what's your name?" you ask him. "Odradek," he says. "And where do you live?" "No fixed abode," he says and laughs; but it is only the kind of laughter that has no lungs behind it. It sounds rather like the rustling of fallen leaves. And that is usually the end of the conversation. Even these answers are not always forthcoming; often he stays mute for a long time, as wooden as his appearance.

I ask myself, to no purpose, what is likely to happen to him? Can he possibly die? Anything that dies has had some kind of aim in life, some kind of activity, which has worn out; but that does not apply to Odradek. Am I to suppose, then, that he will always be rolling down the stairs, with ends of thread trailing after him, right before the feet of my children, and my children's children? He does no harm to anyone that one can see; but the idea that he is likely to survive me I find almost painful.[30]

Odradek, as an object that is transgenerational (exempted from the cycle of generations), immortal, outside finitude (because outside sexual difference), outside time, displaying no goal-oriented activity, no purpose, no utility, is jouissance embodied: "*Jouissance* is that which serves nothing," as Lacan put in his seminar 20, *Encore*. There are different figurations of Thing-jouissance—an immortal (or, more precisely, undead) excess—in Kafka's work: the Law that somehow insists without properly existing, making us guilty without us knowing what we are guilty of; the wound that won't heal yet does not let us die; bureaucracy in its most "irrational" aspect; and, last but not least, "partial objects" like Odradek. They all display a kind of mock-Hegelian nightmarish "bad infinity"— there is no *Aufhebung,* no resolution proper; the thing just drags on. We never reach the Law; the Emperor's letter never arrives at its destination; the wound never closes (or kills me). The Kafkan Thing is either transcendent, forever eluding our grasp (the Law, the Castle), or a ridiculous object into which the subject is metamorphosed and which we cannot ever get rid of (like Gregor Samsa, who changes into an insect). The point is to read these two features together: jouissance is that which we cannot ever attain *and* that which we cannot ever get rid of.

Kafka's genius was to eroticize bureaucracy, *the* nonerotic entity if

---

30. Franz Kafka, "The Cares of a Family Man," trans. Willa Muir and Edwin Muir, in *The Complete Stories* (New York: Schocken, 1989).

there ever was one. In Chile, when a citizen wants to identify himself to the authorities, "the clerk on duty demands that the poor petitioner produce proof that he was born, that he isn't a criminal, that he paid his taxes, that he registered to vote, and that he's still alive, because even if he throws a tantrum to prove that he hasn't died, he is obliged to present a 'certificate of survival.' The problem has reached such proportions that the government itself has created an office to combat bureaucracy. Citizens may now complain of being shabbily treated and may file charges against incompetent officials . . . on a form requiring a seal and three copies, of course."[31] This is state bureaucracy at its craziest. Are we aware that this is our only true contact with the divine in our secular times? What can be more "divine" than the traumatic encounter with the bureaucracy at its craziest—when, say, a bureaucrat tells us that, legally, we don't exist? It is in such encounters that we get the glimpse of another order beyond the mere terrestrial everyday reality. Kafka was well aware of this deep link between bureaucracy and the divine: it is as if, in his work, Hegel's thesis on the State as the terrestrial existence of God is "buggered," given a properly obscene twist. It is *only* in this sense that Kafka's works stage a search for the divine in our deserted secular world—more precisely, they not only search for the divine, they *find* it in state bureaucracy.

There are two memorable scenes in Terry Gilliam's *Brazil* that perfectly stage the crazy excess of bureaucratic jouissance perpetuating itself in its autocirculation. After the hero's plumbing breaks down and he leaves a message to the official repair service for urgent help, Robert De Niro enters his apartment, a mythical-mysterious criminal whose subversive activity is that he listens in on the emergency calls and then immediately goes to the customer, repairing his plumbing for free, bypassing the inefficient state repair service's paperwork. Indeed, in a bureaucracy caught in a vicious cycle of jouissance, the ultimate crime is to simply and directly do the job one is supposed to do. If a state repair service actually does its job, this is (at the level of its unconscious libidinal economy) considered an unfortunate by-product, since the bulk of its energy goes into inventing complicated administrative procedures that enable it to invent ever-new obstacles and thus postpone the work indefinitely. In a second scene, we meet—in the corridors of a vast government agency—a group of people permanently running around a leader (big shot bureaucrat) followed by a bunch of lower administrators who shout at him all the time, asking him for a specific opinion or deci-

---

31. Isabel Allende, "The End of All Roads," *Financial Times*, November 15, 2003, W12.

sion, and he nervously spurts out fast, "efficient" replies ("This is to be done by tomorrow at the latest!" "Check that report!" "No, cancel that appointment!" etc.). The appearance of a nervous hyperactivity is, of course, a staged performance that masks a self-indulgent nonsensical spectacle of imitating, of playing "efficient administration." Why do they walk around all the time? The leader is obviously not on the way from one to another meeting—the meaningless fast walk around the corridors is all he does. The hero stumbles from time to time on this group, and the Kafkaesque answer is, of course, that this entire performance is here to attract his gaze, staged for his eyes only. They pretend to be busy, not to be bothered by the hero, but all their activity is here to provoke the hero into addressing a demand to the group's leader, who then snaps back nervously, "Can't you see how busy I am!" or, occasionally, does the reverse and greets the hero as if he was waiting for him for a long time, mysteriously expecting his plea.

Back to Odradek: in his concise analysis of the story, Jean-Claude Milner first draws attention to a peculiarity of Odradek: he has two legs, he speaks, laughs; in short, he displays all the features of a human being. Although he is human, he does not resemble a human being, but clearly appears inhuman.[32] As such, he is the opposite of Oedipus, who (lamenting his fate at Colonus) claims that he became nonhuman when he finally acquired all properties of an ordinary human: in line with the series of Kafka's other heroes, Odradek becomes human only when he no longer resembles a human being (by metamorphosing himself into an insect, or a spool,[33] or whatever). He is, effectively, a "universal singular," a stand-in for humanity by way of embodying its inhuman excess, by not resembling anything "human." The contrast with Aristophanes' myth (in Plato's *Symposium*) of the original spherical human being divided into two parts, eternally searching for its complementary counterpart in order to return to the lost Whole, is crucial here: although also a "partial object," Odradek does not look for any complementary parts, he is lacking nothing. It may be significant, also, that he is not spherical. Milner deciphers *odradek* as an anagram of the Greek *dodekaedron* [dodecahedron], an object of twelve faces, each of them a pentagon (in his *Timaeus* [55c], Plato claims that our universe is a dodecahedron); it is an anagram divided by two, so Odradek is half of a dodecahedron. Odradek is thus simply what Lacan, in his seminar 11 and in his seminal *écrit*

32. Jean-Claude Milner, "Odradek, la bobine de scandale," in *Elucidation*, vol. 10 (Paris: Printemps, 2004), 93–96.

33. How can we not recall, apropos of the fact that Odradek is a spool-like creature, the spool of the Freudian *Fort-Da* game from "Beyond the Pleasure Principle"?

"Positions de l'inconscient," developed as *lamella*, libido as an organ, the inhuman-human "undead" organ without a body, the mythical pre-subjective "undead" life-substance, or, rather, the remainder of the life-substance which has escaped the symbolic colonization, the horrible palpitation of the "acephal" drive which persists beyond ordinary death, outside the scope of paternal authority, nomadic, with no fixed domicile. The choice underlying Kafka's story is thus Lacan's *"le père ou pire,"* "the father or the worse": Odradek is "the worst" as the alternative to the father.

Although they are not to be directly identified, there is a link between Odradek and the "alien" from Ridley Scott's film of the same name: "The alien's form of life is (just, merely, simply) life, life as such: it is not so much a particular species as the essence of what it means to be a species, to be a creature, a natural being—it is Nature incarnate, a nightmare embodiment of the natural realm understood as utterly subordinate to, utterly exhausted by, the twinned Darwinian drives to survive and reproduce."[34] This disgust at Life is disgust with *drive* at its purest. And it is interesting to note how Ridley Scott inverts the usual sexual connotations: Life is presented as inherently *male,* as the phallic power of brutal penetration which parasitizes on the feminine body, exploiting it as the carrier of its reproduction. "The beauty and the beast" is here the feminine subject horrified at the disgusting immortal Life. As Mulhall points out, *Aliens,* James Cameron's sequel, is the weakest link in the series because of the way it reinscribes the force of the pure fantasy deployed in *Alien* into four interconnected standard Hollywood ideological matrixes: (1) the commando war adventure narrative (a group of Marines goes on the expedition to finish off the alien); (2) the very form of the linear adventure narrative as such; (3) the family ideology (at the end of *Aliens,* Ripley is "cured" when she finds her part in the reconstituted nuclear family of herself, Corporal Hicks, and Newt); and, last but not least, (4) the underlying therapeutic structure of the narrative (in order to get rid of her nightmares, Ripley had to return to her traumatic past and confront it). Truly, as they say it in Slovene, when the Devil has youngsters, he has them en masse. Mulhall is also right in emphasizing how David Fincher's superb and much underrated *Alien*[3] (incidentally, his first feature film) restores the proper balance by erasing these ideological references and returning to the force of the elementary "metaphysical" fantasy of *Alien.* With regard to the opposition between fantasy (nightmarish dream) and reality, relations are inverted: the same scene—that

34. Stephen Mulhall, *On Film* (London: Routledge, 2001), 19.

of Ripley being "raped" and impregnated by the alien—is presented in Cameron as a nightmare and in Fincher as the unbearable reality. Cameron's *Aliens*

begins with Ripley enduring a hypersleep nightmare in which she has been impregnated by, and is about to give birth to, an alien. Cameron presents his film as giving Ripley the therapy she needs to wake from such nightmares; Fincher presents his film as awakening Ripley from Cameron's dream, his fantasy of what constitutes a fulfilled existence for his protagonist, and his fantasy of human life as something that with the right degree of effort on our part can be made to come out right.[35]

Mulhall also detects a caricatural, exaggerated, childish, if not outright comic, character of the alien monstrosity in Jean Pierre Junet's *Alien Resurrection,* the fourth and last installment of the series: the alien universe is here "skewed or off-key, an uncanny parody or caricature of the one we have come to know over the years through the adult human eyes of Ripley's original." And does this not signal that "the vision of human fertility and sexuality which the alien species embodies is best understood as embodying the fantasies and fears of a child"[36]? Thus, one should not be surprised to discern in the overall structure of the *Alien* series the matrix of the old Greek theater performance: three tragedies plus a comedy. What can follow the suicidal tragic act of Ripley at the end of Fincher's *Alien³* can only be a comedy, a total change in register, a fairy-tale narrative with children as its main heroes, like Shakespeare's last plays.

There are two properly sublime moments in Junet's *Alien Resurrection.* In the first one, the cloned Ripley enters the laboratory room in which the previous seven aborted attempts to clone her are on display. Here she encounters the ontologically failed, defective versions of herself, up to the almost successful version with her own face but with some of her limbs distorted so that they resemble the limbs of the Alien Thing. This creature asks Ripley's clone to kill her, and, in an outburst of violent rage, the clone effectively destroys the horror-exhibition by torching the whole room. Then there is the unique scene, perhaps *the* shot of the entire series, in which Ripley's clone "is drawn down into the embrace of the alien species, luxuriating in her absorption into the writhing mass of its limbs and tails—as if engulfed by the very lability of organic being that she had earlier attempted to consume in fire."[37] The link between

35. Ibid., 101.
36. Ibid., 128, 129.
37. Ibid., 132.

the two scenes is thus clear: we are dealing with the two sides of the same coin. However, this fascination with the monstrous alien should not be allowed to obfuscate the anticapitalist edge of the *Alien* series: what ultimately endangers the lone group on a spaceship is not the aliens as such but the way the group is used by the anonymous earthly Corporation, which wants to exploit the alien form of life. The point is here not to play the card of the superficial and simplistic "metaphoric meaning" (the vampiric alien monster "really means" Capital), but to move at the metonymic level: how Capital parasitizes and exploits the pure drive of Life. *Pure Life is a category of capitalism.*

The Inhuman Excess

In *City Lights,* one of Charlie Chaplin's absolute masterpieces, there is a memorable scene (commented on by Levinas, among others) which establishes the link between this object and shame. After he swallows a whistle by mistake, the Tramp gets an attack of hiccups, which leads to a comical effect—because of the movement of air in his stomach, each hiccup makes the whistle blow and thus generates a weird sound of whistles coming from inside the body; the embarrassed Tramp desperately tries to cover up these sounds, not knowing what exactly to do. Does this scene not stage shame at its purest? I am ashamed when I am confronted with the excess in my body. It is significant that the source of shame in this scene is sound: a spectral sound emanating from within the Tramp's body, sound as an autonomous "organ without body," located in the very heart of his body and at the same time uncontrollable, like a kind of parasite, a foreign intruder—in short, what Lacan called the voice-object, one of the incarnations of *objet petit a,* of the *agalma,* that which is "in me more than myself."[38]

We find this object even where one would not expect to find such a thing. If there is a novel which is the absolute classic of literary Stalinism, it is Nikolai Ostrovsky's *How the Steel Was Tempered.* In it, Pavka, a Bolshevik fully engaged first in the Civil War and then, during the 1920s, in the construction of steel mills, ends up his life in dirty rags and totally crippled, immobilized, deprived of limbs, thus reduced to an almost nonbodily existence. In such a state, he finally marries a young girl named Taya, making it clear that there will be no sex between them, just companionship, with her function being to take care of him. Here we in a

---

38. I rely here on Joan Copjec's ongoing pathbreaking work on the notion of shame.

way encounter the "truth" of the Stalinist mythology of the Happy New Man: a dirty desexualized cripple, sacrificing everything for the construction of socialism. This fate coincides with that of Ostrovsky himself, who, in the mid-1930s, after finishing the novel, was dying crippled and blind; and, like Ostrovsky, Pavka—reduced to a living death, a kind of living mummy—is reborn at the novel's end through writing a novel about his life.[39] (In the last two years of his life, Ostrovsky lived in a Black Sea resort house as a "living legend," on a street named after himself, his house a site of countless pilgrimages and of great interest to foreign journalists.) This mortification of one's own treacherous body is itself embodied in a piece of shrapnel that has lodged itself in Pavka's eye, gradually blinding him; at this point, Ostrovsky's bland style suddenly explodes into a complex metaphor:

The octopus has a bulging eye the size of a cat's head, a dull-red eye, green in the center, burning, pulsating with a phosphorescent glow. . . . The octopus moves. He can see it almost next to his eyes. The tentacles creep over his body; they are cold and they burn like nettles. The octopus shoots out its sting, and it bites into his head like a leech, and, wriggling convulsively, it sucks at his blood. He feels the blood draining out of his body into the swelling body of the octopus.[40]

To put it in Lacanian-Deleuzian terms, the octopus stands here for the "organ without body," the partial object which invades our ordinary biological body and mortifies it. It is not a metaphor for the capitalist system squeezing and choking workers in its tentacles (the standard popular use of the metaphor between the two world wars), but, surprisingly, a "positive" metaphor for the absolute self-control that a Bolshevik revolutionary has to exert over his body (and over the "pathological," potentially corrupting, bodily desires). As Kaganovska put it, the octopus is a superego organ which controls us from within. When Pavka, at the low-point of despair, reviews his life, Ostrovsky characterizes this moment of reflection as "a meeting of the Politburo with his 'I' about the treacherous behavior of his body." This is yet another proof of how literary ideology cannot ever simply lie: truth articulates itself in it through displacements. One cannot but recall here Kafka's "Country Doctor": is Ostrovsky's octopus not another name for the Kaf-

---

39. I rely here on the excellent paper by Lilja Kaganovska, "Stalin's Men: Gender, Sexuality, and the Body in Nikolai Ostrovsky's *How the Steel Was Tempered*" (unpublished paper).
40. Nikolai Ostrovsky, *How the Steel Was Tempered* (Moscow: Progress Publishers 1979), 195–96.

kan "undead" wound which, while parasitizing upon my body, prevents me from dying?[41]

However, this is not the whole story: Lacan's formula of the fetishist object is *a* over *minus phi* (castration)—*objet petit a* fills in (and simultaneously bears witness to) the gap of castration. This is why Lacan specifies shame as *respect for castration,* as an attitude of discreetly covering up the fact of being castrated. (No wonder women have to be covered more than men: what is concealed is their lack of penis.) While shamelessness resides in openly displaying one's castration, shame displays a desperate attempt to keep the appearance: although I know the truth (about castration), let us pretend that it is not the case. This is why, when I see my crippled neighbor "shamelessly" pushing toward me his disfigured limb, it is I, not he, who is overwhelmed by shame. When a man exposes his distorted limb to his neighbor, his true target is not to expose himself, but the neighbor: to put the neighbor to shame by confronting him with his own ambiguous repulsion/fascination with the spectacle he is forced to witness. In a strictly homologous way, one is ashamed of one's ethnic origins, of the specific "torsion" of one's particular identity, of being caught into the coordinates of a lifeworld into which one was thrown, with which one is stuck, unable to get rid of it.

The father's/narrator's final words in Kafka's "Odradek" ("the idea that he is likely to survive me I find almost painful") echo the final words of *The Trial* ("as if the shame will survive him"): Odradek is effectively *the shame of the father of the family* (the story's narrator). What this indicates is that Odradek is the father's *sinthome,* the "knot" onto which the father's jouissance is stuck. This, however, seems to complicate the link between shame and castration: for Lacan, is such a partial object, *lamella,* the "undead" organ without a body, not precisely that which escapes castration? Lacan defines *lamella* as an asexual object, as the remainder

---

41. No wonder that we find another Kafkaesque feature in the climactic scene of Vsevolod Pudovkin's *Deserter* (1933), which stages a weird displacement of the Stalinist show trials. When the film's hero, a German proletarian working in a gigantic Soviet metallurgical plant, is praised in front of the entire collective for his outstanding labor, he replies with a surprising public confession: he does not deserve this praise, he says, because he came to the Soviet Union to work only to escape his cowardice and betrayal in Germany itself (when the police attacked the striking workers, he stayed at home, because he believed Social Democratic treacherous propaganda)! The public (simple workers) listen to him with perplexity, laughing and clapping—a properly uncanny scene reminding us of the scene in Kafka's *The Trial* when Josef K. confronts the courts—here also, the public laughs and claps at the most unexpected and inappropriate moments. The worker then returns to Germany to fight the battle at his proper place. This scene is so striking because it stages the secret fantasy of the Stalinist trial: the traitor publicly confesses his crime out of his own free will and guilt feeling, without any pressure from the secret police.

of sexuation. For a human being to be "dead while alive" is to be colonized by the "dead" symbolic order; to be "alive while dead" is to give body to the remainder of Life-Substance which has escaped the symbolic colonization (*lamella*). What we are dealing with here is thus the split between Other and Jouissance, between the "dead" symbolic order which mortifies the body and the nonsymbolic Life-Substance of jouissance. These two notions are in Freud and Lacan not what they are in our everyday or standard scientific discourse. In psychoanalysis, they both designate a properly monstrous dimension—Life is the horrible palpitation of the *lamella,* of the nonsubjective (*acephal*) "undead" drive which persists beyond ordinary death; death is the symbolic order itself, the structure which, as a parasite, colonizes the living entity. What defines death drive in Lacan is this double gap: not the simple opposition of life and death, but the split of life itself into "normal" life and horrifying "undead" life, and the split of the dead into "ordinary" dead and the "undead" machine. The basic opposition between Life and Death is thus supplemented by the parasitical symbolic machine (language as a dead entity which "behaves as if it possesses a life of its own") and its counterpoint, the "living dead" (the monstrous life-substance which persists in the Real outside the Symbolic). This split which runs within the domains of Life and Death constitutes the space of the death drive.

In his reading of Kafka, Benjamin focuses on "a long series of figures with the prototype of distortion, the hunchback": "Among the images in Kafka's stories, none is more frequent than that of the man who bows his head far down on his chest: the fatigue of the court officials, the noise affecting the doormen in the hotel, the low ceiling facing the visitors in the gallery." [42] It is crucial to remember here that, in the encounter of the man from the country and the guardian of the Door of the Law, it is the guardian, the figure of authority, who is hunched, not the man from the country, who stands upright. (This point is noted by the priest in his debate with Josef K. that follows the parable on the Door of the Law in *The Trial:* the priest makes it clear that it is the guardian who is subordinated here, playing the role of a servant.) One should thus not idealize the disfigured "creature" into a pathetic figure of the marginalized, excluded from full humanity, the object of solidarity with the victim—if anything, the creaturely hunchback is the prototype of the servant of Power. Let us not forget who are "creatures" par excellence:

42. Benjamin, "Franz Kafka: On the Tenth Anniversary of His Death," trans. Harry Zohn, in *Selected Writings,* vol. 2, *1927–34,* ed. Michael W. Jennings, Howard Eiland, and Gary Smith (Cambridge, MA: Harvard University Press, 2001), 811.

woman is more "creaturely" than man; *Christ on the cross* is *the* creature; and, last but not least, the *psychoanalyst* is an inhuman creature, not a human partner (and the wager of the discourse of the analyst is precisely that one can establish a social link based directly on this creaturely excess, bypassing the master signifier). Recall here Lacan's *le père ou pire,* "father or the worse": insofar as the analyst is not a father figure (a figure of paternal symbolic authority), insofar as his presence signals and enacts the suspension of this authority, is there not in his figure also something of the "primordial" (one is tempted to say *anal*) father, the One exempted from symbolic castration?

This is how we should approach the topic of Eucharist: what exactly do we eat when we eat the body of Christ? We eat the partial object, the undead substance which redeems us and guarantees that we are raised above mortality, that, while still alive here on earth, we already participate in the eternal divine Life. Does this not mean that Eucharist is like the undead substance of the indestructible eternal life that invades the human body in a horror movie? Are we not, through Eucharist, terrorized by an alien monster which invades our body?[43] In the fall of 2003, a weird case of cannibalism was discovered in Germany: a guy ate his partner. What was so weird was the strictly consensual nature of the act: there was not the usual secret abduction and torture; the killer put announcements on the Web, asking for somebody who was willing to be killed and eaten, and found a volunteer. The two first ate together the cooked penis of the victim; then the victim was killed, cut into pieces, and gradually eaten. If ever there was an act of Eucharistic love, this was it.

Shame thus appears to be precisely what overwhelms the subject when he or she is confronted with what, in him or her, remains *noncastrated*, with the embarrassing surplus appendage which continues to dangle out. Is Odradek not the reminder/remainder of the failure of the father to accomplish his work of imposing the Law (of "castration")? Or are we dealing here, yet again, with the structure of parallax? That is to say, what if the lack and the surplus refer to the *same* phenomenon and are simply two perspectives on it? In his "structuralist" *Logic of Sense,* Deleuze developed how, as soon as the symbolic order emerges, we are dealing with the minimal difference between a structural place and the element that occupies (fills out) this place: an element is always logically preceded by the place in the structure it fills out. The two series can,

---

43. And does the uterus not function in the same way in the old notion of "hysteria" as a disease of the traveling womb? Is hysteria not the illness in which the partial object within the subject runs amok and starts to move around?

therefore, also be described as the "empty" formal structure (signifier) and the series of elements filling out the empty places in the structure (signified). From this perspective, the paradox consists in the fact that the two series never overlap: we always encounter an entity that is simultaneously—with regard to the structure—an empty, unoccupied place and—with regard to the elements—a rapidly moving, elusive object, an occupant without a place. We have thereby produced Lacan's formula of fantasy $ \lozenge a$, since the matheme for the subject is $, an empty place in the structure, an elided signifier, while *objet a* is, by definition, an excessive object, an object that lacks its place in the structure. Consequently, the point is not that there is simply the surplus of an element over the places available in the structure or the surplus of a place that has no element to fill it out. An empty place in the structure would still sustain the fantasy of an element that will emerge and fill out this place; an excessive element lacking its place would still sustain the fantasy of some yet unknown place waiting for it. The point is, rather, that the empty place in the structure strictly correlates to the errant element lacking its place: they are not two different entities, but the front and the back of one and the same entity, that is, one and the same entity inscribed onto the two surfaces of a Möbius strip. At its most formal, "castration" designates the precedence of the empty place over the contingent elements filling it; this is what accounts for the elementary structure of hysteria, of the hysterical question "Why am I what you are saying that I am? Why am I at that place in the symbolic order?" However, correlative to it is the fact of being stuck with an object with no (symbolic) place, an object which escaped castration. One should therefore not be afraid to draw the ultimate paradoxical conclusion: castration and its disavowal are two sides of the same coin, castration has to be sustained by a noncastrated remainder, a fully realized castration cancels itself. Or, to put it more precisely: *lamella,* the "undead" object, is not a remainder of castration in the sense of a little part which somehow escaped unhurt the swipe of castration, but, literally, the *product* of the cut of castration, the *surplus* generated by it.

This link between castration and *sinthome* means that the "undead" partial object is the inscription on the body of what Eric Santner calls "signifying stress": the wound, the disfiguration/distortion, inflicted upon the body when the body is colonized by the symbolic order. This is why animals are *not* "creatures" in this precise sense, they are *not* stuck onto a *sinthome*. However, one should avoid here the temptation to translate this feature into the terms of the traditional philosophical anthropology, according to which, animals are immersed in their environs, their behavior regulated by innate instincts, while humans are "home-less" animals deprived of immediate instinctual support, which is why they need a master to impose on them their "second nature," symbolic norms and regulations. The key difference is that the "cringe" of the *sinthome* is not a cultural device destined to impose a new balance onto the uprooted human being which threatens to explode into untamed ex-cess, but the name of this excess itself: a human being (to come) loses its animal instinctual coordinates by way of getting transfixed/stuck onto an "inhuman" *sinthome*. What this means is that the *differentia specifica* which defines a human being is, therefore, not the difference between human and animal (or any other real or imaginary species, such as gods), but an *inherent* difference, the difference between human and the inhu-man excess that is inherent to being-human.

So what does psychoanalysis do with shame? The first association that pops up is, of course, that the aim of analytic treatment is precisely to *dissolve* the "knot" (the specific "pathological" formula onto which the subject's jouissance is stuck). That is to say, is such a stuckness onto a symptom not the most elementary form of the blockade psychoanaly-sis is dealing with? What prevents us from "freely enjoying sexuality" is not a direct repression, the so-called internalization of inhibitions, but the very excess of enjoyment coagulated into a specific formula which curves/distorts/transfixes our space of enjoyment, closes off new pos-sibilities of enjoyment, condemns the subject to err in the closure of a vicious cycle, compulsively circulating around the same point of (libid-inal) reference. And, within this framework, the function of psycho-analysis would be to bring the subject to *fully assume castration:* to untie the knot, to dissolve this stuckness, and thus to liberate his or her desire. Or, in Deleuzian terms: "stuckness" is the elementary form of *libidinal territorialization,* and the aim of psychoanalysis is to deterritorialize the subject's desire. However, the late Lacan proposes an exactly inverted formula: the aim of psychoanalysis is to get the subject to come to terms with the *sinthome,* with his specific "formula of enjoyment." Lacan's in-sight here is that of the full ontological weight of "stuckness": when one dissolves the *sinthome* and thus gets fully unstuck, one loses the minimal consistency of one's own being—in short, what appears as obstacle is a positive condition of possibility.

What happens in psychoanalysis is thus not the dissolution of symp-tom, but the shift in perspective which inverts the condition of impos-sibility into the condition of possibility. The mode of functioning of *lamella* is therefore that of *suppleance.* When, in his seminar 20, Lacan proposes the formula *"Y'a de l'Un"* (the colloquial French for "There is something of the One"), this One is not the One of a harmonious Whole, or the One of some unifying principle, or of the Master-Signifier, but, on the contrary, the One that persists as the obstacle destabilizing every unity. This One—which is ultimately what Lacan calls the "object small *a*"—has the structure of what Lacan calls *suppleance:* supplementing the lack of what is in itself impossible. Thus, *suppleance* has nothing to do with the standard—false—reading of "suture" as the gesture of filling in the structural lack and imposing a false unification onto the multitude. It is, rather, what Badiou calls the "symptomal knot," the "supernumerary" element which renders palpable the inconsistency of the social totality.[44] Therefore, is *suppleance* not (also) another name for the object-cause of desire qua surplus-enjoyment and, simultaneously, what Freud called the supplementary bonus of forepleasure?[45]

What if, however, this very choice between the dissolution of a symptomal knot and its acceptance as a positive condition is, again, a false one? What if the very structure of a drive (as opposed to instinct) provides a solution? We are stuck on a knot around which drive circulates, yet it is this very stuckness that pushes us again and again forward to invent ever new forms to approach it. Every "openness" has thus to be sustained by a "knot" which stands for a fundamental impossibility. The excess of humanity with regard to the animal is not (only) an excess of dynamism, but rather an excess of fixity: a human remains "stubbornly attached," fixated, to an impossible point, returning to it on account of a compulsion to repeat, unable to drop it even when it reveals itself as unattainable. Consequently, is the "theological" dimension—without which, for Benjamin, revolution cannot win—not the very dimension of the excess of drive, of its "too-muchness"? Is a solution, then, to change the modality of our being-stuck into a mode that allows, solicits even, the activity of sublimation?

Shame and Its Vicissitudes

Lacan's theory effectively outlines a series of "vicissitudes of shame." There is the cynical position (not that of the modern cynicism, but of

---

44. The key question of any psychoanalytic notion of society is: can one base a social link on this *suppleance?* The wager of the analyst's discourse is that one can do it. And the wager of revolutionary politics is that this is how a revolutionary collective functions.

45. As such, it is linked to judgment (in the strict Kantian sense): insofar as the object-cause of desire is that which makes us desire the (direct) object of desire, it is the ground of judgment, i.e., that on account of which we make the judgment that an object is desired by us. (Thus, the "transcendental" status of *objet a* is again confirmed.)

the cynicism of the Ancients, that of Diogenes), the position of shame-lessness, of displaying one's obscene excess publicly (Diogenes, it is re-ported, used to masturbate in front of others). Then there is the sadist pervert who displaces shame onto his other/victim (the sadist assumes the position of the object-instrument of the other's jouissance, in other words, the aim of the sadist's activity is not primarily to impose pain onto the other, but to put the other to shame by way of confronting him or her with the unbearable knot of his or her enjoyment). It is a key fact here that the formula of the discourse of perversion is the same as that of the analyst's discourse: Lacan defines perversion as the inverted fan-tasy, in other words, his formula of perversion is $a \lozenge \$$, which is pre-cisely the upper level of the analyst's discourse. The difference between the social link of perversion and that of analysis is grounded in the rad-ical ambiguity of *objet petit a* in Lacan, which stands simultaneously for the imaginary fantasmatic lure/screen and for that which this lure is ob-fuscating, for the void behind the lure. So, when we pass from perver-sion to the analytic social link, the agent (analyst) reduces himself to the void that provokes the subject into confronting the truth of his desire.

It would be all too easy to establish here a link between shame and the Levinasian notion of responsibility toward the neighbor's face; how-ever, the ultimate limitation of shame is the same as that of Levinas: it relies on some figure of "big Other" whose presupposed gaze makes us ashamed. For example, in *City Lights* the Tramp is ashamed because his hiccup-whistles are noted by those around him. Recall the key moment in a Jerry Lewis film which occurs when the idiot he plays is compelled to become aware of the havoc his behavior has caused. And this holds even for Oedipus: why did he blind himself after discovering the truth about himself? Not to punish himself, but to escape the unbearable gaze of the Other, the gaze which, as Lacan put it in seminar 11, is outside—it does not belong to an eye but to an all-seeing world which photo-graphs me all the time. This is what Oedipus was not able to sustain: the shame of the truth of his being disclosed to the world to see it. What, then, happens to shame once the subject assumes the inexistence of the big Other?

When Lacan defines the Freudian drive as reflexive, as the stance of "*se faire* . . ." (visual drive is not the drive to see, but, in contrast to the desire to see, the drive to *make oneself* seen, etc.), does he not thereby point toward the most elementary *theatricality* of the human condition? Our fundamental striving is not to observe, but *to be part of a staged scene*, to expose oneself to a gaze—not a determinate gaze of a person in reality, but of the nonexistent pure Gaze of the big Other. This is the gaze for which the ancient Romans carved the details in the reliefs at the top of their viaducts, details invisible to the eye of any human standing below; the gaze for which the ancient Incas made their gigantic drawings out of stones whose form could be perceived only from high up in the air; the gaze for which the Stalinists organized their gigantic public spectacles. To specify this gaze as "divine" is already to "gentrify" its status, to obfuscate the fact that it is a gaze of no one, a gaze freely floating around, with no bearer. The two correlative positions, that of the actor on the stage and that of the spectator, are not ontologically equivalent or contemporary: we are originally not observers of the play-stage of reality, but part of the tableau staged for the void of a nonexisting gaze, and it is only in a secondary time that we can assume the position of those who look at the stage. The unbearable "impossible" position is not that of the actor, but that of the observer, of the public.

Along these lines, Gerard Wajcman recently proposed a Lacanian version of the rise of modern subjectivity. According to Wajcman, the medieval human remained inscribed *into* the field of the Other's gaze, into creation under the protection of God's gaze; this gaze is a secondary version of the original fact that, prior to seeing, we are objects of the Other's gaze. Against this background, the break of modernity, the rise of the modern subject, equals the emergence of the space of *intimacy:* the subject asserts itself as the subject of a gaze who masters the world by first seeing it from a safe distance, from a dark place beyond the Other's gaze. Unseen, I see. This is what the Cartesian *cogito* ultimately amounts to: I am insofar as I am not seen, insofar as the core of my being dwells in an "intimate" space that escapes the Other's public gaze. This exemption is an illusion, however, a screen against the fact that, prior to seeing, I am here for the Other's gaze:

Lacan will lift the final veil on all this in order to show the truth: that there is nothing to see. In other words, what is elided in the visible, outside of the gaze and with the gaze, is that nothing in truth looks at the spectator, except himself, his own gaze in the field of the Other. His own gaze *ex qua,* placed outside. But it seems to me that this should be added: that one can do nothing with such a truth except to know it. It would be better for the health of a subject if he had nothing to do with this truth in the real, if he never encountered it, if he never came up against the unveiling of the gaze which would thus be that of his phantasm. Between lie and undesirable truth, Lacan advocates a path for the subject, the path of the subject, ethical, that of a choice of being duped. Choosing the illusion nevertheless implies knowing the truth, not losing the view that it is an illusion. But a vital illusion.[46]

On the next page, Wajcman refers to a psychotic case of a patient of his, Madame R., who lived in a terrifying Real, outside illusion: totally exposed to the Other's gaze, flattened, desubjectivized by it, transparent, deprived of any substance, invisible precisely because she is totally open to the Other's gaze. This is Wajcman's version of Lacan's *les non-dupes errent:* the nonduped—those who refuse to get caught in the illusion of being able to see from a safe distance, to be exempted from the world, and to elude the Other's gaze—pay for this a terrible price of psychotic closure.

However, Lacan's *les non-dupes errent* can (and should) be read in a different, opposite almost, way, as a formula against cynicism: the "nonduped" are not psychotics but cynics who refuse to get caught in the symbolic fiction and reduce it to a mere superficial mask beneath which the "real thing" dwells (power, jouissance, etc.). What cynics do not see is that, as Lacan emphasized (paraphrasing Alphonse Allais), we are naked only beneath our dress. And, effectively, Wajcman himself comes dangerously close to a cynical position insofar as his version of Lacan's "ethical path" (allow yourself to be duped, while knowing that it is only an illusion) cannot but function as another *je sais bien mais quand meme:* I know the truth but I choose illusion. In other words, I choose to act as if I believe in the illusion. This is an "empty" knowledge, a knowledge deprived of symbolic-performative efficiency. It is false because it remains disconnected from truth; the truth is not on the side of my knowledge, but on the side of the illusion in which I let myself get caught. This is how today's ideology functions: a successful businessman who, deep in himself, thinks that his economic activity is just a game in which he participates, while his "true Self" expresses itself in spiritual meditation that he regularly practices, is not aware that this "true Self" is a mere delusion enabling him to successfully participate in the economic activity. He is like a Jew who knows there is no God, but nonetheless obeys the kosher rules.

Here I must raise a series of questions. Is a psychotic really the one who heroically assumes the unbearable truth (that I am seen, exposed; or that I am spoken), in contrast to the "normal" seeing/speaking subject who relies on an illusion? If the nonpsychotic space in which we are

---

46. Gerard Wajcman, "The Birth of the Intimate," *Lacanian Ink* 23 (2004): 64.

exempted from being exposed to the Other's gaze emerged only with the rise of modern subjectivity, and even constitutes that subjectivity, in what way were premodern humans *not* psychotics, although—according to Wajcman—they were fully exposed to the Other's gaze, perceiving themselves as dwelling within the created world sustained by the divine Gaze? Furthermore, is Lacan's point not also that I am only as seen through a blind spot in what I see, through the stain in the field of the visible which is strictly correlative to the subject's existence? Is this not what Lacan's formula $ \diamond a$ (the "impossible" correlation between the void of subjectivity and the stain of the object) amounts to? Is this not also the antipanopticon lesson of the recent trend of "-cam" Web sites, which realize the logic of "The Truman Show"? (On these sites, we are able to follow continuously some event or place: the life of a person in his or her apartment, the view on a street, etc.) Do they not display an urgent need for the fantasmatic Other's Gaze serving as the guarantee of the subject's being: "I exist only insofar as I am looked at all the time"? (Similar to this is the phenomenon, noted by Claude Lefort, of the TV set that is all the time turned on, even when no one effectively watches it. It serves as the minimum guarantee of the existence of a social link.) Thus, the contemporary situation is the tragicomic reversal of the Benthamic-Orwellian notion of the panopticon society in which we are (potentially) observed all the time and have no place to hide from the omnipresent gaze of the Power. Today, anxiety arises from the prospect of *not* being exposed to the Other's gaze all the time, so that the subject needs the camera's gaze as a kind of ontological guarantee of his or her being.

And, last but not least, is the only position outside illusion really the impossible position of a totally desubjectivized self-exposure? Does Wajcman not confound here two quite distinct experiences: the psychotic exposure to the all-seeing gaze of the Other *and* the experience that nothing in truth looks back at me because "there is no big Other," because the Other is in itself inconsistent, lacking? In Lacan's perspective, it is wrong to say that the subject exists only insofar as it is exempted from the Other's gaze; rather, the subject's ($) existence is correlative to the *lack* in the Other, to the fact that the big Other itself is barred. There is a subject only insofar as the Other is itself traversed by the bar of an inherent impossibility. (Here, we should bear in mind that *l'objet petit a* signals and simultaneously fills in the lack in the Other, so that saying that the subject is correlative to *a* equals saying that it is correlative to the lack in the Other.) Far from assuming this lack, the psychotic persists in the illusion of a consistent (noncastrated) Other who is *not* just a fiction, in other words, who is *not* just "my own gaze in the field of the Other."

What this means is that the subject's opacity is strictly correlative to his or her total self-exposure. The first act of Sygne, the heroine of Paul-Louis-Charles-Marie Claudel's *The Hostage,* is that of what, following Freud, Lacan calls *Versagung:* the radical (self-relating) loss/renunciation of the very fantasmatic core of her being. First, I sacrifice all I have for the Cause-Thing that is for me more than my life; what I then get in exchange for this sacrifice is the loss of this Cause-Thing itself.[47] In order to save the Pope hiding in her house, Sygne agrees to marry Toussaint Turelure, a person she despises. Turelure is the son of her servant and wet nurse and has used the Revolution to promote his career; as a Jacobin local potentate, he ordered the execution of Sygne's parents in the presence of their children. Thus, Sygne sacrifices everything that matters to her—her love, her family name, and her estate. Her second act is her final No! to Turelure. Turelure, standing by the bed of the fatally wounded Sygne, desperately asks her to give a sign which would confer some meaning on her unexpected suicidal gesture of saving the life of her loathed husband—anything, even if she didn't do it for the love of him but merely to save the family name from disgrace. The dying Sygne doesn't utter a sound. She merely signals her rejection of the final reconciliation with her husband by means of a compulsive tic, a kind of convulsed twitching that repeatedly distorts her gentle face. There is a key difference between the facial tic which stands for the "non de Sygne" (Lacan), for her refusal to confer meaning on her suicidal act, and the Tramp's hiccups in *City Lights.* His uncontrollable hiccups make the Tramp ashamed in the eyes of the public, while there is no shame in Sygne. Her shattering experience deprives her of that fantasmatic core, the exposure of which would put her to shame; so her tic is just that, a feature that provides the minimum of consistency to her devastated/voided subjectivity.

Thus, it is totally misleading to try to "interpret" Sygne's No! so as to see in it some desperate strategy of retaining a minimum of dignity or privacy, or to perceive it as conditioned by some psychopathological compulsion. Sygne's fate makes it clear how *total exposure equals opacity:* it is precisely when a subject exposes himself totally to me that I experience him as thoroughly impenetrable—although there is no content

---

47. Lacan provided a detailed interpretation of Claudel's *L'otage* in his seminar 8 on transference (*Le séminaire, livre 8: Le transfert* [Paris: Seuil, 1982]); see also my reading of *Versagung* in chapter 2 of *The Indivisible Remainder* (London: Verso, 1996).

hidden from me, the enigma is that of the form itself, of the status of the very gesture of exposure.

Love, Hatred, and Indifference

We should therefore assume the risk of countering Levinas's position with a more radical one: others are primordially an (ethically) indifferent multitude, and love is a violent gesture of cutting into this multitude and privileging a One as the neighbor, thus introducing a radical imbalance into the whole. In contrast to love, justice begins when I remember the faceless many left in shadow in this privileging of the One. Justice and love are thus structurally incompatible: justice, not love, has to be blind; it must disregard the privileged One whom I "really understand." What this means is that the Third is not secondary: it is always-already here, and the primordial ethical obligation is toward this Third who is *not* here in the face-to-face relationship, the one in shadow, like the absent child of a love-couple. This not simply the Derridean-Kierkegaardian point that I always betray the Other because *toute autre est un autre*, because I have to make a *choice* to *select* who my neighbor is from the mass of the Thirds, and this is the original sin-choice of love. The structure is similar to the one described by Emile Benveniste regarding verbs: the primordial couple is not active-passive, to which the middle form is then added, but active and middle (along the axis of engaged-disengaged). The primordial couple is Neutral and Evil (the choice which disturbs the neutral balance) or, grammatically, impersonal Other and I—"you" is a secondary addition.[48]

To properly grasp the triangle of love, hatred, and indifference, one must rely on the logic of the universal and its constitutive exception which only introduces existence. The truth of the universal proposition "Humans are mortal" does not imply the existence of even one human, while the "less strong" proposition "There is at least one human who exists (i.e., some humans exist)" implies their existence. Lacan draws from this the conclusion that we pass from universal proposition (which defines the content of a notion) to existence only through a proposition stating the existence of—not the at least one element of the universal genus which exists, but—at least one which is an exception to the universality in question. What this means with regard to love is that the

---

48. See Emile Benveniste, "The Active and Middle Form in Verbs," in *Problems in General Linguistics* (Miami: University of Miami Press, 1973).

universal proposition "I love you all" acquires the level of actual existence only if "there is at least one whom I hate"—a thesis abundantly confirmed by the fact that universal love for humanity always led to the brutal hatred of the (actually existing) exception, of the enemies of humanity. This hatred of the exception is the "truth" of universal love, in contrast to true love which can emerge only against the background— *not* of universal hatred, but—of universal indifference: I am indifferent toward All, the totality of the universe, and as such, I actually love *you,* the unique individual who stands/sticks out of this indifferent background. Love and hatred are thus not symmetrical: love emerges out of universal indifference, while hatred emerges out of universal love. In short, we are dealing here again with the formulas of sexuation: "I do not love you all" is the only foundation of "there is nobody that I do not love," while "I love you all" necessarily relies on "I really hate some of you." "But I love you all!"—this is how Erich Mielke, the boss of the East German secret police, defended himself. His universal love was obviously grounded in its constitutive exception, the hatred of the enemies of socialism.[49]

This brings us to the radical anti-Levinasian conclusion: the true ethical step is the one *beyond* the face of the other, the one of *suspending* the hold of the face, the one of choosing *against* the face, for the *third*. This coldness *is* justice at its most elementary. Every preempting of the Other in the guise of his or her face relegates the Third to the faceless background. And the elementary gesture of justice is not to show respect for the face in front of me, to be open to its depth, but to abstract from it and refocus onto the faceless Thirds in the background.[50] It is only such

49. And does the same not go for the status of the inhuman? First, there is the inhuman of constitutive exception: the (external, barbarian, etc.) other with regard to which I define my being-human. Then, there is a more radical inhumanity: there is nothing in humans which is not human, and, for this very reason, not-all is human, we are all overwhelmed by an unspecifiable excess of the inhuman.

50. We find a refined case of such a reference to the Third in the famous passage in Koran 7:163–66, which tells the story of a community of fishermen who succumbed to the temptation to fish on the Sabbath; God punishes them by changing them into monkeys. However, when the faithful ones admonish the evildoers for their transgression, a third group protests: "'Why do you admonish people God is about to destroy or to chastise with a terrible chastisement?' they said." The population in question is thus divided into three groups: the first group broke the Sabbath, the second admonished them, and the third thought the admonition pointless. The enigmatic point is that, in describing God's response, the Koran mentions only two groups, those who were punished by being changed into monkeys and those who admonished them and were saved—what became of the third group? Here commentators have agonized, since it touches a sensitive ethical question: are those who, while not participating in the evildoing, keep silent in the face of it, to be reckoned among the damned or among the saved? Are those who preferred silence guilty of implicit endorsement, or, on the contrary, are those who gleefully celebrated the terrible fate of the evildoers hypocritical conformists? The elegance of the Koran is to address this issue in absentia, through its enigmatic silence.

a shift of focus onto the Third that effectively *uproots* justice, liberating it from the contingent umbilical link that renders it "embedded" in a particular situation. In other words, it is only such a shift onto the Third that grounds justice in the dimension of *universality* proper. When Levinas endeavors to ground ethics in the Other's face, is he not still clinging to the ultimate root of the ethical commitment, afraid to accept the abyss of the rootless Law as the only foundation of ethics? Thus, truly blind justice cannot be grounded in the relationship to the Other's face, in other words, in the relationship to the neighbor. Justice is emphatically *not* justice for—with regard to—the neighbor.

What is at stake here is not primarily an external critique of Levinas, targeting its problematic sociopolitical consequences, but the deployment of the inherent insufficiency of his rendering of the encounter of the Other's face as the primordial face. This rendering is wrong in its own terms, as a phenomenological description, since it misses the way the Third is always-already here. Prior to encountering the Other as a face in front of us, the Other is here as a paradoxical background-face; in other words, the first relationship to an Other is that to a faceless Third. The Third is a formal-transcendental fact; it is not that, while, in our empirical lives, the Third is irreducible, we should maintain as a kind of regulative Idea the full grounding of ethics in the relationship to the Other's Face. Such a grounding is not only empirically impossible, it is a priori impossible, since the limitation of our capacity to relate to Others' faces is the mark of our very finitude. In other words, the limitation of our ethical relation of responsibility toward the Other's face which necessitates the rise of the Third (the domain of regulations) is a positive condition of ethics, not simply its secondary supplement. If we deny this—in other words, if we stick to the postulate of a final translatability of the Third into a relation to the Other's face—we remain caught in the vicious cycle of "understanding." One can "understand" everything; even the most hideous crime has an "inner truth and beauty" when observed from within (recall the refined spiritual meditations of the Japanese warriors). There is a weird scene in Hector Babenco's *Kiss of the Spider Woman*. In German-occupied France, a high Gestapo officer explains to his French mistress the inner truth of the Nazis, how they are guided in what may appear brutal military interventions by an inner vision of breathtaking goodness. We never learn in what, exactly, this inner truth and goodness consist; all that matters is this purely formal gesture of asserting that things are not what they seem (brutal occupation and terror), that there is an inner ethical truth which redeems them. *This* is what the ethical Law prohibits: justice *must* be blind, ignoring the inner truth. Recall the famous passage from Graham Greene's *The Power and the Glory:* "When you visualized a man or woman carefully, you could always begin to feel pity—that was a quality God's image carried with it. When you saw the lines at the corners of the eyes, the shape of the mouth, how their hair grew, it was impossible to hate. Hate was just a failure of imagination."[51]

However, what this means is that, in order to practice justice, one *has* to suspend one's power of imagination; if hate is a failure of imagination, then pity is the failure of the power of abstraction. Recall how color-blind people proved useful in World War II: they were able almost immediately to see through camouflage and to identify a tank or a gun behind the protective cover—a proof that this cover worked at the level of color, by reproducing colors that extended smoothly into the surroundings, not at the level of shapes. In the same way, justice is color-blind: in order to perceive the true contours of the act to be appreciated, justice must ignore the entire camouflage of the human face. Far from displaying "a quality God's image carried with it," the face is the ultimate ethical lure, and the passage from Judaism to Christianity is *not* the passage from blindly applying the harsh law to displaying love and pity for the suffering face. It is crucial that it was Judaism, the religion of the harsh letter of the Law, that first formulated the injunction to love thy neighbor: the neighbor is not displayed through a face; it is, as we have seen, in his or her fundamental dimension a *faceless monster.* It is *here* that one has to remain faithful to the Jewish legacy: in order to arrive at the "neighbor" we have to love, we must pass through the "dead" letter of the Law, which cleanses the neighbor of all imaginary lure, of the "inner wealth of a person" displayed through his or her face, reducing him or her to a *pure subject.* Levinas is right to point out the ultimate paradox of how "the Jewish consciousness, formed precisely through contact with this harsh morality, with its obligations and sanctions, has learned to have an absolute horror of blood, while the doctrine of non-violence has not stemmed the natural course towards violence displayed by a whole world over the last two thousand years. . . . Only a God who maintains the principle of Law can *in practice* tone down its severity and use oral law to go beyond the inescapable harshness of Scriptures" (*DF,* 138).

But what about the opposite paradox? What if only a God who is ready to subordinate his own Law to love can *in practice* push us to realize blind justice in all its harshness? Recall the infamous lines from Che Guevara's testamentary "Message to the Tricontinental" (1967): "Hatred

---

51. Graham Greene, *The Power and the Glory* (Harmondsworth: Penguin, 1971), 131.

is an element of struggle; relentless hatred of the enemy that impels us over and beyond the natural limitations of man and transforms us into effective, violent, selective, and cold killing machines. Our soldiers must be thus; a people without hatred cannot vanquish a brutal enemy." [52] And it is crucial to read these lines together with Guevara's notion of revolutionary violence as a "work of love": "Let me say, with the risk of appearing ridiculous, that the true revolutionary is guided by strong feelings of love. It is impossible to think of an authentic revolutionary without this quality." [53] One should confer to the words "beyond the natural limitations of man" their entire Kantian weight: in their love/hatred, revolutionaries are pushed beyond the limitations of empirical "human nature," so that their violence is literally *angelic*. Therein resides the core of *revolutionary justice*, this much misused term: harshness of the measures taken, sustained by love. Does this not recall Christ's scandalous words from Luke ("if anyone comes to me and does not hate his father and his mother, his wife and children, his brothers and sisters—yes even his own life—he cannot be my disciple" [Luke 14:26]), which point in exactly the same direction as another famous quote from Che? "You may have to be tough, but do not lose your tenderness. You may have to cut the flowers, but it will not stop the Spring." [54] This Christian stance is the opposite of the Oriental attitude of nonviolence, which—as we know from the long history of Buddhist rulers and warriors—can legitimize the worst violence. It is not that the revolutionary violence "really" aims at establishing a nonviolent harmony; on the contrary, the authentic revolutionary liberation is much more directly identified with violence— it is violence as such (the violent gesture of discarding, of establishing a difference, of drawing a line of separation) which liberates. Freedom is not a blissfully neutral state of harmony and balance, but the violent act which disturbs this balance.

Marx said about the petit-bourgeois that he sees in every object two aspects, bad and good, and tries to keep the good and fight the bad. One should avoid the same mistake in dealing with Judaism: setting the "good" Levinasian Judaism of justice, respect for and responsibility toward the other, and so on, against the "bad" tradition of Jehovah, his fits of vengeance and genocidal violence against the neighboring people. This is the illusion to be avoided; one should assert a Hegelian "specula-

52. Available online at www.marxists.org/archive/guevara/1967/04/16.htm.

53. Quoted from Jon Lee Anderson, *Che Guevara: A Revolutionary Life* (New York: Grove, 1997), 636–37.

54. Quoted from Peter McLaren, *Che Guevara, Paulo Freire, and the Pedagogy of Revolution* (Oxford: Rowman & Littlefield, 2000), 27.

tive identity" between these two aspects and see in Jehovah the *support* of justice and responsibility. It is here that one should recall Lacan's formula of the ultimate choice facing us: *le père ou pire*. Against fatherly love, against father as the figure of universal, all-embracing justice, the one who "loves us all," we should gather the courage to choose "the worse," to make a difficult bet on the "other father" (in the same way that Miller speaks of the "other Lacan"), father as a *divisive* figure of struggle.

Judaism is the moment of unbearable absolute contradiction, the worst (monotheistic violence) and the best (responsibility toward the other) in absolute tension—the two are identical and simultaneously absolutely incompatible. Christianity resolves the tension by way of introducing a cut: the Bad itself (finitude, cut, the gesture of difference, "differentiation," as the Communists used to put it—"the need for ideological differentiation") as the direct source of Good. In a move from In-Itself to For-Itself, Christianity merely assumes the Jewish contradiction. So if I seem to argue for the step from Judaism to Paulinian Christianity, one should be fully aware that Paul is here conceived as "the first great German-Jewish thinker, equal in stature to Rosenzweig, Freud, and Benjamin."[55] At what point in the historical development of Christianity did this Paulinian moment reemerge most forcefully?

Do the three main versions of Christianity not form a kind of Hegelian triad? In the succession of Orthodoxy, Catholicism, and Protestantism, each new term is a subdivision, split off of a previous unity. This triad of Universal-Particular-Singular can be designated by three representative founding figures (John, Peter, Paul) as well as by three races (Slavic, Latin, German). In the Eastern Orthodoxy, we have the substantial unity of the text and the corpus of believers, which is why the believers are allowed to interpret the sacred Text. The Text goes on and lives in them; it is not outside the living history as its exempted standard and model.[56] The substance of religious life is the Christian community itself. Catholicism stands for radical alienation: the entity which mediates between the founding sacred Text and the corpus of believers, the

55. See Eric Santner's contribution to the present volume.

56. *The Fast Runner*, a unique film retelling an old Inuit legend, was made by Inuits themselves. The authors decided to change the ending, replacing the original slaughter in which all participants die with a more conciliatory conclusion; they claimed that such an ending is more befitting to today's times. The paradox is that precisely this readiness to adapt the story to today's specific needs attests to the fact that the authors were still part of the ancient Inuit tradition—such "opportunistic" rewriting is a feature of premodern culture, while the very notion of "fidelity to the original" signals that we are already in the space of modernity, that we have lost the immediate contact with tradition.

Church, the religious Institution, regains its full autonomy. The highest authority resides in the Church, which is why the Church has the right to interpret the Text; the Text is read during the mass in Latin, a language which is not understood by ordinary believers, and it is even considered a sin for an ordinary believer to read the Text directly, bypassing the priest's guidance. For Protestantism, finally, the only authority is the Text itself, and the wager is on every believer's direct contact with the Word of God as it was delivered in the Text; the mediator (the Particular) thus disappears, withdraws into insignificance, enabling the believer to adopt the position of a "universal Singular," the individual in direct contact with the divine Universality, bypassing the mediating role of the particular Institution. This reconciliation, however, becomes possible only after alienation is brought to the extreme: in contrast to the Catholic notion of a caring and loving God with whom one can communicate, negotiate even, Protestantism starts with the notion of God deprived of any "common measure" shared with humans, of God as an impenetrable Beyond who distributes grace in a totally contingent way.[57] One can discern the traces of this full acceptance of God's unconditional and capricious authority in the last song Johnny Cash recorded just before his death, "The Man Comes Around," an exemplary articulation of the anxieties contained in Southern Baptist Christianity:

There's a man goin' 'round taking names
And he decides who to free and who to blame
Everybody won't be treated all the same
There will be a golden ladder reaching down
When the man comes around

The hairs on your arm will stand up
At the terror in each sip and each sup
Will you partake of that last offered cup
Or disappear into the potter's ground
When the man comes around

Hear the trumpets hear the pipers
One hundred million angels singin'

---

57. For those who know Hegel, it is easy to locate this excessive element: at the end of his *Science of Logic,* Hegel addresses the naive question: how many moments should we count in a dialectical process, three or four? His reply is that they can be counted as either three or four: the middle moment, negativity, is redoubled into direct negation and the self-relating absolute negativity which directly passes into the return to positive synthesis.

Multitudes are marching to the big kettledrum
Voices callin' and voices cryin'
Some are born and some are dyin'
It's Alpha and Omega's Kingdom come

And the whirlwind is in the thorn trees
The virgins are all trimming their wicks
The whirlwind is in the thorn trees
It's hard for thee to kick against the pricks

Till Armageddon no shalam no shalom
Then the father hen will call his chickens home
The wise men will bow down before the thorn
And at his feet they'll cast their golden crowns
When the man comes around

Whoever is unjust, let him be unjust still
Whoever is righteous, let him be righteous still
Whoever is filthy, let him be filthy still

The song is about Armageddon, the end of days, when God will appear and perform the Last Judgment, and this event is presented as pure and arbitrary terror: God is presented almost as Evil personified, as a kind of political informer, a man who "comes around" and provokes consternation by "taking names," by deciding who is saved and who lost. If anything, Cash's description evokes the well-known scene of people lined up for a brutal interrogation, and the informer pointing out those selected for torture. There is no mercy, no pardon of sins in it, no jubilation in it. We are all fixed in our roles: the just remain just and the filthy remain filthy. In this divine proclamation, we are not simply judged in a just way. Rather, we are informed from outside, as if learning about an arbitrary decision, whether we were righteous or sinners, whether we are saved or condemned. This decision appears to have nothing to do with our inner qualities. And, again, this dark excess of the ruthless divine sadism—excess over the image of a severe, but nonetheless just, God— is a necessary negative, an underside, of the excess of Christian love over the Jewish Law: love that suspends the Law is necessarily accompanied by arbitrary cruelty that also suspends the Law. This is also why it is wrong to oppose the Christian god of Love to the Jewish god of cruel justice: excessive cruelty is the necessary obverse of Christian Love. And, again, the relationship between these two is one of parallax: there is no "substantial" difference between the god of Love and the god of excessive-arbitrary cruelty; it is one and the same god who appears in a different light only due to a parallactic shift of our perspective.

One might designate this intrusion of radical negativity as the "return of the Jewish repressed" within Christianity: the return of the figure of Jehovah, the cruel God of vengeful blind justice. And it is when one is faced with this violent return that one should assert the ultimate speculative identity of Judaism and Christianity: the "infinite judgment" is here "Christianity *is* Judaism."